Talk
on the
Wilde
Side

Toward a Genealogy of a Discourse
on Male Sexualities

Ed Cohen

Routledge

New York   London

Published in 1993 by

Routledge
An imprint of Routledge, Chapman and Hall, Inc.
29 West 35th Street
New York, NY 10001

Published in Great Britain by

Routledge
11 New Fetter Lane
London EC4P 4EE

Library of Congress Cataloging in Publication Data

Cohen, Ed, 1958–
    Talk on the Wilde side : towards a genealogy of a discourse on
male sexualities / Ed Cohen.
        p.   cm.
    Includes bibliographical references and index.
    ISBN 0-415-90229-0. — ISBN 0-415-90230-4 (pbk.)
    1. Wilde, Oscar, 1854–1900. 2. Homosexuality, Male—Great
Britain—History—19th century. 3. Authors, Irish—19th century—
Biography. 4. Gay men—Great Britain—Sexual behavior. 5. Trials
(Sex crimes)—England—London. 6. Men—Sexual behavior—History.
7. Masculinity (Psychology) 8. Sex (Psychology)   I. Title.
PR5823.C64   1992
828'.809—dc20
[B]   92-18036
                                                          CIP

ISBN 0-415-90229-0 (HB)
ISBN 0-415-90230-4 (PB)

To my family, my friends, and my teachers,
without whom nothing is possible.

CONTENTS

ACKNOWLEDGMENTS

The way to study the past is not to confine oneself to mere knowledge of history, but through application of this knowledge, to give actuality to the past.

I Ching, #26 "Taming Power of the Great"

This book began as a Ph.d. dissertation more than eight years ago. At that time, I was recovering from a life-threatening illness that shattered the world as I had lived it until then. Fortunately, during my period of physical and mental recovery, I was given the gift of working with Naomi Remen, one of the wisest people I have ever known, who suggested that if I wanted to learn to develop a healthy relationship to my work, I should write about something that "touched" me. In pondering that suggestion, I realized that what I had most viscerally excluded from my academic life until then, and consequently what I most needed to find a way to engage within it, was my identity as a gay man. This realization was soon followed by another: not only did I not know what it meant to experience "my identity as a gay man" either inside or outside academia, but I was becoming increasingly less sure about what it meant to "have" such an "identity" at all. Thus, I decided to devote myself to examining these personal/intellectual issues, embarking on a journey of exploration which has lead me both into the archive and into my "self" in order to give these realizations meaning.

As a result of Naomi's advice, the process of writing this book has been much more than I ever expected: much more arduous, much more interesting, much more rewarding, and much more fun. And the fact that I can write this now is necessarily predicated on the wonderful generosity and support I have received from so many people throughout the years. From the faculty I worked with at Stanford, I received unstinting support, for which I have the deepest gratitude. I was blessed by having Mary Pratt as my advisor from my first days in graduate school. With her quick mind, her generous heart, her undaunted enthusiasm, and her unabashed concern, Mary was not only the best possible kind of mentor, but also is a beloved friend, whose example illustrates both the importance and arduousness of a responsible academic practice. I also had the privilege of working with Regenia Gagnier, whose enthusiasm and support for this project since it was first conceived in her graduate seminar on "Aesthetes and Decadents" helped me to persevere throughout. Regenia's generosity and interest both as a scholar and as a comrade are deeply ingrained in this text. The other faculty at Stanford who also shared of their kindness and erudition are many and I list them here as a mnemonic for a debt of gratitude that I hope I will be able to repay through my own work with students in the years to come: Jean Franco, Bill Todd, Diane Middlebrook, Jack Winkler, Renato Rosaldo, Russell Berman, Judy Brown, Herbie Lindenberger, and David Halliburton.

Over the years I have been cajoled, inspired, stimulated, and admonished to finish "that damn book" by a large number of generous and patient friends. If I merely list them here, it is only because if I tried to describe how much each of them has meant to me it would require writing another book. Marcia Ian, Diana Fuss, Judy Walkowitz, George Chauncey, Cora Kaplan, Casey Finch, Carolyn Williams, Barry Qualls, Wayne Koestenbaum, Maria Damon, Kelly Hurley, Rey Chow, and Chris Craft have all done double duty as friends and readers. Lisa Nolling, Jennie McKnight, Jan Parker, Jane West, Peter Gibian, Kath Weston, Rebecca Mark, Ellen Bruno, Mary Wood, Caroline Streeter, Elaine Holliman, Cheryl Kremkow, Tory Read, Sue Zemka, David Weisberg, Paola Attala, and Monica Dorenkamp have helped keep me (relatively) sane if not joyful. Phillip Brooks, Emilie Conrad-Daoud, Susan Harper, and Mayla Riley have been my teachers in the academy of life. Alan Hill helped me put the final touches on the book by designing a really groovy cover and Beryle Chandler saved me by letting me use her groovy computer. My many wonderful housemates, Liz Kotz, Mary Klages, Karla Millett, Jen Aanastead, and especially Michael Lighty, Barney Stein, and the kitties, have put up with me and this book throughout the many years of its gestation. My grandma, Faye Cohen, has supported me financially and emotionally my whole life. And my parents Sylvia and Art Cohen have taught me the most important lessons of all: how to think and how to dance. In thanks for all, I offer my undying gratitude and love.

PROLOGUE
A Funny Thing Happened
on the Way to the Trials;
or, Why I Digress

During the late spring of 1895, the trials of Oscar Wilde erupted from the pages of almost every London newspaper—and indeed from the pages of almost every newspaper throughout Europe and North America. With a cast of characters that included one of London's most renowned and remarkable playwrights; a famously eccentric member of the British aristocracy; his son, a beautiful and effete young lord; a band of legal luminaries, including the highest ranking barrister in the nation; and a chorus of working-class men of tender age and questionable morals, it is hardly surprising that the sex scandal both captivated public interest and boosted newspaper sales. For more than two months Londoners were treated to daily installments chronicling a drama so fascinating that even Wilde's highly popular West End hits paled in comparison.[1] Moreover, the three trials in which Wilde played a principal part almost too coincidentally appeared to constitute the three acts of a modern tragedy, giving a "natural" aesthetic shape to the already tantalizing events. When the first trial, Wilde's unsuccessful prosecution of the Marquis of Queensberry for criminal libel, was interrupted, even before—and in order to prevent—the defense's presentation of its evidence against him, the stage was set for the ensuing legal proceedings in which Wilde would in turn "ironically" become the prosecuted. By 25 May, when Wilde was sentenced to two years' imprisonment with hard labor, after having been been tried twice and finally convicted on seven counts of engaging in "acts of gross indecency with another male person," his case was already so well known that it had significantly altered the shape of the Victorian sexual imagination. For, by the time of his conviction, not only had Wilde been confirmed as *the* sexual deviant for the late nineteenth century, but he

1

had become the paradigmatic example for an emerging public definition of a new "type" of male sexual actor: "the homosexual."

While I believe that the dénouement of this social drama has been
part of my unconscious cultural and sexual awareness since, as an
adolescent, I first learned "who Oscar Wilde was," I was only properly
introduced to the "tragedy of Oscar Wilde" years later through the
books of H. Montgomery Hyde. Reading Hyde's *The Trials of Oscar
Wilde* for the first time in a graduate seminar on "Aestheticism and
Decadence," I found myself unwittingly seduced into enjoying this
work—although I was prepared to find it didactic and dry—mesmer-
ized both by the powerful rendering of Wilde's courtroom appearances
and by the careful depiction of the legal and cultural forces unleashed
against him.[2] On the one hand, Hyde's book, which presents itself
as "verbatim transcripts with an introduction," evoked for me the
contradictory and compelling ways that Wilde's aesthetic/personal
style directly challenged the dominant interpretations of, among other
things, the patriarchal family, class difference, male sexuality, and the
politics of writing. With its apparently unmediated representations of
Wilde's courtroom performances, *The Trials of Oscar Wilde* seemed
to celebrate the audacity and intelligence of a man who publicly tried
to keep the monologic forces of law and state at bay armed only with
the blades of his wit and witticism. On the other hand, the book vividly
suggested the vigor and determination of those who opposed Wilde,
first in the form of an outraged father, the Marquis of Queensberry,
and then in the guise of the assiduous Crown prosecutors, who saw
themselves as defending the unequivocal values of "home," "class,"
"sex," and "art" against Wilde's willful and exemplary defiance. Thus,
the trials appeared to enact a public renegotiation of the boundaries
within which "private" behaviors were determined as (in)appropriate
in order, conversely, to stablize the very ground of the "public" itself.

Unfortunately, while the social and sexual dynamics crystallized by
Wilde's numerous courtroom appearances quickly emerged from my
reading of this incredibly engaging material, they were disturbingly
unaddressed by Hyde's text itself. In fact, although *The Trials of
Oscar Wilde* enticingly adumbrates these issues through its focused
recounting of what it calls "the legal contest," it leaves the contextual
questions of why and how Wilde's "tragedy" catalyzed public discussion entirely unexplored and undeveloped. In large part, this absence
derives from Hyde's own (now problematic) interpretation of the
"cause" underlying the events he reconstructs: for Hyde, Wilde can
only be understood as a man whose "abnormal sexual drive" (50) led
him to forsake "normal sexual intercourse" (55) in favor of sexual

relations with other men until "he made the fatal mistake of extending the range of his homosexual acquaintances to a different social class from his own" (60). Hence, rather than being able to analyze the conditions under which and within which Wilde was made the subject of legal/social scrutiny, Hyde is forced by his own preconceptions both to apologize for Wilde's "fatal mistake" and to try to explain away Wilde's (sexual) acts. In order to accomplish this exacting task, Hyde therefore introduces his account of the trials with a biographical sketch that portrays the famous playwright and author as a "tragic" figure whose blindness to the fact that his own "genius" could not excuse his "peculiar inverted instincts" (60) left him vulnerable to the execration and punishment of a society that could neither understand nor ultimately even tolerate him.

Because Hyde's works have been the primary source for nearly all contemporary narratives about Wilde's trials and conviction—having presented his account almost without variation in *The Trials of Oscar Wilde, Oscar Wilde: A Biography, Oscar Wilde: The Aftermath, The Other Love* (or, as its American pressing is entitled, *The Love that Dared Not Speak Its Name*), *Cases That Changed the Law*, and his recently published biography of Lord Alfred Douglas—his interpretation of what he characterizes as Wilde's "downfall" has provided *and effectively continues to provide* a de facto "official version" of the case.[3] Thus, as much as I reveled in and was piqued by Hyde's many retellings, my training in literary and social theory led me to be somewhat skeptical about the impact that Hyde's now canonical rendering has had upon the story of Wilde's trials and how they have come to make sense to us. Moreover, because the issues at play in the case seemed to me quite central to how contemporary male sexualities have been (re)produced and (re)presented throughout the century since his conviction, I wondered if there wasn't another way of shaping the story that could avoid Hyde's characterological orientation while illuminating what I imagined to be the larger social and political stakes. In fact, I hoped that by reinterpreting the (con)textual nexus from which the prevailing narratives about Wilde's "tragedy" have emerged, I might be able to elucidate the ways in which Wilde became a crucial figure both for what it meant to be an "English homosexual" at the end of the nineteenth century and for how "English homosexuality" has subsequently come to be figured in this one.[4]

It was with these epistemological desires, then, that I naively flew off to London to find the documents upon which Hyde had based his "complete transcriptions of all three trials,"[5] hoping that once I found them I could immediately begin the textual exegesis that I imagined would be my primary task. As soon as I began making the rounds of document repositories in search of my texts, however, I realized that something was awry. Not only did there not seem to be any transcripts available from any of the proceedings, but many of the other documents relating to the cases were also missing. And when I frantically started to question why this overwhelming absence existed, since it threatened to sink my project even before it had embarked, one very helpful official at the Public Records Office told me, in a most soothing voice designed, I'm sure, to defuse my increasingly visible hysteria: "Don't worry sir. It's not necessarily suspicious." Needless to say, this answer did not exactly assuage me and so in a panic I wrote to H. Montgomery Hyde asking him where he had found the transcripts he used to produce his books. Whereupon he wrote back to me to say, "I did not use any transcripts of the trials in my book and in fact relied on press reports in addition to *Oscar Wilde: Three Times Tried* published anonymously by Stuart Mason (Christopher Millard)"—which it turned out was also based on press reports and personal reminiscences.[6]

So there I was in London with my project in shambles and several months left before I had to return to the United States to complete my dissertation. Now, since I had never really undertaken a historical project of this magnitude—or indeed any magnitude—before, I didn't exactly know what I should do. However, I figured that since everyone else who'd written about the trials had used the newspaper accounts as their basis, I might as well check them out too. Trekking to the British Museum's newspaper dungeon in Collingdale, I began to examine the hundreds and hundreds of columns of tiny newsprint devoted to depicting Wilde's passage through the chambers of the Old Bailey. And the more I read, the more I realized that, far from providing me with "factual" accounts of these complex legal proceedings, as Hyde and others had heretofore assumed, these texts were themselves highly mediated stories whose narrative structures organized and gave mean-ingful shapes to the events they purported to accurately represent. Indeed, what seemed to me most striking about the reporting was that while the journalistic accounts endlessly circled around the very titillating sexual accusations made against Wilde, first indirectly by the Marquis of Queensberry's barrister, and then very directly by the Crown's prosecution, *at no point did the newspapers describe or even explicitly refer to the sexual charges made against Wilde.* Yet, since it was obviously this sexual dimension that made what was unfolding in the Old Bailey's crowded courtrooms both interesting *and* marketable, I began to wonder how it was that everyone could seem to know what it was that Wilde was accused of without it ever having to be positively stated. Thus began the book that you now have before you. . . .

Having started with this major detour, it seemed that the project could hardly have progressed except by way of digression. The more I read the newspapers, the more I realized how amazing it was that they had engendered the meanings now attributed to them; the more I pondered the underlying assumptions that made the stories cohere as stories, the more I understood that in order to prize apart their narrative frames I would have to delve back into the meanings and events that preceded them. And, given what was centrally—if unarticulably—at issue in the case, perhaps this regressive process was ultimately the most appropriate way to proceed, i.e., ass-backward. However, now that I am considering how you as readers will take up this book, I fear that my tendency to take two steps backward for each step forward will frustrate if not infuriate you. So let me quickly offer you a reversible reading map which may help you to plot your way through my emplotments as you will: If you are looking for the analysis of the newspaper accounts of Wilde's trials promised by this book's title, it appears in the last two chapters. They are preceded by a chapter charting the transformations in the meanings ascribed to the criminalization of sexual acts between men. Together these three chapters constitute the second part of the book, entitled "Pressing Issues," which tries to illuminate Wilde's emergence as a paradigmatic figure for a discernibly nonnormative male sexuality at the end of the nineteenth century. The first half of the book, "Against the Norm," on the other hand, attempts to consider the production of the normative, middle-class masculinity with respect to which Wilde came to signify and be signified as its antithesis. Thus, it pushes backward to the seventeenth and eighteenth centuries to explore how class-specific male embodiments of gender were (in the first chapter), then zooms up to and focuses on a mid-nineteenth-century example of how qualitative gender attributes were assigned to somatic signifiers of difference (in the second chapter), before reaching the 1880s and the feminist and evangelical instigation of the legislation under which Wilde was tried and convicted (in the third chapter). While to my mind "Against the Norm" sets up the questions which get worked through in "Pressing Issues," and hence the two parts are inextricably linked, I invite you to chart your own way through this text as your motives guide you. Please keep in mind, however, that I am not primarily (or even secondarily) concerned with providing yet another version of Wilde's trials. Rather, I am interested in exploring how the meanings engendered by their journalistic representations crystallized a variety of social/sexual discourses already at play throughout the nineteenth century in England. In other words, I am trying to explore here how it was that a certain structural opposition between "heterosexual" and "homosexual" came to imbue the ways middle-class masculinities were embodied at the cusp of our own century.

Since the specifics of this text's theoretical and historical projects are developed at length in the introductions to each of the book's two halves, I'll refrain from recapitulating them for you here. Instead, let me close this first of the many digressions you will encounter as you move through this material by simply wishing you "bon voyage."

PART I

AGAINST THE NORM

It is the value of all morbid states that they show us under a magnifying glass certain states that are normal—but are not easily visible when normal.

Nietzsche

Unlike their Continental colleagues, who had by the 1890s become quite prolific on the topic, medical experts in Britain seemed hesitant to broach the subject of sexual relations between men directly. Indeed, until 1897, when *Sexual Inversion* appeared as the first volume published in Havelock Ellis's series *Studies in the Psychology of Sex* (and was shortly thereafter removed from circulation),[1] the only references to male "homosexuality" in English texts were translations from German, French, and Italian medical works.[2] Coined in 1869 by the Austro-Hungarian translator and littérateur Karl Maria Kertbeny and popularized in the writing of the German sexologists, the word "homosexual"—the now ubiquitous, quasi-scientific denotation both for sexual intimacies between men and for the men who engage in them—made its first widespread British appearance in Charles Chaddock's 1892 translation of Krafft-Ebing's seminal *Psychopathia Sexualis*.[3] Here, as the descriptive assessment of a "contrary" or "inverted" "sexual nature," "homosexual"[4] came to signify a pathological deviation from monogamous, procreative sexual intercourse within marriage, which Krafft-Ebing unhesitantly called "the sexual instinct." That this new characterization of sexual relations between men not only (negatively) confirmed the dominance of the "instinctual" sexual norm but also, to some extent, produced it can be seen in the concurrent emergence of the word "heterosexual." For, coined by symmetry with and in opposition to "homosexual,"[5] "heterosexual" also made its first English appearance in the 1892 translation of *Psychopathia Sexualis* as a description of the desired, "virile" outcome that therapeutic treatment *should* produce in the "pathological" male: "the object of post

9

hypnotic suggestion is to remove the impulse to masturbation and homo-sexual feelings and impulses, and to encourage hetero-sexual feelings with a sense of virility."[6] In this (con)text, "heterosexual" emerges only as the "impulse" toward autoerotic and homoerotic behaviors and feelings are negated, so that the abnormal male is "encouraged" to conjoin proper sexual feelings (i.e., feelings that direct sexual desire toward a person of the "opposite" sex) with proper gender attributes (e.g., "a sense of virility").

From the inception of its English usage, then, "homosexuality" has been clinically defined as marking out the boundaries of sexual and gender norms: as that presence whose absence (re)produces the possibility of social and sexual "reproduction." The section heading introducing Krafft-Ebing's initial formulation clearly establishes the term as a signifier of what it lacks: "*Great Diminution or Complete Absence of Sexual Feeling for the Opposite Sex, with Substitution of Sexual Feeling and Instinct for the Same Sex (Homo-sexuality or Contrary Sexual Instinct).*"[7] Introducing "homo-sexuality" in parallel with its more explicitly comparative equivalent, "contrary sexual instinct,"[8] the title phrase sets out the parameters of Krafft-Ebing's discussion. Based on the "natural" determination of an "opposition" between male and female (itself predicated on the privileging of "male" as the unmarked term and "female" as its "opposite"), nonpathological, noncontrary "sexual feeling" stabilizes relations *across* sex. Thus, the "diminution" or "absence" of this "feeling" signals a pathological deviation from "a definite sexual personality and consciousness of desire . . . which, consciously or unconsciously, have a procreative purpose."[9] Desire for members of the "same" sex is depicted here as a substitution that displaces/replaces the absent or diminished (reproductive) feeling for the "opposite sex," situating itself in this gap as a simulacrum of—or "contrary" to—"instinct." In this medico-juridical text, then, "homosexuality" mimes the self-evident plenitude of the male/female dichotomy (here ideologically legitimated as "natural") in order to become its negative double. That "homosexual" and "heterosexual" are born(e) into the English language together, each simultaneously legitimating and undermining the other, illustrates how such normative characterizations reproduce, and are reproduced by, larger cultural assumptions that are concomitantly inscribed within them as their "natural" confirmation.

Since by and large the binary pairing homosexual/heterosexual still continues to define the poles between which male gender identities are plotted both "scientifically" and colloquially, the legacy of this late nineteenth-century sexological formulation continues to impinge on male experiences even today. In a recent article noting the enduring effects of this opposition in structuring the meanings given to contemporary men's lives, Tim Calligan, Bob Connell, and John Lee explain that "the homosexual/heterosexual dichotomy acts as a central symbol in *all* rankings of masculinity. Any kind of powerlessness, or refusal to compete, among men readily becomes involved with images of homosexuality."[10] Homosexuality, it seems, continues to bear within it the mark of absence—the absence of power, of success, indeed, of all the ideological markers that masculine privilege engenders within a patriarchally organized, capitalist world system. For, unlike the terms "gay" and "lesbian," which were popularized by the political struggles of the late 1960s and early 1970s and which explicitly seek to affirm same-sex relations (whether sexual or not), "homosexual" remains intimately linked to its nineteenth-century sexological origins.[11] Moreover, having long ago leapt from the relatively obscure pages of medico-forensic texts onto the pages/screens of the contemporary mass media, the popular deployments of "homosexuality" today continue to reassert the normative potential of "procreative heterosexuality" along with the corresponding normative gender expectations in new, more expansive ways.

Consider for a moment one of the most egregious contemporary examples of "homosexuality's" normalizing function: In the early to mid-1980s, the first American mass media reporting on the emerging AIDS epidemic focused on the incidence of infection among those "high risk groups" that Paula Treichler has succinctly labeled "the four H's": homosexuals, hemophiliacs, heroin addicts, and Haitians.[12] Yet, in these press depictions, the horrifying images of dying "homosexuals" quickly came to serve as the metonymic embodiments of this risky list so that the disease was effectively constructed in the popular imagination as hovering just beyond the limits of sexual/social normalcy—a limit whose breach five years into the epidemic gave rise to a distinctly different social category: "heterosexual AIDS."[13] Following upon earlier newspaper accounts which portrayed as "innocent victims" those people who unwittingly contracted the human immunodeficiency virus (HIV) through blood transfusions or treatments for hemophilia, the appearance of "heterosexual AIDS" negatively suggested that those who tested positive for HIV could be clearly identified as either sexually "normal" or "pathological" despite the fact that the "origin" of the syndrome would be the same in all cases: i.e., the transmission of a human retrovirus. However, while such putative distinctions have been repeatedly challenged by the medical and scientific explanations of the illness—not to mention the explanations and descriptions offered by

AIDS activists and people with AIDS themselves—they continue to provide the standard frame for journalistic representations.

Thus, the recent *New York Times* coverage of AIDS, to take just one highly influential and widely disseminated instance, continues to reiterate the attempt to draw a *cordon sanitaire* around the "normal" heterosexual population. In her reporting of the Fifth International AIDS conference in Florence (June 1991), *Times* correspondent Gina Kolata explains:

> In this country, it is still uncertain whether there is an independent AIDS epidemic among heterosexuals. Although the AIDS virus spreads heterosexually and the total of heterosexual AIDS cases is rising steadily, such cases still appear linked to the infected pool of intravenous drug abusers, meaning the epidemic has not yet taken on a life of its own among heterosexuals who do not use drugs.[14]

The terms of this description clearly demonstrate the ways the popular representations of AIDS are invested in defining the boundaries of the "epidemic" by sexually specifying the "types" of individuals who manifest HIV related illnesses. In so doing, they mask the semantic work involved in producing such conceptual demarcations and instead make such categorical distinctions seem intrinsic to the "natural history" of the disease. In the *New York Times* article, this naturalizing occurs in the slippage between Kolata's use of the adverb "heterosexually" as a metonym for the unnamed sexual practices through which AIDS "spreads,"[15] the adjective "heterosexual" as a designation for a particular group of people who have been diagnosed as "having" AIDS, and the noun "heterosexuals" as a signifier for the majority population of "this country" which may or may not be manifesting "an independent AIDS epidemic." That the distinctness of the "heterosexual" is asserted here through its many grammatical guises suggests that embedded in this way of imagining and representing the complex constellation of somatic events, relationships, and meanings we call "AIDS" is a corollary interest in drawing (sexual) boundaries between kinds of people.[16]

In undertaking so much ideological labor in order to protect the sanctity of "heterosexuals"—or at least of "heterosexuals who do not use drugs"—such popular representations not only function implicitly to produce AIDS as a "naturally" "homosexual" disease in the American social imaginary, but conversely serve to reanimate the always available meanings of homosexuality *as a disease*. Hence, the significance of this contemporary reinvestment in a disease model of sexuality must be understood *both* as a way of making sense of the fear and uncertainty occasioned by an emerging epidemic and as a way of remapping the shifting boundaries of gender and sexuality that were destabilized by the politicized (sexual) practices of the feminist and lesbian/gay movements. For, when these political/sexual challenges to normative masculinity and to normative "heterosexuality" crystallized as visible alternatives to—if not interruptions of—the heretofore prevailing patriarchal and familialist expectations, they made available possibilities that did not symmetrically imagine women as the "opposite" of men, or lesbians and gay men as the "opposite" of "straight" women and men. In reasserting the underlying links between pathology and homosexuality, then, the popular discourse on AIDS once again seeks to "fix" the meanings of gender and sexuality in order to reinscribe them within the discernible boundaries of the bourgeois family. As Simon Watney has remarked, "homosexuality, understood by AIDS commentary as the 'cause' of AIDS, is always available as a coercive and menacing category to entrench the institutions of family life and to prop up the unstable identities those institutions generate."[17] What the recent evocations of the "hetero/homo" opposition within the discourse on AIDS illustrate, therefore, is the extent to which this conceptual divide continues to imbricate the normativity of gender and sexuality in order to make sense of *and thereby contain* any threats to the entrenched privilege and authority that (re)produce white, Western, patriarchal capitalism—to give the beast a name.

Since this book grows out of the intellectual foment of contemporary feminist and lesbian/gay politics, it attempts to interrupt the assertions of normative masculinities by tracing the emergence of the homo/hetero divide back beyond its point of entry into the English language and culture to explore the conditions that made both its appearance and proliferation possible. In order to produce this disruptive effect, I begin by examining a number of British (con)texts throughout the nineteenth century within which the normativity of male gender and sexuality were construed as a "problem." For if, as Derrida tells us, "in a classical philosophical opposition we are not dealing with the peaceful coexistence of a *vis-à-vis*, but rather with a violent hierarchy,"[18] then the emergence of "homosexuality" under the mark of pathology and powerlessness is clearly governed by the violent assertion of "heterosexual" superiority. By overturning the silent privilege of remaining unmarked, which has heretofore been accorded to definitions of "normal" male sexuality, the first half of this book seeks both to challenge the implicit hierarchy that such privilege establishes and to illuminate the cultural contradictions that the production of the norm attempts to mask. Thus, rather than focusing here on the emergence of "homosexuality" per se as a category of "deviance," I seek instead to analyze the shifts in the discursive (re)production of normative male gender and ("hetero")sexuality as the background against which "the homosexual" could appear. This initial section, then, addresses a variety of institutional texts that sought to demarcate the realm of "normal" or "healthy" male sexual activity in order to demonstrate the transformations in the nineteenth-century bourgeois conceptualization of masculinity. In particular, these next three chapters try to sketch out the ways class, national, generational, and gender ideologies crystallized into the normative figure of a "healthy" adult, middle-class male who imaginatively embodied the category for which Wilde would eventually become one of the most recognizable and most execrable of "others."

1

EMBODYING THE ENGLISHMAN
A Theoretical Fiction

[A] man's body is given to him to be trained and brought into subjection and then used for the protection of the weak, the advancement of all righteous causes and the subduing of the earth which God has given to the children of men.

Thomas Hughes, *Tom Brown at Oxford*

On 16 June 1895, a little over three weeks after Oscar Wilde's conviction and sentencing for committing seven "acts of gross indecency with another male person," the popular Sunday newspaper the *Weekly Sun* published a full front page review of Max Nordau's controversial book *Degeneration*.[1] Introducing Nordau's text as a "wise, sound, and necessary warning against the tendencies and perils of the age," the anonymous author of the essay sketched the broad outlines of this timely work by quoting—at great length—Nordau's impassioned attacks on the "diseases," "manifestations," and "quacks" that he believed to be characteristic of *fin-de-siècle* Europe. Since Nordau's book primarily attempted to extend the theories of "degeneration" articulated by B. A. Morel and Caesar Lombroso[2] from the realms of "psychiatry, criminal law, politics, and sociology" into the sphere of "art and literature," the passages quoted in the *Weekly Sun* illustrated Nordau's belief that the most notable products of nineteenth-century literary and artistic "genius" were often actually the products of "diseased" intellects:

All these new tendencies, realism, or naturalism, "decadentism," "neo-mysticism," and their sub-varieties, are manifestations of degeneration and hysteria. . . . [E]veryone capable of logical thought will recognize that he commits a serious error if, in the aesthetic schools of the last few years, he sees the heralds of a new era. They do not direct us to the future, but point backwards towards the past.

15

> Their word is no ecstatic prophecy, but the senseless stammering
> and babbling of deranged minds, and what the ignorant hold to be
> outbursts of gushing, youthful vigour and turbulent constructive
> impulses are nothing but the convulsions and spasms of exhaustion.

Drawing upon a concept whose imbricated sexual and characterological meanings assumed a critical role in the coverage of Wilde's trials
(as we will see in chapter 5), this quotation summarizes Nordau's
attack on contemporary artistic and literary "tendencies." In it we
find the biologistic assumptions underlying Nordau's cultural analysis
made explicit: the writings of the "decadents," he thought, were not
"ecstatic prophecy" but dangerous anachronism; "the senseless stam-
mering and babbling of deranged minds," they were the symptomatic
"manifestations" of those popular late-Victorian diseases, "degeneration" and "hysteria," and hence merely "convulsions and spasms of
exhaustion." To an audience familiar with the century's frequent social
applications of both Darwinian and Lamarckian evolutionary theory,
these metaphors impugning the health of the current "aesthetic
schools" undoubtedly signified all that was antithetical to an uncom-
promised progressive development, a development that was itself identified with the "natural" destiny of the English middle class.[3] Indeed,
the reviewer underscores the somatic implications of this middle-class
ideology with a lame pun, troping upon the authority accorded to
medical discourse generally and to pathology specifically, by noting
that in Nordau's book "the literary men, and many of the musical
prodigies of our time are analyzed—perhaps, I should say dissected,"
before going on to quote extensively from Nordau's attacks on Swin-
burne, Verlaine, and Mallarmé. The article then closes with the regret
that there is "not room for some more of the strong, fierce sketches of
the decadents who figure in this remarkable volume," including Tol-
stoi, Wagner, and Zola.

Although the review makes no explicit reference to Wilde (who is
briefly considered in Nordau's book as an "ego-maniacal" example of
a British "aesthete")[4] or to the events of Wilde's sensational trials, it
follows so closely upon their conclusion and touches so directly upon
the issues they raised that it undoubtedly evoked many resonances of
these unparalleled legal proceedings for its readers. Indeed, the topical-
ity of Nordau's book was frequently made explicit in the course of the
press reports on the trials, so that it became a familiar reference for
the general condition of which Wilde was increasingly deemed a specific
and noteworthy example.[5] It should come as little surprise, then, that
in concluding the *Weekly Sun*'s front-page treatment of *Degeneration*

with an unqualified affirmation of the book's "healthy" masculinity, the author appears to capitalize on these connections by implicitly juxtaposing the latter to the diseased un-manliness so recently made evident (on other front pages) by Wilde:

> [I]t is a manly, healthy, and badly-needed protest against some of the inanities and—the word is not too strong—bestialities which raise their brazen and brutal heads in the literature of our time; and it is entitled, therefore, to the admiration of every honest, pure, and manly man.

With its emphatic reiteration and its unhesitating execration, this final passage explicitly interpellates the "manly man" by hailing him to condemn "the inanities and . . . bestialities which raise their brazen and brutal heads in the literature of our time." Since Wilde, who had frequently been criticized for his "inanities," was undoubtedly one of the most famous contemporary British litterateurs even before his trials, and since the imputation of "bestialities" to both his writing and his life had been the stuff of newspaper headlines for the three months preceding this review, there can be little doubt that the "literary" reference here is intended to signify Wilde as the object—or at least as one of the most recognizable objects—of the "manly, healthy, and badly-needed protest." In this context, the coincidence of the attributes "manly" and "healthy" as emphatically laudatory qualities serves to define the positive position from which Wilde and other men "like" him can be judged as falling away; thus it implicitly characterizes those who are the objects of this "badly-needed protest" as both less "healthy" and less "manly." Yet in unproblematically positing the "admiring" reader of Nordau's book as an "honest, pure, and manly man," the reviewer unwittingly introduces a gap between the qualifying adjectives and the noun they modify. Indeed, the insistent reiteration suggests that the former only correspond to the latter to the extent that the man in question concurs in abjuring the "inanities" and "bestialities" that Wilde and his literary cohort now come to signify. In other words, even though it produces a sententious crescendo designed to affirm the triumph of "pure" masculinity, the repetition at the heart of the review's concluding phrase (un)necessarily foregrounds the contingent correspondence between what it designates as an anatomically defined male sex and what it deems to be the proper forms of male gender. For in punctuating this review with what—in the rhetorics of Lacan and Derrida—we might call its *point de capiton*, the review's ultimate invocation calls forth the very problem it seeks to "fix": i.e., that men are not "naturally" "manly."

The coincidence that I have been briefly exploring here between the highly publicized conclusion of Wilde's legal ordeals and the *Weekly Sun*'s front-page review of Nordau's *Degeneration* suggests that by the end of the nineteenth century there existed a heightened public awareness of the potential disjunction between male sex and "manly" gender. Moreover, it indicates a desire on the part of many (would-be) "manly men" to "fix" this semantic/sexual discrepancy by differentiating themselves from those whom they perceived to be "like" Wilde. In rhetorically attempting to suture the attributes signified by the reiterative formulation "manly man" to the bodies of those men who would claim (or aspire) to possess such "manly" qualities as their own "property," the newspapers produced a way of stabilizing "proper" masculinity by defining it in opposition to another kind of masculinity which seemed to threaten it—if only by having different "properties." Nevertheless, the ambiguities contained in this oppositional construction of male "propriety" were not easily resolved, semantically or otherwise, since by the 1890s it proved impossible to sustain the unqualified affirmation of the "manly man" without simultaneously castigating those who had come to be defined as his "other(s)."[6] Indeed, it is precisely because such oppositional formulations of masculinity were so ubiquitous during the last half of the nineteenth century that it now becomes important to ask retrospectively: What exactly is meant by a "manly man" and (how) did such a man "essentially" differ from other kinds of men? What difference does "manly" make to "man" so as to modify his "nature" in a discernible way? And why is this reiteration, "manly man," deemed to stabilize what it concomitantly—if only covertly—demonstrates as the instabilities of "maleness"? These questions, in turn, underscore a corollary set of issues also at play in these (con)texts: i.e., why is a "manly man" believed to be "healthier" than one who is not? How can "manliness" both be and not be an attribute of male bodies? And what difference does "proper" masculinity make to the "healthy body" of the middle-class Englishman?

In seeking to elucidate the ways that male "propriety" emerges as a defining attribute of "healthy" middle-class masculinity in nineteenth-century England, these questions suggest that such an emergence must be seen within the constellation of national, class, generational, and gender practices that coalesced into an effective economic, political and sexual hegemony by the second half of the century.[7] To be sure, this hegemonic process unfolded across several hundred years and cannot be adequately subsumed under such rubrics as "the rise of the bourgeoisie," "the triumph of the British Empire," or "the consolidation of patriarchal capitalism." Nevertheless the lineaments of such large-scale transformations can be partially traced from the writings on and about the (male) body. For, as I will attempt to suggest in this book, it was by increasingly assigning qualitative attributes to somatic signifiers of difference that middle-class English men were able to produce and naturalize the multiple effects of privilege and authority that accrued to them throughout the course of the nineteenth century. Or, in other words, by taking the "properties" of what they designated as "the body" to be the "natural" ground of differences between individuals, middle-class English men were able to legitimate as "healthy" those practices through which they constituted and consolidated their positions as economic, political, and sexual subjects—over and against all "others."

Before beginning to unpack these rather abstract formulations, I want to call attention to an initial difficulty that should not be overlooked, since it underlies and sustains the very problem I seek to explore: i.e., the concept of the "middle-class Englishman." The issues here are in part empirical and in part epistemological. Demographically, it is difficult to say exactly who fell into the category of "middle-class men" during the Victorian period in England. Unlike the aristocracy and landed gentry, on the one hand, whose positionings were historically predicated on birth and inheritance, or agricultural laborers and the industrial working classes, on the other hand, whose social situations were largely determined by the material constraints circumscribing their lives, the definition of the middle-class(es) was often ambiguous.[8] If, as Raymond Williams has suggested, "the essential history of the introduction of class [in the eighteenth century], as a word which would supersede older names for social divisions, relates to the increasing consciousness that social position is made rather than merely inherited," then the relational designation "middle class" was necessarily marked by the instability of its historically fabricated boundaries.[9] Indeed, the "emergence" of the "English middle class" as a readily recognizable social and economic grouping over the course of the eighteenth and nineteenth centuries provides one of the best historical examples that—as Marcia Ian has recently noted—"the world is both made and made up."[10]

Without too much quibbling, however, we might say that the denizens of the Victorian middle class were those who had been able to advance themselves financially and socially in the accelerating, expanding, and industrializing British economy. Hence it included a wide array of individuals from merchant princes and entrepreneurial wizards, to an ever-growing number of professionals, bankers, bureaucrats, and civil servants, to local shopkeepers, artisans, teachers, clergy, and clerks, along with their families. The Victorian economist Leone Levi in his *Wages and Earnings of the Working Classes* (1884) characterized this range as extending from "mechanics and skilled artisans [who] are as far removed from common laborers and miners as clerks and curates are from those who have reached the highest places in the liberal professions or wealthy merchants or bankers, all of whom pass under the category of the middle classes."[11] Given this practice of specifying the contents contained within the "category" of the middle class(es) by listing occupational titles, it is not surprising that the category's definition crystallized primarily as the accretion of such designations. Indeed, the difficulties that this categorical proliferation presented for assessing the composition of the middle class(es) can be found in the very attempts that were made to take account of such definitions. For example, in considering how to enumerate the "professions"—which were after all a major means for consolidating class identity among bourgeois men throughout the nineteenth century— the 1841 census listed only the ancient professions: law, medicine, and the church. By 1861, schoolmasters, professors, civil engineers, actors, authors, journalists, and musicians were added to the ranks, and in 1881, architects, land agents, and surveyors made the list.[12] However, even as the number of occupational designations expanded to give some sense of the changing demographic contours, census data did not differentiate among the income and status levels within relatively broad categories (e.g., "persons engaged in numerous branches of manufacture") so that it proved (and still proves) impossible to specify exactly whom the Victorian middle class(es) consisted of.[13]

Moreover, even if one did manage to occupy a position that—in Levi's terms—"passed" as middle class, there was no guarantee that one would continue to occupy such a position throughout the course of one's life, let alone that one's children would throughout theirs. The fluctuating episodes of economic crisis and boom—occurring long before the cyclic characteristics of the capitalist economy had been charted—gave rise to a precarious instability of class definition that was endemic to the Victorian era: "For the world of the established bourgeoisie was considered to be basically insecure, a state of war in which they might at any moment become casualties of competition, fraud, or economic slump."[14] As the years of economic expansion (1851–53, 1856–57, 1863–65, 1871–73) alternated with years of economic contraction (1839–42, 1857–58, 1866–67, and the so called "Great Depression" of 1873–95) and "crisis" (1836, 1847, 1857, 1866, 1890), the susceptibility of the middle class(es) to rapid financial advances and reversals fostered an anxiety about social status that was thoroughly embedded in the social imaginary. As Walter Houghton has remarked:

> The major [middle-class] worry was "failure." In a period when hectic booms alternated with financial panics and there was no such thing as limited liability, the business magnates and the public investor were haunted by the specters of bankruptcy and the debtor's jail.[15]

While the impact of bankruptcy on the middle-class as a whole is hard to determine exactly, due to the limitations of contemporary statistical sources, the complexities of and changes in nineteenth-century bankruptcy laws, and the numerous cases of financial insolvency which fell outside the legal purview, nevertheless the realities of bankruptcy impinged on the middle class(es) both materially and symbolically. As Barbara Weiss has recently demonstrated, not only was bankrupty a constant political concern in Parliament where members sought to adjudicate responsibility for the casualties of the Victorian economy, but it was a ubiquitous theme in the cultural artifacts of the period. Indeed, bankrupty seems to have (re)presented in its very existence the contradictions which undermined the certainty of class stability:

> By its very nature, [bankruptcy] challenged the most cherished ideals of the period. The capitalist system was supposed to reward the virtuous, the prudent, the energetic, the thrifty; the prosperity of England was therefore proof of national righteousness. Widespread economic failure, on the other hand, was a reality which simply could not be ignored. Bankruptcy was a glaring defect in the otherwise gilded surface of Victorian prosperity, a defect that suggested the possibility of a void beneath, and the specter of this ugly reality seems to have haunted the Victorian imagination.[16]

As these examples suggest, the problem of determining who fell in or out of the category "middle class(es)"—either empirically or epistemologically—is complicated by the movements both within and across the concrete and conceptual divides which gave this category definition at any particular moment. Yet, in spite of all these variations and fluctuations, there appeared to be something that allowed the Victorian bourgeoisie to perceive its own unity as a class, or, at least, that allowed bourgeois individuals to imagine and thereby effectively orchestrate such a unity. In their book *Family Fortunes*, Lenore Davidoff and Catherine Hall elucidate this process of self constitution as it took place in the last decades of the eighteenth and first decades the

nineteenth centuries. While the engendering of bourgeois subjects is in
no way reducible to any one set of practices, Davidoff and Hall suggest
that the techniques for self-observation and self-control promulgated
by Protestant religions—especially those of the evangelical and dis-
senting varieties—provided the basis for "establishing the cultural
practices and institutions which were to become characteristic hallmarks of the middle classes." Indeed, they go on to claim, "it was
religious and moral practice which provided the basis for distinctive
middle-class demands for status and power."[17] Although similar characterizations of the social and economic effects produced by Protestant-
ism(s) have been popular at least since Weber, the specificity of Davidoff and Hall's conclusions derives from a comprehensive analysis
of the ways religious disciplines established techniques for self-awareness and personal transformation that simultaneously called upon individuals to intervene in and change the world. Thus, they provide an
explanation for Eric Hobsbawm's succinct observation that during the
nineteenth century the qualification "middle class" was predicated on
a way of living that stressed the significance of individual achievement
and superiority:

> [T]he main characteristic of the bourgeoisie as a class was that it
> was a body of persons of power and influence, independent of
> traditional birth and status. To belong to it a man had to be "some-
> one"; a person who counted *as an individual,* because of his wealth,
> his capacity to command other men or otherwise to influence them.[18]

There are several things to note about this statement. First, it articulates
class as a relation of power, so that the affirmative definition of those
in the middle class is predicated on the ability to effect the actions
of those "beneath" them. Second, it emphasizes the importance of
individual achievement so that the aggregation, "middle class," appears as an epiphenomenon of the independent actors who coalesce
(abstractly?) as "a body of persons." And third, it is unabashedly
gendered male.[19]

The appearance of what we commonly refer to as a "middle-class
man," then, is predicated on the overdetermined coincidence of these
attributes. It situates a male person in relation to other people (male
and female) as an agent who has power over their actions and who is,
moreover, positioned in relation to other such agents as an "equal"
only to the extent that he is another adult man. Articulated in this way
it becomes easier to understand that the (re)production of the middle-

class Englishman was a far from "natural" process. Indeed, the practices *both material and imaginary* through which the middle-class Englishman was born(e) into his nineteenthth-century economic and cultural contexts constitute a complex social technology which operates specifically here as what I will term a "mode of embodiment." Hence, in noting that what we colloquially designate by the "middle-class Englishman" is not only empirically indeterminate but epistemologically unstable, I wish to consider how this designation comes to be "fixed"—in the sense of being both pinned down and repaired—as it is embodied.

The historical "fiction" that Michel Foucault offers in the first volume of *The History of Sexuality* provides a starting point for my consideration.[20] In this seminal work, Foucault outlines his understanding of how the eighteenth- and nineteenthth-century bourgeoisie articulated its own self definition within a complex set of practices, institutions, and discourses through which it attached itself to its own ("proper") sexuality. Contrasting this emerging regime with the aristocracy, whose continuity had heretofore been guaranteed through systems of alliance that assured the transfer of property and position would follow along lines of "blood," Foucault argues that the "[middle] class must be seen rather as being occupied, from the mid-eighteenth century on, with creating its own sexuality and forming a specific body based on it, a 'class' body with its health, hygiene, descent and race. . . ."[21] In Foucault's narrative, the middle-class body becomes the site of a technological "implantation" through which "sexuality" was "included . . . in the body as a mode of specifying individuals."[22] "The notion of sex," he suggests, "made it possible to group together in an artificial unity, anatomical elements, biological functions, conducts, sensations and pleasures, and it enabled one to make sense of this fictitious unity as a causal principle, an omnipresent meaning, a secret to discover everywhere."[23] Yet, more than simply including sex "in" the body in order to discern the "truth" of the individual, sexuality also provided a means of constituting "the body" as the property of a class:

> [O]ne of [the bourgeoisie's] primary concerns was to provide itself with a body and a sexuality—to ensure the strength, endurance and secular proliferation of that body through the organization of a deployment of sexuality. This process, moreover, was linked to the movement by which it asserted its distinctiveness and its hegemony. There is little question that one of the primordial forms of class consciousness is the affirmation of the body. . . .[24]

In this historical context, Foucault sees the "affirmation of the body" as a "political ordering of life"[25] that both produces and orders the shifting articulations of power which become visible and intelligible, beginning in the eighteenth century, as the effects of "class." The idealized, "healthy" body, Foucault suggests, formed the basis for legitimating this constellation of social practices in so far as it "naturally" impressed the individual within social aggregations such as "population" and "the life of the species," which conversely made sense of—and indeed created the sense of—a social whole.[26] Hence, the affirmation of the middle-class body served to progressively link an affirmation of (species) life to a specific, political investment in life, an investment that concomitantly legitimated the continued (re)production of bourgeois Europeans' privilege by casting it as a result of the "healthier" body. It is this affirmative principle that Foucault characterizes as "dynamic racism," depicting it as the "bud" that would bear the strange fruits of nineteenth-century imperialism.[27]

In trying to come to terms with Foucault's persuasive "fiction," however, we should be careful not to read this political "dynamic" too one-dimensionally: as if we believed that the middle class through some act of seizure claimed "the body" as its own, wresting "it" away from those who had previously held "it" in thrall, only to colonize "it" in turn. Rather we must understand that what we (perhaps too unproblematically) continue to designate as "the body" is itself an effect, produced within the same historical constellations that engender those "differences" that we politically apprehend as attributes of "it" (e.g., class, gender, race, nationality, or age).[28] While Foucault is not centrally concerned with investigating how the (re)production of social differences simultaneously gives rise to modes of embodiment that serve as both their ground and their guarantee, his analysis nevertheless leads us to explore this process: "It [the middle class] provided itself with a body to be cared for, protected, cultivated, and preserved from many dangers and contacts, to be isolated from others so that it would retain its differential value. . . ."[29] If the (re)production of "the body" as a repository for "differential value" seems central to the English bourgeoisie's self-affirmations as a class, though, this is not only because "it" provided the space for implanting technologies that generated the predominant social, political, and economic orderings of life. Instead the production of a "differential" (class) body was also necessary precisely because the members of the middle class legitimated their claims to social, political, and economic subjectivity based on their embodiments of these technologies. It was as the site upon which—or "within" which—these various practices coincided that "the body"

The body defined individuality [handwritten]

took on its significance as the locus for defining the "individuality" of Victorian, middle-class Englishmen.

To some extent, the very possibility of perceiving social, political, economic, or sexual distinctions between "individuals" as embodied attributes calls upon an earlier conceptual tradition that sought to delimit the purviews of religious and state power by imagining the individual as the site of what we might now call a (presocial) "self." As Charles Taylor explains, starting in the seventeenth century there emerged new ways of imagining, and hence positioning, individuals within collective formations which for the first time in modern European history were not predicated upon the assumption of prior social or spiritual connections:

> Previously that people were members of a community went without saying. It didn't need to be justified relative to a more basic situation. But now the theory starts from the individual on his own. Membership of a community with common power of decision is now something which needs to be explained by an individual's prior consent. . . . [W]hat cannot now be taken for granted anymore is a community with decisional powers over its members. People start off as political atoms.[30]

Moreover, from the mid-seventeenth century onward, British political philosophers relied upon what they designated as "the body" to ground such notions of individual autonomy and subjectivity. Indeed, as this body came to define the accepted social perimeter of the self, it simultaneously served to delimit the contact zone between the individual and the collective. Thus, as what were perceived to be properties of the body came to be understood as properties of the individual, the former were attributed to the latter as a "natural" consequence and were understood to precede—or indeed to precondition—all social influences. In taking the body to be the "natural" location of the autonomous self, then, these philosophical arguments provided the conceptual basis for what we have come to deem the "individualism" of eighteenth- and nineteenth-century British bourgeois culture.

self and other. [handwritten]

In part, this way of understanding the individual can be traced back to the writings of Thomas Hobbes, which were occasioned by the English civil wars. In his widely disseminated texts, Hobbes predicated his theories of political subjectivity on a "materialist" analysis of not only the (human) body but all physical bodies—the most complex being the "artificial" body called the state or society. Hence his attempts to define the principles from which human aggregations can be organized and ordered into functioning systems depends upon an assessment of the "natural" conditions that ensue from human embodiment. As George Sabine indicates in his now-canonical interpretation of Hobbes: "The rule behind all behavior is that the living body is set instinctively to preserve or heighten its vitality. In a word, the physiological principle behind all behavior is self-preservation, and self-preservation means just the continuance of individual biological existence."[31] Hobbes's evaluation of human behavior, it seems, reads back into "the living body" those qualities that are assumed to ensure its integrity as the locus of individual life. In this system of thought, the body is defined as the individual's ultimate temporal and spatial limit so that human existence appears to cohere through—and against—an unceasing attempt to forestall the inevitable end of biological-as-bodily life. Therefore, the singularity of the embodied individual in the face of his or her own (potential) death becomes the basis upon which all collective undertakings are to be imagined and from which notions of individual agency are derived.[32]

A little more than forty years after Hobbes, John Locke developed the implications underlying such a somatically defined individualism into a political philosophy that had far-reaching consequences in England for the production of "liberal" theories about human subjectivity over the next two hundred years. Writing amid the developing Enlightenment challenges to earlier ecclesiastically derived political paradigms, Locke rejected theological explanations which interpreted human "differences" (both inter- and intra-species) as epiphenomena of "soul." Instead, he adopted a term, "identity," that had previously been used in algebra and logic to characterize the now problematic distinction/relation between "body" and "mind."[33] In this context, "identity" provided an effective way of understanding the sameness of what was concomitantly being construed as "difference" (body/mind) precisely because it mobilized the idealizing effects derived from earlier philosophical and mathematical (con)texts. Moreover, the idealization worked simultaneously in two directions so that, just as "mind" came to signify the transcendental qualities of reason that enabled this self-reflexive undertaking (most infamously illustrated by Descartes' *cogito*), "body" served to naturalize the essential and autonomous unity of the thinking being: "it is not the idea of a thinking or rational being alone that makes the idea of a man in most people's sense, but of a body, so and so shaped, joined to it. ..."[34] Hence Locke's famous explanation in his *Essay Concerning Human Understanding* (1690) predicates "identity" as an enduring quality of the person on the enduring sameness of "the body":

Identity of the same Man consists . . . in nothing but a participation of the same continued Life, by constantly fleeting Particles of Matter, in succession vitally united to the same organized Body. He that shall place the identity of man in anything else, but like that of other animals, in one fitly organized body, taken in any one instant, and from thence continued, under one organization of life, in several successively fleeting particles of matter united to it, will find it hard to make an embryo, one of years, mad and sober, the same man, by any supposition, that will not make it possible for Seth, Ismael, Socrates, Pilate, St. Austin, and Caesar Borgia to be the same man.[35]

As Locke's definition suggests, "identity" evokes the "sameness" of human differentiation *across time* by collapsing the processes of (self-)/transformation *through time* into an unchanging and highly idealized notion, "the same organized Body." This dehistoricizing gesture correspondingly organizes a matrix of intelligibility and visibility that produces the idealized body as both the ground and the guarantee for making qualitative distinctions between human beings. The knowledge effects produced by this somatic idealization support the more wide-reaching—and perhaps historically significant—inference that if one's "identity" presupposes the "sameness" of one's somatic differentiation, then conversely one's somatic difference(s) must "naturally" define the "sameness" of one's "identity."

The political implications engendered by this conceptual elision between body and self became crucial in the late-eighteenth and early-nineteenth centuries as social thinkers sought both to make and to make sense of the cultural and economic changes that attended the consolidation of industrial capitalism in England. For, as C. B. Macpherson illustrates in his now-classic analysis, much of the political theorizing developed after the seventeenth century by thinkers like Smith, Malthus, Ricardo, Bentham, Mill, and others, was predicated on a set of fundamental assumptions about the disposition of bodies as they mark out the locus of the self. In Macpherson's famous formulation, this trajectory within Western political discourse gives rise to what he calls "possessive individualism," a mode of social (re)production in which (male) individuals are perceived as proprietors of their fleshly incarnations who achieve integrity primarily as the "owners" of themselves:

[S]eventeenth-century individualism contained [a] central difficulty which lay in its possessive quality. Its possessive quality is found in the conception of the individual as essentially the proprietor of his own person or capacities, owing nothing to society for them. The

individual was seen neither as a moral whole, nor as a part of a
larger social whole, but as owner of himself. The relation of owner-
ship, having become for more and more men the critically important
relation determining their actual freedom and actual prospect of
realizing their full potentialities, was read back into the nature of
the individual.[36]

While Macpherson himself focuses upon the utility which this "proprietary" formulation has had for the social legitimation (or "naturalization") of bourgeois political economy, his insights also suggest some
important corollaries. If "individuals"—or as his text literally and
perhaps intentionally indicates—if *men* are imagined as existing in
an essentially proprietary relation to themselves, they are constituted
simultaneously as possessors and possessions of themselves, thereby
reproducing the isomorphic dissection of mind/body that the concept
of "identity" seeks to reconcile. This dichotomous positioning then
organizes an economy in which and through which the bourgeois
(male) individual comes to understand his "identity" as what is
"proper" to him, i.e., his possessive relation to himself. Yet since what
is specifically designated as "property" in this relation is the body and
its labor (Locke writes: "Every Man has a *Property* in his own Person.
This no body has any Right to but himself. The *Labour* of his Body,
and the *Work* of his Hands, we may say are properly his."),[37] somatic
materiality implicitly becomes the unchanging ground upon which
(male) identity can be both erected and possessed.[38] In this process of
self-construction, then, the slippage between bodies as property and
the properties of bodies comes to overdetermine what Macpherson
felicitously terms "the nature of the individual." Thus, as the body
comes to define the proper locus of human individuation and (male)
individuality, its somatic properties are increasingly utilized in order
to legitimate the interpretation of social and sexual differences as
"natural."

While it is far beyond the scope of this discussion to elaborate fully
the consequences that such somatically defined individualism had for
the development of Victorian middle-class life, or even of middle-
class masculinity, let me very briefly consider how it was famously—if
pessimistically—elaborated by Thomas Malthus in order to adumbrate
the ways the (male) body becomes the locus for the production of a
class-specific mode of embodiment. Written precisely at the cusp of the
eighteenth and nineteenth centuries[39] and drawing upon theoretical
insights derived from both Hobbes and Locke, Malthus's renowned
Essay on the Principle of Population crystallized contemporary ways

of imagining the human body and inscribed them within a social theory that envisioned this body as a critical nexus for the nation.[40] In fact, Malthus's text was so successful at disseminating this political inscription of the body that his conceptual crystallization prevailed both politically and epistemologically throughout the next fifty years,[41] whereupon it was taken up and transformed by Darwin's version which prevailed for at least the next fifty.[42] The first edition of the *Essay*, appearing in 1798, developed Malthus's remarkably dismal premise that if otherwise "unchecked" by "misery and vice," the "fixed laws of our nature"—which demanded both the nourishment of food and the gratification of sex—would produce a national population that would outstrip the national means of subsistence.[43] Yet, according to Malthus, the "wants of the body" are also the "stimulants" that spur "the brain of infant man into sentient activity" so that they necessarily underlie all forms of social productivity.[44] This formulation, as Catherine Gallagher has aptly noted, simultaneously positions the body as absolutely central to and absolutely problematic for the social formation.[45] In other words, the body with its need for daily nutriment and its "necessity" for "passion between the sexes," becomes the crux of an analysis that seeks to explain why the (bodily) capacity for economic and biological (re)production can simultaneously give rise to abject poverty and starvation. However, the analysis works only by attributing this paradox to the "laws of nature" inhering in human bodies themselves. Thus, Malthus imagines "the body" at and as the intersection of economic and biological processes, thereby fleshing out earlier proprietary notions of the body as "property" and conversely grounding social distinctions within a somaticized "natural history." Indeed, he provides a consummate example of Foucault's observation that:

> In the eighteenth century, the development of demography, of urban structures, of the problem of industrial labor, had raised in biological and medical terms the question of human "populations," with their conditions of existence, of habitation, of nutrition, with their birth and mortality rate, with their pathological phenomena (epidemics, endemic diseases, infant mortality). [Thus] the social "body" ceased to be simply a juridico-political metaphor (like the one in Leviathan) and became a biological reality. . . .[46]

By drawing together these eighteenth-century "developments" into a coherent and persuasive explanation for social problems like poverty, malnutrition, disease, and unemployment, Malthus's work therefore establishes the body as a nexus that both naturalizes the unequal distribution of resources within the nation and articulates individual difference(s) as a function of biological processes.

Recognizing that "it is undoubtedly a most disheartening reflection that the great obstacle in the way to any extraordinary improvement in society is of a nature we can never hope to overcome,"[47] Malthus devotes the concluding chapters of the *Essay*'s first edition to reconciling his bleak "naturalism" with the beneficence of "the Diety." Hence he argues that "evil exists in the world not to create despair but activity" and so derives all "higher" virtues and achievements from physical abjection.[48] Significantly, however, when Malthus rewrote the *Essay* for the second edition (upon which all subsequent editions were based) in 1803, he dropped both this argument and these chapters entirely. Instead he sought to allow for the evasion of his somatic paradox that (individual) life breeds (collective) death by introducing what he believed to be another way out: "moral restraint." Adding an entire book devoted to exploring the implications of this "virtuous" check on population, the *Essay*'s second edition offers a completely different concluding vision than the first: instead of impending mass death through starvation and disease, Malthus now envisions the transvaluation of (lower-class) bodies through personal discipline. As Gertrude Himmelfarb succinctly notes: "The de-naturalization or socialization of the lower classes [in the revised editions of Malthus's *Essay*] was [to be] the first step in their *embourgeoisement*, their initiation into the middle classes."[49] Indeed, the entire principle of "moral restraint," which Malthus summarily defines as "the abstaining from marriage til . . . in a condition to support a family, with a perfectly moral conduct during that period," is predicated on a somatic technology specifically designed to produce middle-class men.[50] In a chapter succinctly entitled "Of the Only Effectual Mode of Improving the Condition of the Poor," Malthus opines:

> The happiness of the whole is to be the result of the happiness of individuals, and to begin with them first. No cooperation is required. Every step tells. He who performs his duty faithfully will reap the fruits of it, whatever may be the number of others who fail. This duty is intelligible to the humblest capacity. It is merely that he is not to bring beings into the world for whom he cannot find the means of support. When once this subject is cleared from the obscurity thrown over it by parochial laws and private benevolence, every man must feel the strongest conviction of such an obligation. If he cannot support his children they must starve; and if he marry in the face of a fair probability that he shall not be able to support his children, he is guilty of all the evils which he thus brings upon

himself, his wife, and his offspring. It is clearly in his interest, and will tend greatly to promote his happiness, to defer marrying til by industry and economy he is in a capacity to support the children he may reasonably expect from his marriage. . . .[51]

According to Malthus's revised perspective, then, the only possibility for averting the poverty, destitution, and death necessitated by the body's (re)productive capacities requires men to learn to control their bodies so that they mitigate one of the "fixed laws of our nature," i.e., "the impulses of our passions." In other words, what Malthus proposes as the only way to forestall the (national) calamities brought on by what he deems to be the biological requirements of the human body is to engender a particular mode of embodiment in which men "rationally" organize their somatic processes so that they refrain from "bring[ing] beings into the world for whom [they] cannot find the means of support." Indeed, Malthus goes so far as to suggest:

> if the true and permanent cause of poverty were clearly and forcibly brought home to each man's bosom, it would have some influence on his conduct. . . . In searching for objects of accusation, [however] he never adverts to the quarter from which his misfortunes originate. The last person that he would think of accusing is himself, on whom in fact the principal blame lies. . . .[52]

Here Malthus elides his famous contention that the causes of poverty are biologically induced with his understanding that a man's body and its "products" are his property and therefore his responsibility. Hence Malthus's suggestion that the individual man both deserves the "principal blame" and serves as the "true and permanent cause" of poverty derives not from any moral culpability or incapacity (as will be claimed somewhat later in the century), but rather from the failure to comprehend the economic consequences of his biological ability to (re)produce. In proffering "moral restraint" as a "mode of improving the condition of the poor," then, Malthus avers that the coincidence of individual and social "happiness" depends upon creating a way of disposing the male body so that its biological/sexual capabilities (and requirements) are aligned with the socially designated (gender) functions of an adult, middle-class man: income generator, husband, progenitor, patriarch, etc. Since this formulation attempts to resolve the contradictions raised by situating the (biological) body at the center of the social formation, it obviously foregrounds the imbrication of biological and economic practices; more significantly, however, it does so only by proposing that the proper disposition of male bodies will subsume the former within the latter. It is this imbricated relationship of social and somatic masculinity that will come to define the identity— if not the "normality"—of the Victorian middle-class Englishman.

While much recent (feminist) historiography has attended to how the meanings attributed to women's bodies served to (re)produce (middle-class) male dominance in nineteenth-century Britain, there has been less focus on the ways male bodies (re)produced significance and power in the period. In part, this absence can be attributed to the fact that while women's bodies were often clearly marked as "problematic" (for men?), thereby becoming the subjects of inquiries, observations, speculations, coercion, or violence, adult men's bodies were often taken to be the unmarked sites of political, economic, and sexual subjectivity. Indeed, it was precisely this somatic elision that came to define the locus of middle-class masculinity: "The . . . early nineteenth-century concept of 'manhood' had political as much as sexual connotations. Manhood was to become a central part of claims to legitimate middle-class leadership."[53] Yet the significance of "manhood" as a political and sexual category was linked not merely to anatomical distinctions, but rather to the ways these distinctions achieved biological, economic, and social significance. As Davidoff and Hall remark, "[middle-class men's] identity depended upon their ability to operate as economic agents. To become adult men within their own terms they must provide a livelihood which made possible a domestic establishment where they and their dependants could live a rational and morally sanctioned life."[54] This definition of adult, middle-class, male "identity," much like Malthus's admonition to men quoted above, indicates that even though the (re)productive capacities of men's bodies did not engender the same kind of discursive avalanche throughout the nineteenth century as women's bodies did, they were nevertheless thoroughly "problematic." For a middle class Englishman's process of maturation depended upon his embodying a disposition that would ensure that he was both productive and reproductive—and that the former preceded the latter. Predicated on this mode of embodiment, he could assume his privilege as a political, economic and sexual subject.

The writings of Isaac Taylor in the first decades of the nineteenth century provide one example of how this somaticized version of bourgeois masculinity was disseminated. Author of such popular texts as *Self Cultivation Recommended; or, Hints to a Youth Leaving School* (1817), *Advice to Teens; or, Practical Help Towards the Formation of One's Own Character* (1818), and *Character Essential to Success in Life Addressed to those Approaching Manhood* (1820), Taylor assiduously sought to articulate a methodology that would ensure that young middle-class men safely negotiated the passage into an adulthood befitting their "station." Hence, his copious—if somewhat repetitive and banal—advice consisted primarily of ceaselessly admonishing his putatively youthful readers to "make something" of themselves lest they fall into idleness and waste. Troping relentlessly on the horticultural implications of "cultivation," Taylor attempted to define the developmental principles by which pliant and capricious adolescent males could be shaped into sturdy and reliable adult men. For Taylor, the key to this successful transformation lay in teaching the young man to "regulate [his] conduct" in order to bring his body and his will into alignment with his "duty."

> His very nature demands of him this care and cultivation. In vain are admirable powers given to him if he will not use them; in vain is he raised far above the brute, if he continues prone, and will not seek after more than they do. Why has he firm limbs, if he will not stand? If he will not teach his right hand her [sic] proper cunning, it is given to him in vain. Why has he powers of understanding, of reasoning, if he will not think? Capacities are wasted on him, if he will not store them well; and keep them in continual and useful employ.[55]

Here Taylor deploys the metaphors of husbandry to emphasize the technical aspects of male self-(re)production. Like the empty field or the undomesticated animal, the potential inhering in a young male's "nature" "demands" the application of his labor. Indeed, it is precisely this "continual and useful employ[ment]" that transforms the adolescent's male body (i.e., his "nature") into a man's—not a "brute's"—and simultaneously defines the mode of embodiment "proper" to his class position. As a "minister of the gospel," Taylor gives voice to concerns that typify the Protestant articulations of middle-class masculinity in the period; hence his understanding of "self-cultivation" foregrounds the coincidence of Christian and class expectations as essential to the fulfillment of the adult man:

> [R]egular habits and principles will give greater facility of action; will attain the result more expeditiously; and give to the whole character something more of manliness, than can be hoped for without such aid. The very name of acting upon [this] principle, will possess the minds of observers, and make them hope well of a person rising to eminence, by steps so firm, so legitimate, so successful.[56]

The supplemental "manliness" engendered by the application of "regular habits and principles" augments the young man's "natural" maleness so that it is transformed into something else: the ground for eminence, legitimacy, and success. These qualities, which define the apotheosis of bourgeois masculinity, consequently appear to derive from a process of self-regulation that engenders a mode of embodiment *distinctly recognizable* to those who can further the young man's career. For, it is only by visibly bodying forth these standards for middle-class propriety, Taylor implies, that the middle class male is positioned to accumulate the property that will ensure his standing as a bourgeois Englishman.

While this circular process of self-(re)production was increasingly embedded in the representations that defined middle-class standards for male behavior throughout the first half of the century, it had not yet taken on the full somatic salience it was soon to incarnate. Indeed, until the middle third of the century, the concepts of "self-cultivation," "self-governance," or "self-control" largely signified practices of supplementation through which biological masculinity could be qualified or channeled into forms appropriate to—or indeed, necessary for—the emerging designations of class. However, by the 1840s and 1850s, this somatic supplementarity was elided with the somatic itself, engendering the body as the (symbolic) origin of, if not the source for, class distinctions. Once the qualities deemed necessary to the articulations of social difference(s) were attributed to the body rather than being understood to be (re)produced within it, they appeared to emanate "naturally" from those who exhibited them. In order to elucidate this historical imbrication of the somatic and the social, the next chapter will consider how the slippage between them functioned to inscribe the values of middle-class masculinity onto and into the bodies of adolescent males by focusing on the discourses and practices that perhaps most materially affected the young man's relation to himself: those concerning the prevention and treatment of masturbation.

2

TAKING SEX IN HAND
Inscribing Masturbation and the
Construction of Normative Masculinity

> The duty of work is written on the thews and muscles of the limbs,
> the mechanism of the hand, the nerves and lobes of the brain—the
> sum of whose healthy action is satisfaction and enjoyment.
> Samuel Smiles, *Self Help*

The proliferation of texts written about masturbation in nineteenth-century Britain is truly remarkable, even for a culture dedicated—as Michel Foucault has suggested—to putting sexuality into discourse. Perhaps the most amazing fact about the writings on masturbation is that they did not just emanate from one or two institutional contexts, but were produced in incredible quantities by and for doctors, educators, evangelists, mothers, fathers, adolescents, military officers, quacks, and alienists alike. Similarly, they appeared in a wide variety of forms: books, pamphlets, religious tracts, medical articles, newspaper advertisements, self-help literature, stories, cartoons, and jingles. "Self-abuse," "onanism," "the secret vice," "schoolboy immorality," or, as the subtitle of one tract comprehensively described it, "the Vice of Boyhood, the Blight of Youth, the Curse of Men, the Wreck of Manhood, and the Bane of Posterity"[1]: these names sketch out one of the primary categories through which the middle-class males of nineteenth-century England would come to understand and explain, both for themselves and for others, the condition of their embodiment.

From the late eighteenth century onward, the increasing circulation of texts about masturbation guaranteed that, once they reached puberty (if not even before), middle-class male bodies would be continually subjected to a wide array of institutional gazes that sought to give precise (sexual) meanings to their minute behavioral patterns. These probing speculations assiduously sought to detect, evaluate, and root

35

out those particular deviations from "healthy," continent, a.k.a. "Christian" standards that signified the lurking presence of the youthful masturbator—that is, to those who knew how to look for him. But of course it was precisely the massive literature about masturbation that was supposed to ensure such knowledge became common. Conversely, it was the ubiquitous (and most certainly unstoppable) potential for adolescent masturbation that became one of the specific catalysts for the growing interpenetration of institutional practices directed toward inscribing social values onto/into male bodies. As doctors, teachers, clergymen, and parents strove to further each other's efforts to regulate the ways in which the young middle-class male shaped his embodiment and made it meaningful, there developed an increasingly intricate web of supports between these authorities aimed at circumventing the "solitary offender" through combinations of moral suasion, physical coercion, religious judgment, and personal fear. Indeed, by weaving an ideological web of medical, pedagogical, religious, and familial practices around the adolescent male body, nineteenth-century British bourgeois culture transformed the ubiquitous potential for male autoeroticism into a set of physiological, psychological, and moral symptoms that revealed the execrable existence of "the masturbator." Moreover, this new pathological definition not only (re)produced a kind of male youth whose "self-abuse" legitimated the watchful gazes of those who devoted themselves to his governance, but it also inscribed the "material" experiences of all middle-class male children within a mode of embodiment that earnestly sought to transform their relationships to themselves. For whatever other effects it may have been been intended to foster in postpubescent English males, the discursive construction of "the masturbator" imbricated both their (material) bodies and their material (class) culture in order to shape them into future middle-class Englishmen.

The story of the masturbator begins, necessarily, with his family, since this is the location where he is born(e) into his body and his culture. If, as Mark Poster succinctly characterizes it, "the family is the social space where generations confront each other directly and where two sexes define their differences and power relations,"[2] then the middle-class Victorian family in particular was a highly charged nexus of definition and differentiation both between/across generations and between/across sexes. Indeed the nineteenth-century bourgeois family is memorable for establishing new standards both for women ("the housewife") and for children ("the adolescent") that were distinct enactments of their class practices.[3] For the Victorian middle class(es), the family served symbolically and psychologically as a necessary compliment to—even though it was usually represented as the antithesis of—the evolving relations of production that characterized the fluctuating if ultimately expanding economy of nineteenth-century England. As bourgeois women withdrew from the "public sphere" of the workplace into the "private sphere" of the middle-class home, thereby specifying their difference from working-class women, and just as pointedly, indicating their husbands' distance from working-class men, women's domestic roles took on increasing importance as articulations of class and gender.[4] Similarly, the role of children in the middle-class family underwent significant redefinition during the late eighteenth and early nineteenth centuries as they ceased to be expected to contribute to the household's economic productivity and came to be increasingly valued as signifiers of social status and class perpetuation.[5] These restructured familial dynamics became the hallmarks of the middle class(es) throughout the nineteenth century so that the domestic de(em)ployment of women and children functioned both ideologically and materially—almost as much as economic resources did—to evoke the designation "middle class." Of course, these are in no way independent factors: the ability of a woman to hire servants or to decide how many servants to hire and the ability of a male child to be educated outside the home relied entirely on the income level of the family, as the large body of contemporary literature on budgeting for a middle-class life style testifies.[6] However, the cultural significance of these practices as indices of class position was determinant above and beyond mere income levels.[7]

In particular, as the economic importance of a male offspring's contributions to family income declined, his symbolic importance increased—both as a potential heir, who by his very existence justified and inspired his father's desire for increasing capital accumulation, and as a future standard-bearer of class privilege, whose formative identity underwrote the development of bourgeois political and cultural practices.[8] This new significance was most directly expressed in the emerging stress on economic expenditure for, or quite literally "investment in," institutionally organized, secondary education for middle-class male children. Indeed, by the second quarter of the nineteenth century secondary education for boys outside the home itself became metonymically known as "middle-class education."[9] The origins of this practice within the middle class(es) can be charted across the first decades of the 1800s when the bourgeois educational norm moved away from a late-eighteenth century ideal of "domestic education" as propounded in the pedagogical writings of such influential figures as Rousseau, Locke, and the Edgewares. During the first third of the new century, this earlier standard for education, which prescribed that children (potentially of both sexes) be taught in the home, preferably by parents themselves if possible, or by a hired tutor if not, was increasingly abjured in favor of one in which sons were "schooled" outside the family residence. As educational historian F. Musgrove has suggested, this "public" method of education superseded the earlier "private" practice because the latter, which had been appropriate for the more stable social configurations of the eighteenth century in which "middle-class families were not, in general, seeking for their sons a way of life and occupation different from their fathers'," could not (re)produce the upward mobility expected of the British bourgeois male in the nineteenth century.[10]

Not surprisingly, then, the new educational demands of the middle-class(es) soon gave rise to significant changes in the character of "public schooling" which had heretofore been oriented primarily toward educating the male children of aristocratic and landed families. By the 1830s, for example, there ensued major renovations in the pedagogical practices at the nine "great schools" that had historically served Britain's elite, a process most notably exemplified by Thomas Arnold's famous revamping of Rugby. Indeed, this particular institutional transformation was subsequently to become even more significant when Thomas Hughes retrospectively immortalized it in his classic boys' novel, *Tom Brown's School Days* (1857), which remained a popular seller throughout the rest of the century. As Hughes portrays this restructuring—in his unabashedly didactic prose—it sought to redress the excessive behaviors that had been cultivated by the ruling classes throughout the eighteenth century and to instill instead standards for male propriety that would inculcate techniques of self-governance and self-control.[11] Coincident with these changes in long-established educational practices, there emerged almost simultaneously a new and competing type of institution, the "proprietary school," whose founding capital was raised by the purchase of shares entitling the bearer to nominate one boy (usually a son) to the school. By and large these institutions modeled themselves on—and indeed strove to be assimilated into—the ranks of "public schools"; yet they also put (market) pressure on the older schools to conform to the new demands for a pedagogy that would satisfy the large numbers of middle-class boys.[12] The first of these changes, then, saw the reorganization of those ancient educational bastions of the upper class, which in contemporary opinion had become come "hotbeds of vice," into more disciplined, moral, Christian, and ultimately middle-class environments. The second provided vastly increased opportunity for middle-class offspring to partake of such elevating pedagogical experiences, and challenged the established schools to address this newly expanded market.[13] Together these educational developments redefined the experience of middle-class adolescents, such that "public schooling" became a vital aspect in the transformation from the limitations of childhood to the privileged position of a mature bourgeois male.

In *Tom Brown's Universe*, J. R. de S. Honey argues persuasively that the reason public and certain exclusive proprietary schools were so successful in facilitating this transvaluation of middle-class English boys into middle-class Englishmen was that they established a lasting sense of community both symbolically (through shared ritual and experience) and institutionally (through the development of "Old Boys" networks). Yet while such educational practices undoubtedly engendered recognizable social commonalties, there was also underlying this sense of "community" an evolving perception of "manliness" whose embodiment engendered norms for adult male behavior. For in many respects, the inculcation of standards for male behavior became the primary pedagogical project of the middle class. Certainly it was materially inscribed in both the old ("public") and the new ("proprietary") schools, where boys were educated in exclusively male institutions whose same-sex environments were explicitly designed to mold them into men—even as the mold itself was changing. During the third and fourth decades of the century, the masculine educational standard (as put forth most eloquently by Dr. Arnold's example) was a Christian ideal "of openness and transparent honesty as opposed to the baser elements suggested by such words as subtlety, refinement, luxury or ostentation."[14] This model stressed moral and intellectual strengths as the criteria by which boys attained a mature masculine identity, while simultaneously disassociating itself from the more boisterous attributes most often associated with the "manliness" of the 18th-century aristocracy (e.g., hunting, riding, drinking, and "wenching").[15] However, by mid-century, these "high-minded" moralizing criteria began to be supplemented by more "muscular" ones as Charles Kingsley's "muscular Christian" became a popular paradigm for the educated middle-class male.[16]

Kingsley's ideal was one that saw healthy minds as products of healthy bodies—*mens sana in corpore sano*. The establishment of this right relationship of body and mind in young boys would, in his opinion, result in healthy, "manly" men. However, Kingsley's concept of "manliness" no longer conveyed simply the sense of "the fulfillment of one's potentialities in the living of a higher, better and more useful life" but was defined (in opposition to "effeminacy") as embodying "robust energy, spirited courage, and physical vitality."[17] In short, Kingsley's "manly" ideal was the embodied apotheosis of industriousness and (re)productivity that defined the perfect bourgeois male. Kingsley makes this distinction explicit in his later essay "The Science of Health" (1879) where he constructs responses to the remarks of a fictional interlocutor in order to contrast his somatized philosophy with the earlier moralizing—mentally identified—masculine ideology. This fictional exchange so clearly exemplifies Kingsley's concept of "manliness," especially as it was taken up throughout the rest of the century, that it is worth quoting here at length:

> There may be those who would answer—or rather, there would certainly have been those who would have so answered thirty years ago, before the so-called materialism of advanced science had taught us some practical wisdom about education, and reminded people that they have bodies as well as minds and souls—"You say, we are likely to grow weaklier, unhealthier. And if it were so, what matter? Mind makes the man, not body. We do not want our children to be stupid giants and bravos; but clever, able, highly educated, however weakly Providence or the laws of nature may have chosen to make them. Let them overstrain their brains a little; let them contract their chests, and injure their digestion and eyesight, by sitting at desks, poring over books. Intellect is what we want. Intellect makes money. Intellect makes the world. We would rather see our son a genius than an athlete." Well: and so would I. But what if intellect alone does not even make money ... unless it is backed by an able, enduring, healthy physique, such as I have seen, almost without exception in those successful men of business whom I have had the honor and pleasure of knowing? What if intellect, or what is called intellect, did not make the world, or the smallest wheel or cog of it? What if, for want of obeying the laws of nature, parents bred up neither a genius nor an athlete, but only an incapable unhappy personage, with a huge upright forehead, like that of a Byzantine Greek, filled with some sort of pap instead of brains, and tempted alternately to fanaticism and strong drink? We must, in the great majority of cases have the corpus sanem if we want the mentum santum; and healthy bodies are the only trustworthy organs for healthy minds. (*Health and Education* 16–17)

This rhetorical exchange between "mental" and "muscular" ideals underscores the subtending interest that unites them: both Kingsley's parodic voice and his narrative persona agree that the essential (male) goal is making money. What they disagree about is how this goal is best achieved. Kingsley's emphatic identification with "successful businessmen" allows him to suggest that those who deny his physicalist masculine ideal in favor of a more mental standard are unproductive, if not counterproductive. He associates the cranial development of the unhappy male offspring—here denied even the label of masculinity and referred to instead only as a neuter "personage"—of such a misguided parent with that of a "Byzantine Greek" suggesting through this phrenological metaphor that this child's growth into "unnatural" ("for want of obeying the laws of nature") manhood will lead to the fall of the British empire just as it has caused the downfall of the great empires of the past—a suggestion he underscores by concluding the same paragraph with a reference to the "physical degradation in Imperial Rome, in Alexandria, in Byzantium." Thus, Kingsley's elaboration of "muscular" masculinity as the norm for middle-class male development situates this standard not only in relation to the economic interests of class, but also ideologically identifies these interests with those of nation and empire.[18]

Yet, while Kingsley's articulation of this ideology was undoubtedly influential in generating new representations of male norms, it was not merely this discursive elaboration that lead to the shift in popular middle-class conceptions of "manliness." Perhaps just as significant was the introduction during the 1850s of two decisively new pedagogical techniques designed to discipline the bodies and minds of adolescent males: the examination and organized athletics. Together, these new educational practices reshaped the public schools and their newly founded competitors (for sporting trophies as well as for admissions to the universities, the military and the civil service) into factories for the production of middle-class men. From mid-century onward, young middle-class males were subject to a wide range of classificatory, disciplinary, and competitive activities both in the schoolroom and on the playing fields designed to transform them from offspring who were symbolically valued for their masculine potential into economically and sexually (re)productive men who would perpetuate the middle class.

The widespread adoption of the examination in secondary education during the 1850s and 1860s reflected shifts in the institutional structures into which boys passed after the completion of their schooling. At this time, Oxford and Cambridge placed new significance upon examinations as criteria both for admission and for graduation. Similarly, the army and the civil service began to move away from older systems of commission purchases and patronage, to a more "meritocratic" system dictated by exam results.[19] As the examination penetrated the fields of professional employment most readily accessible to a young bourgeois male (e.g., teaching, the clergy, medicine, the military, public administration), they necessarily took on an expanded role in the schools whose ostensible mission was to prepare him for such employment. However, the introduction of compulsory examination as a periodic assessment of educational "success" also carried with it the additional function of "normalizing" the examined student by critically positioning him in relation to an institutional standard, to other students, and to his "class" as a whole.[20]

The coincidence between the introduction of organized sports into secondary education and the dissemination of the examination further reinforced the disciplinary regime to which young middle-class males were subjected, in this case articulating it explicitly as a mode of embodiment. Compulsory athletics were initially instituted in order to increase control over public school boys who, heretofore largely unsupervised outside the classroom, were given to engaging in a variety of disruptive activities in communities surrounding the schools (vandalism, fights, petty theft, etc.). Yet they soon came to rival academics as the main focus of secondary education throughout the last half of the nineteenth century. Indeed, such games quickly came to provide a primary source of self-affirmation both for the schools and for the individual participants. In some cases, the clearest example being the Scottish school Loretto under headmaster H. H. Almond, the educational institution was transformed into a virtual training camp. Both intramural and extramural events became a regularly scheduled and often required part of male middle-class education, developing their own material culture manifest in the uniforms, elites, prizes, and physical and dietary regimes that came to characterize the practices of late-nineteenth-century public and proprietary schools.[21]

While this attention to athletics was undoubtedly aimed at conditioning adolescent male bodies and facilitating their transformation into healthy adult men,[22] it was also designed to define a certain ideology of masculinity whose embodiment the middle-class boy was to become. This underlying project of defining male gender identity was an explicit aspect of organized school games from the very beginning of the pedagogical interest in the playing fields. As the prospectus of the Harrow Philathletic Club (1853) made clear, the main benefit of a sports club would be to disseminate throughout the school "a stronger feeling of interest in manly exercises and amusements than now exists,"[23] since athletics appeared to provide an excellent means for inculcating such a "manly" ideology. By establishing a structured set of practices through which boys would compare themselves to one another, compete with each other, and be ranked according to their physical abilities and by investing these practices with the symbolic and moral values most closely ("naturally") associated with "manhood," the cult of the playing field provided the terrain over which adolescent males assumed the middle-class norms for adult masculinity. Through athletic training and competitions, their maturing bodies were marked with the signs of maleness and this "masculinizing" function came increasingly to justify the existence—if not the expense—of secondary education for boys. As one contemporary analyst observes:

> Many a lad who leaves an English public school disgracefully igno-rant of the rudiments of useful knowledge, who can speak no language but his own, and writes that imperfectly, to whom the noble literature of his country and the stirring history of his forefathers are almost a sealed book, and who had devoted a great part of his time and nearly all his thoughts to athletic sports, yet brings away with him something beyond all price, a manly straightforward char-acter, a scorn of lying and meanness, habits of obedience and com-mand, and fearless courage. Thus equipped, he goes out into the world, and bears a man's part in subduing the earth, ruling its wild folk, and building up the Empire. . . .[24]

This ideological connection of "manly straightforward character" with Britain's imperialist project (over and against any intellectual prepara-tion) simultaneously defines imperialism as the "natural" domination of the British male by virtue of the superiority he has cultivated in his educational (sporting) activities and articulates a concept of masculin-ity which is inextricably bound up with nationalist interests.[25] This normalization of adult masculinity is rooted in somatic training even as it mitigates the importance of intellectual development. Thus, to the extent that the introduction of organized athletics was coincident with the introduction of the examination in British secondary education for boys, it enveloped them, body and mind, in a web of practices that structured their expectations and experiences as males amid the grow-ing bureaucratic, industrial, and imperialist institutions of Victorian Britain.

It is in this context of the accelerating normalization of middle-class adolescent male experience, then, that the concern with "schoolboy immorality" must be located. Until the middle of the century, the use of words such as "immorality," "vice," and "sin" to describe the activities of secondary school students seemed to refer almost exclu-sively to nonsexual practices such as lying, cheating, stealing, bullying, indiscipline, or drunkenness. However, as J. R. de S. Honey has demonstrated in his exhaustive survey of the literature produced by headmasters during the second half of the century, after the 1850s there was an ever-increasing awareness of and campaign against the "solitary vice" and its far more serious companion, the "dual vice."[26] As the topic of frequent sermons, lectures, advice sessions, and disciplinary actions, masturbation became a primary focus for the enactment of pedagogical authority over middle-class adolescent boys. Dormitories were partitioned, younger boys forbidden to consort with older boys, pupils were required to engage in strenuous physical activities (in the hope they would drop into bed exhausted and *just* sleep), and schedules were reorganized to limit the amount of free time, all in the (assuredly unsuccessful) attempt to curtail adolescent masturbation.

However, while the subject provided innumerable opportunities for the articulation of a moral code that mentally and physically enveloped the youthful male body, the verbal references to autoeroticism were often so oblique as to be unintelligible, even to those with much practical experience. The example of Edward Thring, headmaster at Uppingham, whose sermons contained a catalogue of the symptoms and consequences of ill-defined "secret acts," "hidden pleasures," and "hidden impurity," illustrates the general antimasturbatory tenor of these pedagogical texts:

> And so the poisonous breath of sin keeps tainting and corrupting all the freshness and purity of young life; and the corruption spreads, and gets into the very soul, destroying all its power to do true work, and win even earthly credit; and the face loses its frank and manly expression; and the poison begins to be seen outwardly; and after disappointing father, mother, and family, and himself most of all, the wretched victim either sinks down to a lower level and lives on, or often finds an early grave, killed by his own foul passions.[27]

This euphemistic description which metaphorically associates "sin" with the physiological effects of "poison," metonymically equates the "corruption" of the young boy's "soul" with the loss of "frank and manly [facial] expression," suggesting that there exists a parallel between the spiritual and physical degradation evoked by the unnamed, yet unmistakable, "foul passions." This trope, which establishes a tension between the physical and the moral, underlies most of the pedagogical pronouncements against masturbation, as Edward Lyttleton, headmaster of Eton makes clear in his pamphlet *The Causes and Prevention of Immorality in Schools*: "That stern struggle between the moral and the physical is one of man's greatest trials; a trial which it may be presumption voluntarily to encounter, yet a trial which is at some time or other laid upon most men . . ." (42). However, Lyttleton's recognition that the existence of physical desire "is at some time or other laid upon most men" in no way interrupts his Christian morality, which interprets such desire as a "trial." This totalizing interpretive schema, which largely characterized the clerical writings on "schoolboy immorality," encumbered the pedagogical discussions of male masturbation with a self-censorship that severely limited its utterances to indirections and euphemisms.[28] Thus, as prolific as educational authorities were on the matter, their texts remained at best metaphoric, moralizing, fear-inducing sermons, leaving the elaboration of a more explicit analysis of the effects of masturbation to their medical colleagues.

From its earliest examples, the medical discourse on male masturbation complimented the pedagogical practices disciplining the adolescent male body.[29] Doctors, in their expanding role as the guardians of "public health," increasingly supported teachers and parents in the efforts to raise and educate healthy future generations of middle-class Britons.[30] Masturbation, which was portrayed as undermining not only the reproductive potential of this future but also the productive capacities of the individual adolescents, provided an opportunity for parents, doctors, clergy, and teachers to act in concert in order to guarantee the health and the perpetuation of their class.[31] The first known medical work devoted solely to the "problem" of masturbation was the Swiss physician Samuel Tissot's *Tentamen de morbis ex manustrupratione*, which appeared in Latin in 1758, and which was expanded and translated into French, reappearing in 1760 as *L'Onanisme, ou Dissertation physique sur les maladies produit par la masturbation*. Tissot's monograph quickly attained popularity in this version, and was translated into English and German and later Italian. The fact that it was seldom out of print for the next seventy years and was reprinted as late as 1905 attests to its widespread appeal.[32] Indeed, his famous maxim that "the loss of one ounce of it [seminal fluid], enfeebles more than [the loss of] forty ounces of blood" was repeated popularly over the next century and a half.[33]

In Tissot's analysis, masturbation caused the "unnatural" loss of seminal fluid, leading to a dissipation of vital bodily energies which, in turn, gave rise to a variety of somatic and mental illnesses. Based on his notion that semen "is an extremely important secretion, called *huile essentielle*, quintessence of animal fluids, or more exactly *rectified spirit*, the dissipation of which leaves other humors feeble"[34] and his understanding that orgasm is a form of seizure that is itself harmful to the brain, leaving "its functions . . . necessarily deranged"[35] and causing a harmful flow of blood away from other vital organs,[36] Tissot produced an exhaustive list of the debilitating side effects of self-abuse. Among other consequences, he believed, masturbation caused a weakening of the digestive system, a loss or exaggeration of appetite, vomiting, and indigestion; he claimed that it destroyed the nervous and respiratory systems, leading in severe cases to epilepsy, or in more lucky circumstances only to general lassitude, debility, vertigo, loss of sleep, bad dreams, hypochondria, hysteria, dry cough, rheumatic pains of the limbs, pimples, hemorrhoids, and/or the impairment of memory and the senses.[37]

More significant, however, than these now seemingly ludicrous claims about the physiological effects of masturbation was the way Tissot effectively elided the somatic and social "symptoms" he retrospectively attributed to male autoeroticism. For, in so doing, Tissot established a paradigm that prefigured the behavioral claims of those middle-class physicians who followed him by arguing that one of the most harmful consequences of masturbation was that it undermined a young man's ability to work effectively:

> It [masturbation] very much injures numerous young men; since even when their faculties are not exhausted, their use is perverted. Whatever be their pursuit, they succeed in nothing without a degree of attention which is impossible, on account of this destructive habit. Among those who have no business, (and of these there are too many,) there are some not fit for this; and an air of distraction, embarrassment and stupidity, causes only a disagreeable feeling of laziness. We might also mention that this inability to confine the attention added to the diminution of the faculties entirely incapacitates [them] for taking any stand in society. This sad state reduces man below the level of the brute, and justly renders him an object of contempt more than of pity.[38]

The symptomatology that Tissot develops to characterize the consequences of masturbation (e.g., "an air of distraction, embarrassment, and stupidity," "a disagreeable feeling of laziness") implicitly constructs masturbation as antithetical to the qualities upon which bourgeois social productivity is predicated.[39] His parenthetical aside castigating those "who have no business" and his determination that the "solitary debauchee's" diminished capacity "entirely incapacitates [him] for taking a stand in society" underscore his assumption that there are essential "productive" capacities that distinguish "man" from "brute"—capacities that he perceives are directly threatened by the masturbating youth. Thus, drawing upon the medical authority engendered by his "scientific" descriptions of the (supposed) physiological consequences that masturbation brings about in the adolescent male, Tissot simultaneously normalizes a set of ideological assumptions about the productive "nature" of male behavior. Concomitantly, by portraying these assumptions as natural "human" functions, he implicitly defines masturbation—an act that apparently defies the (re)productive potential of male sexuality[40]—as falling away from this norm.

This strategy of ascribing a set of somatic consequences to autoerotic practices and then defining these symptoms as the antitheses of normal male social behavior characterized much of the medical literature on masturbation produced in the nineteenth century. Doctors drew up compendious lists of symptoms that would befall the unhappy victim of the solitary vice, symptoms that became increasingly likely to include some form of mental derangement:

> Mental wanderings, incoherence of ideas, peculiar grazing sensations occasioned by the passage of the urine, pains extending from the neck of the bladder to the glans of the penis and margin of the anus, shivering, palpitations, sinking sensations, gastric and intestinal symptoms, diarrhoea, anaesthesia, frightful sensations like those occasioned by electricity, amblyopia or dilopia ending in amaurosis, impairment of hearing, perversion of sense of taste and smell, pains in the head and vertigo. It is scarcely to be marvelled at that anyone so direly afflicted should fall, as we are told he does, "into a state of extreme wasting;" that his skin "acquires a yellowish, leaden hue;" that his eyes "become encircled with a blue ring;" and that he winds up by falling into a state of "brutish stupidity," insanity, and locomotor ataxy. The wonder is that his spirit does not take flight altogether long before matters reach a crisis like this.[41]

Lists like this, then, became the basis for moralizing conclusions about the "proper," "normal," "healthy," or "true" uses of the male sexual organs. These conclusions took on considerable weight, especially as doctors were increasingly legitimated as "the" medical expert throughout the century, displacing earlier noninstitutionalized herbalists, midwives, surgeons, barbers, apothecaries, etc.[42] Moreover, as doctors assiduously sought to enter the public sphere as authorities, claiming expertise as the arbiters of "public health," their prognostications assumed value not only as medical advice, but also as the basis for addressing social problems and setting moral standards.[43] Perhaps the most widely known and socially influential example of such antimasturbatory medical moralizing is found in William Acton's *The Func-*

tions and Disorders of the Reproductive Organs. Acton, who was one
of the most famous physicians of the period, in part as a result of his
avid political support for the Contagious Disease Acts during the 1860s
and 1870s,[44] produced this medical text in 1857 in order, he claimed,
to redress the insufficiencies in "many of the so-called standard works
[which] altogether ignore the subject, as if sexual functions did not
exist."[45] Acton's book was so popular that it was reprinted in a second
edition the following year; was translated into French in 1863; and
went through a variety of British and American pressings during Acton's lifetime and well after his death.[46] Highly acclaimed on its first
appearance by the British medical establishment, as the following review in *The Lancet* illustrates, the book received much laudatory
medical attention, although the circumspect wording of the praise
points to the very evasions about "sexual functions" that Acton identified: "In the work now before us all the essential detail upon its subject
matter is clearly and scientifically given. We recommend it accordingly,
as meeting a necessary requisition of the day, refusing to join in that
opinion which regards the consideration of the topics in question as
beyond the duties of the medical practitioner."[47]

Significantly, then, Acton's work, which was so instrumental in
advancing the medicalization of sexual behavior, is devoted exclusively
to the examination of male sexual function.[48] Given its overt problematization of male sexuality, it is easy to discern the normalizing project
of the book, made explicit in its very structure: Acton divides the text
into two parts, the first entitled "Normal Functions of the Reproductive
Organs" and the second "Functional Disorders of the Reproductive
Organs," providing an explicit juxtaposition of the "healthy" norm to
the corresponding deviations. In a note to the first sentence of the
introduction ("For the due performance of the functions of generation,
I shall suppose that the male organs are perfect") which itself makes
the connection between biological sex and reproduction unambiguous,
he glosses the word "generation" in order to weld this connection even
more securely: "the words 'sexual,' 'reproductive,' 'generative' will be
used synonymously; there are some instances in which distinctions may
be made between them, but these are so slight, I need not further
allude to them." The establishment of this linguistic equivalence, which
condenses male sexuality, human reproduction, and biological generation, underlies Acton's medical assessment of "normal functions of the
reproductive organs" and preemptively defines the "healthy" ideal that
the text endeavors to describe.

Beginning with the sexual development of postpubescent males,
Acton sets out a normative description for the development of

"healthy"—i.e., productively *and* reproductively inclined—men under the guise of an explanation of physiological processes. His account of the biological developments at puberty is inseparable from his assessments of the conditions for proper socialization, such that the latter comes to define the proper "channeling" of the former:

> At PUBERTY, when "life is in excess, the blood boils, the desires are impetuous and tormenting—nature is almost an accomplice," we expect to find the young man a reasoning being. If he is not, those who have been about him during his youth are to blame, as they should have directed his inclinations in the right channels. The boy, long before this epoch of his life, should have been taught that his mere inclinations and instincts are not to be blindly followed. He should have been informed that *the indulgence of sexual desires is (for him) not natural*—that if indulged in the gratification will be followed by the worst consequences.[49]

Here Acton juxtaposes the establishment of "reason" to "mere inclinations and instincts" in order to illustrate the proper hierarchy of psyche over soma that he believed to define the healthy function of the maturing male. In his schema, the improper comprehension of this "rational" domination over "sexual desires" opens the boy to "the worst consequences," whose elaboration is deferred to the second half of the book. That the consequences of natural (i.e., biological) maturation are deemed "not natural" for the adolescent male demonstrates the degree to which "nature" itself is an ideological construct that grounds the proscriptive definitions of "normal function."

Acton underscores the necessity for rationally controlling the body to healthy male development by claiming that "self-control" and "volitional power" are essential to the maintenance of proper mental function. Adopting the physicalist rhetoric of "muscular Christianity," he advocates a "sort of mental gymnasium . . . for the development, regulation, and cultivation of those faculties of mind upon the regular exercise of which depends our intellectual advancement," and criticizes the contemporary educational institutions for failing to instill these essential standards: "If I may judge of the generation now growing up, I should say that modern education has not sufficiently attended to these necessary duties; and yet it is this self-regulation and restraint upon which hangs much of our future success and happiness."[50] Given his personal, professional, and political concern, Acton does not hesitate to advance suggestions for the improvement of pedagogical practices, directing his attention primarily if not exclusively to the bastions

of middle-class education, the public schools and universities. Moreover, he unambiguously connects these institutional practices both to
the medicalization of adolescent male bodies and to the nationalistic
interests of the state. Thus, he uses the authority derived from this
ideological conjunction to make two concrete suggestions that he believes to be of critical social importance, both of which entail increasing
the control over male youths: first, he advocates programs of "muscular
development," à la Kingsley, whom he quotes at some length, and
second, he (almost obsessively) admonishes parents "to watch their
children."

It is this last suggestion that seems to have preoccupied Acton, as he
repeats it in various guises throughout the text, giving the responsibility
for the development of proper adolescent "self-control" over to the
parents. This parental responsibility, according to Acton, defines the
proper relationship between the young male and his parents, such that
the failure to establish such domestic governance leads to the child's
inability to assume the full attributes of his class. Acton forcefully
makes this connection in a rhetorical interlude in which he constructs
a fictive encounter between debauched adolescents and their parents:

> The young men of the day are accused of leading immoral lives, and
> giving way to their sexual gratifications; but may they not answer
> the objectors with a great deal of truth, "Have you, our parents and
> guardians (who have all the experience of age), brought us up to
> exercise that self-control which you now for the first time inculcate?
> Can self-command and restraint be mastered in a minute? Have you
> considered, or do you believe that our hitherto unchecked volition,
> our strongest passions and instincts, can be not only reined and
> curbed, but brought to a dead stand, at a word of command? Is not
> what you would have incompatible with Nature's laws? and does
> not experience show how few in a thousand are able to attain your
> present state of respectability and enjoyment? You lavish on our
> infancy and youth all that love and affection could bestow—you
> cultivated all our intellectual faculties, and all our senses—ignoring
> the strongest, and now you say, too late, as manhood is flowering,
> 'Restrain these passions.' Your advice is too late—we walked in
> the way of nature, and now you call us licentious, vicious, and
> immoral."[51]

The force of Acton's rhetoric here is directed toward the class interests
of parents: he simultaneously invokes those characteristics that the
bourgeois parents would affirm as intrinsic to their self-definition as a
class ("your present state of respectability and enjoyment," the "lav-

ish" attention to the "cultivation" of their children) and then uses these characteristics to indict their failure to ensure that their children will continue to live up to their class position. By phrasing this criticism as if it were coming from the "licentious, vicious, and immoral" children themselves, Acton implicitly compares the decadent future that the maturation of these degenerate offspring would yield to a still-"healthy" present in which the "respectable" parents maintain their authority, in order to urge the consolidation of this patriarchal power in the interests of the future of the class and the nation. Thus, the admonishment he places in the mouths of the youths, "we walked in the way of nature," signifies Acton's understanding that the social values underlying bourgeois respectability are predicated upon the proper shaping of the body's "natural" qualities in order that these qualities then come to cohere as a mode of embodiment that articulates standards for class, gender, and age.

In light of this significance, Acton emphatically underscores what is at stake in proper parental intervention when he considers "normal [sexual] functions in adult age." After ruminating on the strength of "sex-passion" by considering zoological examples such as the fecundity of aphids, flesh flies, cod, the amazing luminescent means of sexual attraction in glow worms, and the developmental cycles of bucks and cocks, Acton offers what is to his mind the only acceptable conclusion to such desire for the middle-class male: "My advice to all young men above twenty-five, who are in good health, is to marry as soon as possible. Everything tends to prove that the moderate gratification of the sex-passion in married life is doubtless followed by the happiest consequences to the individual."[52] In this advice, of course, marriage is defined as the legitimated access to heterosexual intercourse and as such is urged upon the needy male as the only "respectable" option for relieving his pent-up seed.[53] Arguing against the gratification of male sexual passion outside middle-class marriage, Acton challenges the effective Victorian norm that allowed "respectable" bourgeois males to engage in (usually cross-class)[54] extramarital intercourse with servants or prostitutes[55]:

> The occasional indulgence of the sexual feelings is not, in the first place, medically desirable, as stimulating without satisfying the appetite. And each casual intercourse, again, is attended with this danger: —that it may initiate a more permanent liaison, often fraught with painful consequences. If it once assumes regularity, a man may form ties most difficult to break. The class of persons who accept his attentions on these terms without marriage, is beneath

him in station and education. He finds himself in a false position. If
the female is true to him alone, there is often great inducement to
make her what in common parlance is called, "an honest woman."
Should a real marriage ensue, the ill-fated youth finds he has learnt
too late a bitter lesson for the rest of his life. The requirements of
society are such that men only can, or do virtually, visit at his house,
even if his social position is good. His family may try to make the
best of matters, but the well-educated female declines to look over
the new-promoted wife's antecedents.[56]

This somewhat lengthy passage makes clear the assumptions that underlie Acton's construction of "normal" adult male sexuality. Moving
swiftly from the "medical [in]desirability" of "occasional indulgence"
to its real "danger"—i.e., the threat to the potential for a legitimate
middle-class marriage recognized by "society" and "family"—Acton's
text illustrates that his medical discussion of male sexual behavior is
inseparable from his advocacy of bourgeois standards of propriety.
This positioning directs Acton's use of his medical authority to inscribe
the expectations for middle-class domesticity on the male body itself,
underscoring the threats that unbridled sexual expression posed not
only, or even especially, to its physiological function (although he
does briefly consider "disease") but more significantly to the gendered
expectations of his class.

These expectations, then, underlie Acton's discussion of male masturbation, which he considers under the heading "functional disorders
in youth." In Acton's account, the problem begins at school: "When
such a boy goes to school, his elder associates may initiate him into
the habit of masturbation, which he takes to soon and easily."[57] Once
introduced to "the habit," unless he is quickly dissuaded, "the habit is
. . . engrafted on the boy":

His health fails, he is troubled with indigestion, his intellectual
powers are dimmed, he becomes pale, emaciated, and depressed in
spirits; exercise he no longer has taste for, and he seeks solitude. . . .
At a later period the youth cannot so easily minister to his solitary
pleasures, and he excites his organs the more as they flag under the
accustomed stimulus. He becomes shy and timid, particularly in the
presence of women.[58]

Here Acton connects the supposed physiological effects of masturbation with a wider range of deviant patterns of social behavior. The
practitioner of the "solitary vice" becomes literally encased in his habit
such that his entire life becomes an enactment of "solitude." This self-

isolation not only undermines the development of a proper engagement with others, but more significantly causes him to "invert" his properly masculine sex role becoming "shy and timid, particularly in the presence of women." By assigning to the habitual masturbator characteristics conventionally associated in Victorian bourgeois ideology with the "feminine" and by portraying him as frightened by women, Acton implicitly "unsexes" the "solitary offender," creating him as the antithesis of the earlier described "normal" male. Acton makes this juxtaposition explicit in his concluding plea to parents and teachers for vigilance in preventing such acts of "self-abuse":

> [T]hose interested in a youth should in the mildest, but still in a firm way, point out the consequences to which such habits lead, and he should be taught to look upon masturbation as a cowardly, selfish, debasing habit, one which should preclude those who indulge in it from associating with boys of proper spirit, distinguished as they are by a love of manly amusements compatible with health. . . . It is from a want of attention in parents, and those who direct the studies of youth, to the commencement of this evil habit, and of a little seasonable advice and judgement, that many a man's career, commenced under the most favorable auspices, has been thwarted, and his physical powers and growth checked.[59]

In this quotation, Acton implicitly deploys the qualities attributed to the healthy male norm in order to castigate the masturbating boy: the practice is described as "cowardly," "debasing," and "selfish," invoking by way of negation a "manly" ideal (much akin to Kingsley's) that is "heroic," "uplifting," and "selfless." Thus, the practicer of the "evil habit" should be precluded from "healthy" physical association with "good" boys who are well on their way to becoming "manly" men. The economic consequences of this deviation from normal function are suggested in the image of "many a man's [thwarted] career," not a consequence to be taken lightly by members of a class whose continuity from generation to generation was often tenuous and whose anxiety about rising expectations was high (see chapter 1).

This economic anxiety underlies much of the literature on masturbation, such that the two sets of concerns came to be intertwined, each guaranteeing the validity of the other. In his now classic article on the subject, "The Spermatic Economy," G. J. Barker-Benfield convincingly argues that "the interpenetrative confusion of sexual and economic terms represented the two overriding preoccupations of nineteenth-century Western man, sex and money, which were rapidly becoming the only measures of his identity."[60] Using a variety of American sources, Barker-Benfield suggests that behind the very vocal medical concern with the consequences of masturbation lay a functional equivalence between the financial and somatic "economies": the body, like the society generally, was defined as a closed system with limited energies and resources that could be put into circulation. If energy was dissipated at one point in the system, it depleted the total energy available to the system as a whole: "The discharge of sperm, it was generally believed, 'obliterated,' 'prostrated,' and 'blotted out' all of 'the energies of the system.' Instead of 'concentrating' those energies onto the non-sexual ends of success, the masturbator concentrated what was left of them onto his penis and testicles."[61] Thus, Barker-Benfield contends that "the deeper anxiety was spermatic loss, with its concomitant losses of will and order. Such a belief made any uncontrolled expenditure of sperm potentially dangerous."[62] While Barker-Benfield very suggestively characterizes the metaphorical parallels between the textual representations of spermatic loss and economic loss as underlying the larger discursive (re)production of male sexuality in nineteenth-century America, his analysis unnecessarily reifies male experience as a static consequence of American individualism and expansionism. However, what the literature on masturbation demonstrates most convincingly is that all of these categories were in shifting and overlapping relationships of contiguity, such that the unfolding of the discourse on masturbation must be seen as one practice among many through which (class defined) male gender identities were enacted. In fact, since the medical assessment of masturbation itself was far from fixed, its "scientific" representations provide an excellent example of the ways in which doctors helped to produce specific class expressions of male embodiment.

From mid-century onward, medical assessments of masturbation increasingly emphasized the mental and moral consequences of auto-erotic behavior, which gradually superseded the long lists of physiological symptoms characteristic of the earlier writings on the subject. As E. H. Hare has shown in his article "Masturbatory Insanity: The History of an Idea," this shift was accompanied by a concomitant transformation in the characterization of effects of "self-abuse" from one that sought to attribute a set of consequences to specific *acts* to one that defined the signs of a particular type of *actor*:[63]

> The careful study of the supposed effects of masturbation had another consequence; it led to the delineation of a cluster of signs thought to be indicative of "the masturbator." Youths who devel-

oped an insanity associated with masturbation were observed to have displayed characteristic personality traits before they became frankly disordered, and these traits were held to be the early effects of the habit of masturbation which, if continued long enough would lead to their exaggeration into insanity. (8)

This movement away from an examination of acts to a definition of an actor, resituated the concern with masturbation: no longer were doctors solely concerned with the "health" of the adolescent body— even to the extent that definitions of "health" were themselves indices of class identity—but were attempting to define this body as the site of the individual's essential "nature" seen as a product both of gender and class. By redefining the "subject" of the medical gaze from the second-order signs ("symptoms") of an underlying "cause" ("self-abuse") to the first-order signs of a perhaps yet-to-be-manifest result ("masturbatory insanity"), doctors effectively widened the scope of their surveillance. Whereas the earlier definition had been concerned with detecting and "curing," or, more hopefully, preventing masturbation—supposing a direct connection between the practice and the practicer—the new definition established "the masturbator" as existing apart from or even preexisting his disease, "masturbatory insanity." The masturbator defined a biographical entity with "characteristic personality traits" whose existence was anomalous, dangerous, and "unnatural"—a hidden destructive potential lurking beneath the apparently serene surface of Victorian middle-class domesticity. Parents, pastors, doctors and teachers were admonished to be increasingly vigilant in observing their adolescent male charges, in order that they might detect any deviation from the norm that would suggest the development of greater future departures. Thus, through the definition of "the masturbator" and his illness, "masturbatory insanity," doctors in effect consolidated the medical-pedagogical-parental discipline over the young male body.

The first description of "masturbatory insanity" as a separate classification of human experience was offered by the eminent Scottish physician, David Skae, in his inaugural statement as president of the Association of Medical Officers of Asylums and Hospitals for the Insane. Taking this opportunity to publicly address his fellow physicians on the question of putting "the classification of the various forms of insanity on a rational and practical basis," Skae asked, "Why should we attempt to group and classify the varieties of insanity by *mental* symptoms, and not as we do in other diseases, by the *bodily diseases*, of which those mental perversions are but signs?"[64] In response to this rhetorical question, which makes explicit the evolving distinction between classifying insanity as a "mental symptom" or as a "bodily sign," the Scottish M.D. offered to derive a nosography of mental illnesses from what he called their "natural history," that is, from their origins and development in human physiology. To this end, Skae provides a list of twenty-five "manias" (of which over half pertain explicitly to sexual or reproductive "disorders") that in his experience exhaustively mapped out the field of mental disturbances and of which the third "natural family" he assigned to "the masturbators."

Significantly, Skae begins his description of "masturbatory insanity" by noting that: "Although I designate this family by the cause only which originates the insanity, yet I think that it cannot be denied that that vice produces a group of symptoms which are quite characteristic, and easily recognized, and give to the cases a special natural history" (315). Hence, even though the "insanity" of masturbation violates the taxonomic schema that Skae is striving to produce (since he is unable to define the condition by a set of "bodily diseases" that determine it), still he chooses to designate it as one of his "natural families" given the "easily recognizable" quality of the symptoms. The appeal to the common sense of his audience ("yet I think it cannot be denied . . .") implies a reliance on the popular conceptions of "that vice" in order to provide its explicit medicalization. Masturbation, though it belies the descriptive standards that are explicitly being established in the text, merits inclusion because, we infer, "everybody already knows that it is sick." Not surprisingly then, Skae's characterization of the specific qualities of "masturbatory insanity" simply reiterates the lists of the earlier literature on the subject:

> The peculiar imbecility and shy habits of the youthful offender, the suspicion, and fear, and dread, and suicidal impulses, and palpitations, and scared look, and feeble body of the older offenders, passing gradually into dementia, or fatuity, with other characteristic features familiar to all of you, and which I do not stop to enlarge on, all combine to stamp and define this as a natural order or family. (315)

While this litany of ills that mark the behavior of "the masturbator" does not differ significantly from those presented by any of a number of other authors—though its anaphoric use of "and" does give it a unique rhetorical flourish—its placement in the larger nosographic system unifies and subsumes these "characteristic features familiar to all of you" into a distinct expression of a particular type, a "natural order," of individuals, whose existence, Skae asserts is both ubiquitous and undeniable.

In a paper given ten years later, as the prestigious "Morisonian Lecture on Insanity for 1873," Skae reiterates his definition of the "Insanity of Masturbation," once again placing in the context of a larger systematization of mental illness. Here, Skae underscores the coincidence of popular and medical conceptions of masturbation by deriving his description from the popular press:

> The Insanity of Masturbation scarcely requires comment or illustration—it must be familiar to you all. The premonitory signs may be taken from any newspaper from an advertisement headed "Debility," or some such name, readily recognized by the unhappy victim, and going on to tell how a certain doctor cures "Nervous debility, mental and physical depression, palpitation of the heart, noises in the head and ears, indecision, impaired sight and memory, indigestion, loss of energy and appetite, pains in the back, timidity, self distrust, groundless fears, and muscular relaxation." Add to these symptoms the dislike of female society, the inability to look you straight in the eye, the fear of being impelled to commit suicide, culminating in a true suicidal and sometimes homicidal impulse, and you have a pretty accurate bird's-eye view of this form of insanity.[65]

In this passage Skae illustrates two fundamental aspects that underlie the medicalization of masturbation: first, the degree to which it reweaves contemporary assumptions about masturbation and male sexuality produced popularly throughout mid-Victorian Britain into a specific category of "mental illness"; and second, the extent to which doctors were seeking to preempt the encroachment on their authority by a wide variety of "quacks" and to take over what must have been a highly lucrative business in "cures."[66] Together these considerations suggest that the discursive production of "the masturbator" as a distinct subset of male experience encoded a constellation of institutional factors that ascribe to a medical definition those ideological descriptions of "healthy" masculine behavior generated within the family and the schools (among others) discussed above. In this light, it is not surprising to note that Skae concludes his brief consideration of "masturbatory insanity" by counterpoising "self-control" and "reason" to the "impaired memory, energy, silly vanity, and self satisfaction" of the "persevering" masturbator in a virtual reiteration of the distinctions voiced by Acton and even Tissot.

However, while Skae was the first to define "masturbatory insanity" and its concomitant victim, "the masturbator," it was up to the most

famous late-Victorian psychologist, Henry Maudsley, to give them
their clearest expression.[67] Maudsley's paper on the subject, "Illustrations of a Variety of Insanity," delivered before the Harveian Society
of London, 5 March 1868, ostensibly undertakes to extend Skae's plea
for a redefinition of "mental diseases" on a more "rational" and
"scientific" basis. To this end, Maudsley affirms Skae's suggestion that
the classification of "mental derangement" ought to proceed from its
"natural history"—i.e., its bodily symptoms, "natural course," probable termination, and suitable forms of treatment—which would emphasize the "bodily disorder" associated with "mental symptoms."[68]
Yet, after briefly introducing this theoretical frame, Maudsley quickly
and passionately launches into the central concern of his text, which
seeks "to illustrate the features of the mental derangement which is
produced in men by self-abuse, and thus to sketch the features of a
well-marked group" (151).

Maudsley's analysis begins with a description of the emergence of
sexual potency in the adolescent at puberty: "You are aware that no
change which takes place in a person's mental character—in his tastes,
feelings, aims, and conduct, is so marked as that which takes place at
the time of puberty, when the sexual nature is developed. There is a
complete revolution in mental being. . . ."(151–52). This use of the
political metaphor, "revolution," to characterize the emergence of "the
sexual nature"—a metaphoric equivalence repeated four times in the
course of two paragraphs—underscores the ideological nature of
Maudsley's endeavor. Writing twenty years after the 1848 upheavals
swept across Europe—and gave new contemporary meaning to the
term "revolution"—Maudsley uses this description to denote the psy-
chological/physiological changes that beset the pubescent male. By
linking the development of male sexual function to (the fear of) political
revolution, he implicitly suggests an underlying relationship between
establishing a normative sexual identity and (re)producing a stable
body politic that he then juxtaposes to his understanding of "revolution": "A revolution of any kind cannot of course take place without
some amount of disturbance; old combinations must be broken up and
new one's formed, and there will be more or less agitation in the
process. But the tumult in the mind at the time when the sexual system
is establishing itself claims the special attention of psychologists" (152).
If, as Elaine Showalter has asserted, "the physiological obsessions of
late Victorian psychiatry were in perfect conformity with the body
metaphors of late Victorian social analysis,"[69] then Maudsley's claim
for the special interest of psychologists in the "tumult in the mind" of

developing male adolescents must be placed within the larger context of a somatically based social analysis that sought to derive cultural distinctions from biological underpinnings. Thus, Maudsley's interest in describing the "characteristic insanity" of masturbating youths reflects not only a particular medical project of developing a nosology of this "disease," but also the larger medical project of (re)producing and legitimating bourgeois ideology generally and reciprocally affirming its own authority within this dominant order.

Maudsley's specific articulation of this dual project begins by establishing a Darwinian basis for refuting earlier Cartesian understandings of mind/body relations. He asserts that the "new birth of feelings, desires and thoughts" that marks the advent of puberty "proves, if proof on such a point were necessary, how mental life, as the final achievement of organization, really comprehends the whole bodily life" (152). This assertion, which casts the human (especially male) intellect as the "highest" achievement of evolution, leads Maudsley to juxtapose the "metaphysician [who] may separate the mind from the body by an absolute barrier" to the "physician who has to deal practically with the thoughts, feelings, and habits of men, who has to do with the mind, not as an abstract and ideal entity on which to speculate, but as a force in nature which he must study and influence" (152). Designating himself as both a student and master of "nature," Maudsley establishes his own authority to speak as an expert by virtue of his "practicality"—a discursive maneuver that simultaneously enables him to use "common knowledge," i.e., ideologically produced definitions of normative sexual behavior, as the basis for his interpretation of masturbatory insanity.

After this metacritical interlude, Maudsley proceeds to locate the origins of "the miserable sinner whose mind suffers by reason of self abuse" in the dramatic changes that occur at puberty. Drawing on a connection suggested in Skae's nosography between masturbatory insanity and "a mania of pubescence" (also called "hebephrenia," "puerile insanity," or "developmental insanity"),[70] Maudsley notes that:

> The period during which this fermentation is going on is at best a very trying period for a youth; if there be in him any natural instability of nerve element, owing to the curse of a bad descent, or to some other cause, it is easy to perceive that the natural disturbance of the mental equilibrium may pass into the actual destruction of it; that a physiological process in a feeble mental organism may end in pathological results. (153)

This assessment of the hazards that beset the maturing male evokes the precarious quality of "normal" development: if there is any "natural instability of nerve element, owing to the curse of a bad descent" then the pubescent "revolution" may very likely lead to the "destruction" of the "mental equilibrium." If we consider this assessment, for a moment, in light of the somatic metaphors that Herbert Spencer used to describe the organicism of social organization in which the governing males were the "head," the workers the "hands," and middle-class women the "heart,"[71] then we can understand more fully the larger class and gender implications of this potential mental overthrow.

Adding to this sinister threat is the latency that may mask the outbreak of such potentially dangerous symptoms: "Insanity may have its real origin at this critical period, though it may not actually break out for years afterwards" (153). Employing another metaphor suggesting the parallel with the lurking threat of political upheaval, Maudsley's assertion of a "real" origin for a disruption that may "break out . . . years afterwards" locates the critical period at a specific biographical/ biological moment through which all males must pass. Thus, it effectively organizes the interpretation of all adult male experience by making it always already susceptible to the symptoms of masturbatory disease. By alleging that "masturbatory insanity," as a form of "degeneration," exists even though its only indication is that it manifests symptoms at some point in the course of a lifetime (which can then be retroactively attributed to undue excitation at a critical period of physical development), doctors produced a fear of such potential outbreaks leading many middle-class men to a constant self-assessment lest they unwittingly stray from the paths of "health." The enactment of this fear is to be found in the copious literature on "spermatorrhoea," a "disease" which consisted of undue seminal emissions either while sleeping or awake, sometimes manifesting itself in conditions that would, in contemporary sexological discourse, probably be described as "impotence" or "premature ejaculation." The fundamental issue here, however, is that the only way an adult male could be determined to be afflicted with this "disease" was if he turned himself in—which many did—for medical treatment, suggesting that the dissemination of medical criteria for sexual "normalcy" were widespread and used as elements of individuals' conceptions of their own experience.

The key to the normative function of "the masturbator," then, can be found in the medical elaboration of the symptoms that reveal the presence of his hereditary weakness—of which the main symptom was the manifestation of un(re)productive, or anti-authoritarian attitudes by middle-class male. Elaborating upon the "offensive egotism" that envelops the self-abuser "in his own narrow and morbid feelings," Maudsley articulates in no uncertain terms the truly repugnant qualities of the masturbator:

> His mental energy is sapped, and though he has extravagant preten-
> sions, and often speaks of great projects engendered of his conceit,
> he never seriously enters into any occupation nor works systemati-
> cally at the accomplishment of any object, but spends all his time in
> indolent and solitary self-brooding, and is not wearied of going on
> day after day in the same purposeless and idle life. (154–5)

Maudsley's characterization underscores the collapsing of somatic and sociological analysis in the discursive production of the masturbator: positing masturbation as an underlying physiological cause (masturba-tion "saps" mental energy), he exclusively defines the consequences of this cause by using the masturbator to personify the violation of normative expectations for "productive" or "industrious" middle-class male behavior. This personification establishes the masturbator as the embodiment of antisocial impulses ("indolent and solitary self-brood-ing") who, in the fused sexual and economic metaphor, "spends his time" on himself and not on making money. Maudsley then extrapo-lates from these sociological symptoms to portray the habitual mastur-bator as the negation of the "true" middle-class male: "His manner is shy, nervous, and suspicious, his dress often untidy or slovenly; there is a want of manliness of appearance as of manliness of feeling" (154). Unmanly in appearance and feeling, the masturbator is a species apart; by his behavior he excludes himself from the expectations that simulta-neously define his gender and his class, such that, Maudsley concludes, "we have little doubt of the nature of the mental degeneration which is beginning" (154).

However, this "degeneration" clearly derives from the ideological assumptions which underlie the normative definitions of mid-Victorian middle-class masculinity, as Maudsley amply illustrates in his citations of cases.

> The first class of patients of this kind to which I may direct attention
> is that comprising youths of about 18 years of age. They are brought
> for medical advice by their parents or other relatives, because they
> are not doing any good at the business to which they have been put,
> and their masters complain that they can make nothing of them.
> They show no interest, and put no energy in what they are set to do;
> they are forgetful, moody, careless, abstracted, perhaps muttering to
> themselves, and waste a long time doing badly very simple things,

> or fail to do them. It is thought at first that their conduct is the result
> of laziness, viciousness, and a desire to shirk work; but after a while
> it becomes apparent that there is something wrong in them, and
> those who have superintendence of them are convinced there is some
> failure of mind. (154)

The focus on late-adolescent youths as the first category of consideration indicates the concern that doctors, parents, employers, and, as
we saw above, educators alike had at this vulnerable period during
which the middle-class youth was to be transformed into the middle-
class adult. Maudsley's description reveals the extent to which doctors
and parents were acting in concert to ensure the "healthy" development
of male offspring. He appropriately portrays the young male as the
object of adult actions (he has been "brought," "put," "made nothing
of," and "set to"), thereby demonstrating the degree to which concern
for the male child conjoined a constellation of authorities charged with
his "superintendence." It is by acting in violation of this "superintendence" that the male child manifests the symptoms of his masturbatory
insanity: Maudsley's examples include young men "entirely wanting
in reverence for their parents, or in proper feeling for others" as well
as "another who considered the business in which he was employed
beneath his dignity"; in addition, he cites the case of "one youth, who
spent most of the day leaning against a door-post, or in wandering
about in a vacant and abstracted way, [who] maintained that he had
always done his work well" (154–55). To a large extent, it seems that
the definition of the masturbator is closely linked to disturbances in
the acceptance of authority by male youths, but rather than being seen
as protests against or interruptions in the circuits of surveillance and
normalization that enveloped them, these disturbances are recouped
within the field of power by the medical interpretation of young men's
disaffection as "something wrong in them."[72]

That counterhegemonic behavior by middle-class males youths—the
supposed perpetuators of class privilege—was located at the level of
somatic dysfunction enabled the authorities charged with their control
to dismiss the potential threat to class/gender hegemony by situating
such individuals outside the terrain of the "healthy" middle-class.
Referring to a case of "self-abuse" as "an illustration of how completely
all proper feeling had been destroyed by the evil habit"—an evaluation
whose moral implications are hardly subtle—Maudsley proceeds to
consider the case as "a striking illustration of the utter moral perversion
of these patients" that underscores the connection between "perversion" and "degeneration":

> Good moral feeling has been acquired gradually by cultivation
> through generations, as the highest mental endowment of human
> kind; the loss of it is one of the first symptoms of that degeneration
> of mankind which insanity marks, and the loss of it in its most
> offensive form one of the most striking symptoms of insanity caused
> by self-abuse. (155)

By depicting the masturbator as the negation of "the highest mental
endowment of mankind," Maudsley personifies him as the "degeneration of mankind" in its most threatening form. The very middle-class
male who in his perfect form, having attained "good moral feeling,"
bodies forth the essence of evolutionary progress, is, then, at but a very
short remove from this degraded and "offensive" specimen. Only by
total self-control and by internalizing the proper moral behavior, can
the vulnerable male forestall this potential doom; any slip early in life
forebodes possible decay.

> The natural evolution of [mental health] in consciousness is pre-
> vented by reason of the vice having been begun so early. Conse-
> quently, we have degenerate beings produced, who, as regards moral
> character, are very much as eunuchs are represented to be—cunning,
> deceitful, liars, selfish, in fact, morally insane; while their physical
> and intellectual vigor is further damaged by the exhausting vice.
> (156)

Aligned with "eunuchs," the "morally insane" masturbator is discur-
sively "unmanned": his actions inhibit the "natural evolution" of those
states of consciousness appropriate for his class and sex and as a
consequence he exists only as a "degenerate being." Created as the
antithesis of "normal" middle-class male development, the masturbator signifies the hidden potential for the short circuiting of the "natural
evolution" that leads to the ascendency of the middle-class. However,
the vehemence of the rhetoric, as well as the urgency of the warnings,
suggests that beneath both the supposed affirmation of the continent
middle-class male as the perfection of evolutionary progress and the
negative characterization of his "degenerate," "exhausted," masturbating "other" lurks a powerful anxiety about the certainty of middle-
class male privilege.

This anxiety is forcefully exhibited in Maudsley's description of the
second category of males vulnerable to the ravages of masturbation:
the should-be married men. Whereas adolescent males were positioned
as the subjects of familial, occupational, educational, and medical
authority, the adult male is meant to be interpellated as the patriarchal

capitalist par excellence. To the extent that he does not fulfill his class/
gender responsibilities by engendering his own middle-class family
unit, the unmarried adult male threatens "natural evolution" by demonstrating that it is not so "natural." In order to explain the existence
of the unmarried man without contradicting the prevailing familial
ideology, Maudsley declares these single men "deranged":

> But when the mental failure caused by self-abuse occurs at a later
> period of life—when the vicious habit, though it may have com-
> menced early in life, has not produced its disastrous consequences
> until the sexual life has entered into the circle of ideas and feelings,
> then the features of the mental derangement witness to the perversion
> of the sexual instinct. (156)

In Maudsley's text—as in Acton's before him—the "sexual instinct"
is collapsed into "reproductive instinct," so that any nonreproductive
sexual expenditure, embodied in this case by the masturbator, necessarily threatened to interrupt the class/gender logic that fused these "instincts" into one. In order to reassimilate this threat into an affirmation
of the "natural" (read "ideological") order, Maudsley labels such
potential violators "perverts" and locates them outside of nature:

> In any case, the manner of a masturbator under these circumstances
> [i.e., in relation to marriageable women] indicates to an experienced
> eye a lustful feeling without the power of natural restraint or of
> natural gratification. In fact, his behavior betrays the actual state of
> things—a morbid sexual feeling; in the excitement of which he finds
> pleasure, and a want of restraint or manliness, which is an indication
> of real sexual impotence. (156)

The contradictory assumptions that underlie this assessment reveal
much about the ideological underpinnings of Maudsley's project. First,
he identifies "the masturbator" not by any knowledge of his actually
having masturbated (which is the case for almost all of the descriptions
of the category) but rather by his "manner," especially in relation to
women. This manner, which under proper hermeneutic assessment by
an expert or "experienced eye"—a somatic metaphor that desexualizes
the observer lest it be thought he himself had any experience of the
subject at hand—reveals an individual entirely identified with his sexual
"nature." Yet this "nature" is "unnatural," wanting in "the power of
natural restraint or of natural gratification," that is, lacking the proper
enactment that would signify its (ideological) connection to middle-
class assumptions about (reproductive) behavior. Maudsley terms this

improper display of sexual identification without reproductive intention "a morbid sexual feeling," using the terminology of physiological deviation to resituate the violation of sociological norms at the level of the biological body ("nature"). However, Maudsley then continues on to establish an equivalence between "restraint" and "manliness" that implies that the masturbator's (presumed) over-"excitement" of his sexual capacity in fact "is an indication of a real sexual impotence," such that the autoerotic experience of his "sex" (organs) situates the masturbator outside his (reproductive) "sex" and thereby culturally "unsexing" him. This discursive strategy, which excludes the masturbating male from his "natural" sexual/gender identity by describing his overidentification with his "sex," effectively defines the masturbator as the negation of "manliness," in turn legitimating the "naturalness" of the normative middle-class reproductive and familial ideologies of masculinity.

The reinforcement of these normative "manly" ideologies underlies the remainder of Maudsley's discussion of the masturbator. Portrayed as having "abundant self-conceit, but not self-knowledge; a spasmodic sort of self-will but not true will," the masturbator is in every way the antithesis of the "true" male. Primarily, his problems occur in relation to women: he is unable to bring himself to marry or if he does, Maudsley claims, "it is the lady who marries him," signifying the inversion of—in Freud's terms—his sexual aim. Unlike earlier writers on self-abuse, Maudsley does not see marriage as a solution but only an exacerbation of the problem:

> Certainly marriage need not be recommended to the confirmed masturbator in the hope or expectation of curing him of his vice. He will most likely continue it afterwards, and the circumstances in which he is placed will aggravate the misery and the mischief of it. For natural intercourse, he has little power or no desire, and finds no pleasure in it; the indulgence of a depraved appetite has destroyed the natural appetite. Besides if he be not entirely impotent, what an outlook for any child begotten of such degenerate stock! Has a being so degraded any right to curse a child with the inheritance of such a wretched descent? Far better that the vice and its consequences should die out with him. (158)

The reiteration of the contrast between "natural" male behavior ("natural intercourse," "natural appetite") and the "degenerate stock" of the masturbator, indicates the underlying familial ideology that shapes Maudsley's definitions. His emphatic denial of the "right" of "a being so degraded" to reproduce—if possible—prefigures the eugenic arguments that arose in late-Victorian sociological and medical discussions.[73] Using the discourse of "degeneration," he produces a "type" of individual whose characteristic behavior embodies all that violates normative middle-class expectation for "maleness"—so horrifying that it would be "far better that the vice and its consequences should die out with him"—and in so doing he legitimates the "naturalness" of these norms. That this "naturalization" is defined in terms of the male's erotic experience of his own body locates the basis for the ideological production of normative behavior within the psychosomatic frame of nineteenth century mental science. Thus, Maudsley's characterization of the masturbator is much more than a nosological description of a "degenerate" form of male experience, it is also the product of an organic intellectual of the British middle class who uses his medical authority to legitimate a class-based ideology of male gender identity.

While this extended analysis of Maudsley's formative text has been designed to examine the discursive strategies through which the masturbator was produced within mid-Victorian medical writings, it is in no way exhaustive of the literature on the subject.[74] However, Maudsley's article does map out the ways in which the masturbator is personified as the antithesis of the "natural" bourgeois male throughout the rest of the century. For example, D. Yellowlees's entry on the subject in D. Hack Tuke's *Dictionary of Psychological Medicine* (1892), which focuses on the postpubescent practices of young men, defines the condition in terms of "moral and mental degeneration."[75] Relying almost exclusively on a vocabulary of "will" and "self-control" (reminiscent of Maudsley's famous book, *Body and Will*), Yellowlees describes the struggle between "the vice" and "manliness and self-reliance" for "mastery" of the young male body. The description of this moral contest, characterized in military terms as the adolescent's battle "to conquer himself," provides Yellowlees the opportunity to articulate in a medical (con)text the moral ideology underlying middle-class standards for "healthy" male behavior. More directly, E. C. Spitzka's compilation of cases from his New York practice (published for an Anglo-American audience in the *Journal of Mental Science*) presented one of the most extensive examples of the clinical deployment of "masturbatory insanity," one that highlighted the connection between the "mental illness" and violations of occupational and authoritarian expectations for middle-class male behavior.[76] Spiztka's examples include cases such as that of a seventeen year old who was brought to his attention "when in addition to [making occasional grimaces] he refused to leave his bed, and ceased to attend to his business duties, and displayed a state of mind inimical to his parents . . . ," or that of "Graves [who] was a little of everything, a poor joiner, an indifferent tinker, and a worse machinist." The synopsis of Case 9 makes clear the physical/social implications of the disease, "Indirect heredity, masturbation, spinal irritation, voluptuous sensations, outbreaks of fury, purposeless and insane project making" which the first sentence of the description reiterates: "F. S--, aged twenty-three, has no settled occupation. . . ." Also, Spitzka notes recovery when these "unproductive" practices have been reformed, such as those of another twenty-three-year-old man whose symptoms included "impertinence to his mother" but who upon showing improvement "began to take an interest in his father's business."

This assessment of the economic consequences of masturbatory insanity's psychosomatic etiology finds its complement in the literature on "spermatorrhoea." Unlike, "masturbatory insanity," which derived its discursive coherence from the recognizable and widely known autoerotic practice, "spermatorrhoea" defined a nebulous and indistinct set of symptoms all related to forms of nonprocreative spermatic loss (including masturbation, wet dreams, premature ejaculation, and other assorted forms of seminal "expenditure"). While it is beyond the scope of this chapter to survey the extensive literature on the syndrome[77] (which has long since been rendered fictitious), it is appropriate to conclude by all too briefly considering spermatorrhoea as the confirmation of the dissemination of medical views on masturbation.

In works such as John Laws Milton's *On Spermatorrhoea* (1858), M. L'Allemand's *On Spermatorrhoea* (1849), and Robert Bartholow's *On Spermatorrhoea* (1866),[78] the "disease" evolved in close conjunction with the literature on masturbation, such that the latter was often (usually) presented as an efficient cause of the former. The configurations of symptomatic behavior of masturbation and spermatorrhoea were similar both in terms of physiological and psychological manifestations, except spermatorrhoea was confined exclusively to adult males and thus evoked the additional issues of "impotence" and "business failure" (rather than the late-adolescent concerns of "unmanliness" and "unproductiveness"). However, whereas masturbation was the incitement for the intervention of a complex of medical, pedagogical, and familial authorities in the life and on the body of the young middle-class male, spermatorrhoea was the occasion for heightened self-surveillance by the adult male. Men where cautioned to scrutinize every bodily discharge lest it contain spermatic fluid (often such loss was thought to accompany urination or defecation). They were enjoined to control themselves even in sleep, where unbeknownst to the rational mind, lascivious thoughts might unleash flows of seminal fluids. Medical authorities provided the worried male with regimes of diet, exercise, sleep, bathing, travel, work, and marriage all in an effort to stem this egregious loss. They developed varieties of painful therapies including passing specially designed instruments ("bougies") through the penis, cauterizing the urethra, blistering the glans, injecting tinctures of various sorts, and circumcision, as well as developing an apparatus that the fearful victim would encase himself in in order to inhibit unwitting ejaculations which occurred in sleep. While it is unclear as to how many men actually subjected themselves to such sexual surgery or sexual technology, it seems evident from the copious literature as well as from the wide variety of treatments that not a few did so. The implications of this self-subjection seem to indicate that, while young men were to be the subjects of a constellation of institutional gazes, as they grew older many of these males internalized this surveillance such that they themselves undertook to continue these normalizing strategies to ensure the "healthy" continuation of their own sexual identity.

Since the purpose of this lengthy chapter was to sketch out part of the Victorian discursive formation within which "the masturbator" took on his specific identity in order to suggest the ways in which middle-class norms of male gender identity enveloped the bodies of adolescent males, it now seems appropriate to consider how these norms coalesced in other contexts in order to discern the parallel developments in late-Victorian discourse for adult males. In particular, the next chapter will focus on the public discussions of prostitution and venereal diseases during the final third of the century in order to examine the problematization of the sexual "double standard" that seemed to legitimate various forms of "male lust." For, it was from this explicitly political context that there emerged not only a public discourse about the "nature" and consequences of men's sexual relations with women, but also a new legal classification for sexual relations between men.

3

MARKING SOCIAL DIS-EASE
Normalizing Male "Continence" and the (Re)Criminalization of Male Sexuality

> We call a man a criminal, not because he violates any eternal code
> of morality—for there is no such thing—but because he violates the
> ruling code of his time.
>> Edward Carpenter, "The Defense of Criminals"

Even as mid-Victorian medical, pedagogical, religious, and familial authorities were busy producing normative proscriptions that defined a nonmasturbating, married, industrious, and (re)productive body as the "healthy" standard for middle-class masculinity, there existed a contradictory but equally valid—if not even more pervasive—practice among a large sector of the middle-class male population that tacitly accepted extramarital, cross-class sexual activities, primarily with prostitutes or servants.[1] Moreover, this widespread divergence between continent "manly" ideals and profligate "male" practice had as its corollary another familiar duality: while middle-class men negotiated a somewhat flexible, nonmonogamous, sexual standard, middle-class women were rigidly bound, both ideologically and materially, to premarital virginity and chastity within marriage. Together these two sets of parallel practices—each simultaneously supporting and (re)producing the other—constituted what was contemporarily known as the sexual "double standard." In his famous article on this multivalent Victorian sexual ideology, Keith Thomas succinctly describes the situation: "if society was to allow men comparative sexual freedom and at the same time keep single women virgin and married women chaste, then a solution had to be found which would gratify the former without sacrificing the latter. The answer lay in prostitution and the widespread view that a class of fallen women was needed to keep the rest of the world pure."[2] While Thomas's formulation implicitly—but somewhat misleadingly—attributes the "double standard" to the agency of certain unnamed, presumably male, social actors who perpetuated it in order to protect a privileged asymmetry between men and women ("if society was to allow . . . a solution had to be found . . ."), his characterization clearly illustrates the constellation of class and sexual ideologies that imbued this asymmetry. Men were perceived "naturally" to experience a "lust" that made the imposition of premarital virginity and chastity within marriage "unnatural"—especially as the marriage age of bourgeois men continued to rise throughout the middle third of the century.[3] Both single men, who could not yet afford to marry and thereby secure a legitimated form of sexual access to women, and married men, whose sexual appetites led them to seek sexual experiences outside their marriages, were effectively permitted to violate the bourgeoisie's explicitly "familialist" sexual norms.[4] In this way, then, the very ideologies that sought to contain all sexual gratification within the middle-class family were ironically, if not consciously, undermined *in defense of the family itself.*

This circularity of legitimations was, in turn, grounded on another class-based assessment of female sexual "nature." While claiming that middle-class women's passions were "naturally" restricted to their homes and families (often, but not necessarily always, to the exclusion of sexual enjoyment),[5] middle-class sexual ideology concomitantly sexualized and eroticized the bodies of working-class women.[6] These representations portraying working-class women as both sexually active and attractive permitted middle-class men virtually unrestricted legal (if not licit) sexual access to working-class women's bodies by confirming that they were both in their different ways seen to be "naturally" sexual—unlike their mutual "other," the middle-class woman.[7] To take just one widely disseminated example, in his famous mid-century assessment of prostitution, which appeared in the fourth volume of *London Labour and the London Poor* (1861–62), Henry Mayhew goes to great lengths to provide a credible, detailed depiction of the varying conditions among those women engaging in "the disgraceful trade." From the outset, however, the ideological parameters of Mayhew's discussion indicate that what is at stake in his writing is not just the description of "London's Underworld," but also its implicit distinction from the realms of bourgeois propriety, as his definition of the prostitute makes clear: "Literally every woman who yields to her passion and loses her virtue is a prostitute, but many draw a distinction between those who live by promiscuous intercourse, and those who confine themselves to one man."[8] Here Mayhew indicates that while there may be varying qualities of "prostitution" that can be designated by a woman's relationship to her male patrons, the determining factor that *defines her as a prostitute* is that she defies the strictures that constitute bourgeois femininity, i.e., the defense of her "virtue" and the refusal of her "passion." It is important to stress that this characterization of female propriety is distinctly middle class, since as Mayhew's own earlier pieces on needlewomen—written as part of his series for the *Morning Chronicle* (13 and 23 November 1849)—illustrate, workingclass women engaged in various forms of nonmarital sexual relationships to support themselves and their children both financially and emotionally.[9] Yet while Mayhew carefully circumscribes the world of prostitution so that by definition it cannot intersect with the world of middle-class women, his own investigations require that he move between the two, consorting with the very women he seeks to describe. More than just a proximate relationship, however, Mayhew's interactions with the women he interviews become simulations of erotic encounters, with Mayhew on several occasions reporting that he plied women with liquor and/or paid them in order to obtain their stories. Thus Mayhew, the investigator, effectively becomes a surrogate for the prostitute's male clients in order to obtain the narratives that he can then use to characterize the very women whom he defines as prostitutes. In other words, by moving outside the domestic realms of middleclass femininity in order to characterize its emphatically nonbourgeois antithesis, Mayhew himself both (re)produces and enters into the very eroticized dynamic which he retrospectively determines to be the locus of prostitution.[10]

This kind of sexual alignment between the middle-class male and the working-class female not only shapes mid-Victorian discussions of prostitution but also underlies the discourse on what was deemed to be a coincident and corollary problem: venereal disease. As these issues were brought increasingly into public discussions throughout the last half of the century, and especially as they were conjoined as the paradigmatic examples of "social diseases" in the growing literature on "public health," they served as an important locus for the renegotiation of relations between sex, gender, and class. One primary impetus for this renegotiation was the passage during the 1860s of a series of parliamentary measures known collectively as the Contagious Diseases Acts (C. D. Acts), which empowered local police and health authorities to detain and examine women who were "known" to be "common prostitutes" for signs of venereal infection.[11] Outraging large numbers of individuals who abhorred the explicit sexual scapegoating of working-class women, these acts became the target for a coalition of middle-class feminists, evangelicals, and radical working-class men who sought their repeal from the early 1870s until the mid-1880s.

Repealers—or "abolitionists" as they called themselves—viewed the C. D. Acts both as a tacit state license for prostitution (i.e., as the state's attempt to make prostitution "safe" by making those men who consorted with prostitutes less vulnerable to venereal diseases) and as an unwarranted intrusion on the rights and the bodies of working-class women. In their arguments against the Acts they therefore sought to challenge the prevailing sexual asymmetries that underlay such legislation, thereby providing the catalyst for a public rearticulation of late-Victorian sex/gender ideologies. In particular, the journalistic, medical, legal, evangelical, and feminist writings of the repeal movement sought to initiate a public (re)negotiation of the conceptual relations between gender and class in order to articulate new standards for middle-class male sexuality. However, beyond this specifically ideological agenda, the objectives of the repeal movement also lead them to attempt to codify these standards for male propriety legislatively, both by vociferously demanding that the C. D. Acts be rescinded and then by seeking new legislation that would regulate male sexual access to women. Although it took more than a decade for them to achieve these aims, the abolitionists were successful on both counts: the C. D. Acts were suspended in 1883 before being fully repealed in 1886 and in 1885 the Criminal Law Amendment Act defined new statutory limits on male sexuality. This act, fully titled, "An Act to make further provision for the Protection of Women and Girls, the suppression of brothels, and other purposes," quite clearly grew out of the popular momentum produced by the repeal campaigns and was primarily concerned with limiting access to female prostitution and raising the age of consent for young women.[12] Nevertheless, as amended in order to include the now infamous section 11, also known by its author's name as the "Labouchere amendment," it also became the occasion for reclassifying the legal status of sexual acts between men for the first time since "sodomy" was made a civil offense in Britain in 1533 (see chapter 4). Thus, the legislative effects initiated (though not entirely orchestrated) by the campaigns to repeal the Contagious Diseases Acts effectively came to link the legal status of same-sex practices between men to the larger cultural agitation over male sexuality and to the concomitant ideological transformations it provoked. Since this was the statute under which Oscar Wilde would be tried and convicted ten years later, an elucidation of the conditions that preceded its passage will provide an important insight into the discursive formation from which this new legal definition arose, especially as it would come to be most publicly embodied by Wilde himself.

Given the imbrication of normative male sexuality and concepts of men's "health" discussed in the last chapter, it should hardly be surprising that the story of the rise and fall of the C. D. Acts and the attendant changes in the legal circumscription both of male sexuality and of sex between men[13] evolved in tandem with new governmental strategies designed to defend "public health." Indeed, citing the incidence of "venereal diseases" became an important way of linking normative notions of sexuality to the promotion of personal "health," in turn legitimating public strategies to police individual behaviors. Throughout the nineteenth century the proliferation of venereal diseases became one of a number of health issues that accompanied the rapid expansion of urban population. The growing number of urban centers as well as the number of urban inhabitants provided a fertile breeding ground for a wide variety of serious illnesses that manifested themselves in series of deadly epidemics throughout the first half of the nineteenth century.[14] This marked threat to human life and especially the lives of the urban poor who primarily inhabited overcrowded, poorly venti lated, improperly constructed housing with inadequate water and sewage facilities (not to mention inadequate food), precipitated the conjunction of medical and state apparatus in an effort to preserve "public health."[15]

"Public health," thus, became the basis for the widening penetration by government and medical authorities into the daily lives of the British people. Beginning in the 1830s with the statistical works of William Farr, whose efforts resulted in the first public assessments of rampant mortality and morbidity rates among the general population, concern for the health and living conditions of urban dwellers led to the passage of the Public Health Act in 1848. This act established a General Board of Health and empowered local authorities to establish local health boards to address the growing problems of city life; however, since it relied exclusively upon local impetus to undertake improvements, and since these improvements were often opposed as examples of intolerable state interference, the 1848 act ultimately effected little change.[16] It was not until 1866, the same year the second of the C. D. Acts was passed, that the Sanitary Act became the first piece of national public-health legislation to instigate compulsory adherence to new codes of sanitation.

According the Anthony Wohl, this compulsory aspect signaled an important shift in state strategies to assure the lives of the citizenry: "The [Sanitary] Act marked an important stage in the development of the state in preventative medicine. No longer did it merely direct and advise local authorities. It could now compel action, and in that sense take charge of the direction and tempo of reform throughout England."[17] Following upon the establishment of the metropolitan police force in 1839, the new powers vested in health authorities gave rise to increased surveillance, assessment, and intervention in the lives of the urban population. Through this confluence of legislative actions, the British state could for the first time directly address (in a very material sense) the bodies and the lives of a civilian population in the name of preserving its physiological well-being. Of course, as already suggested in the specific case of middle-class boys and men, "health" is a very potent ideological construct and the ramifications of this new strategy of state intervention can be understood, as Michel Foucault has argued, as a part of the larger dispersion of a new regime of power that invests the body in the name of preserving its life.[18] Hence, more than just ameliorative proposals, the legislative developments designed to contain the multiple threats of "disease" in England introduced new possibilities for surveying, interpreting, regulating, and controlling a wide array of social and sexual practices.

In particular, the new policy of state intervention on behalf of "public health" explicitly shaped the passage of legislation aimed at containing those conditions that came to be specifically designated as "social diseases": prostitution and venereal disease. Since taken together—as was often the case—they simultaneously represented symbolic and somatic threats to the bourgeois family, both prostitution and venereal disease became the focus from mid-century onward of a (sometimes nearly hysterical) public concern that, in turn, legitimated new forms of state practices to contain them. While the actual figures remain somewhat dubious, it seems clear that the growth of urban centers accelerated both the numbers of women entering prostitution (either as a sole or partial means of self-support) and the numbers of individuals who contracted venereal diseases[19]; however, the unreliability of actual statistics often gave rise to overblown notions of the perceived threats. As Keith Nield has recently suggested: "Exaggeration of the numbers of prostitutes, a notorious feature of the literature of prostitution in mid-century, was a function of the despair widely felt about worsening urban conditions and an expression of middle-class fears about the corrosive character of this *lumpenproletariat*."[20]

The projection of middle-class fears about "public health" onto both prostitution and venereal diseases illustrates the manner in which "health" became a critical criterion for normative definitions of middle-class behavior. As the descriptions of "degeneration" appearing throughout the period suggest, the symptomatology of venereal disease provided the archetype for a hereditary illness that manifests itself in the decay of the ideal, "healthy," human body.[21] Since middle-class men's patronage of prostitutes increased the potential for rapidly transmitting this degeneracy across class lines, it directly threatened one of the most important supports of class difference: the geopolitical demarcation of the urban space into distinct class environments. As one contemporary account declared: "Married men—the fact is as notorious as it is grievous—are, in numberless instances, regular frequenters of brothels, and by their means syphilis is introduced into the bosom of families; and the most virtuous women, and the most innocent children, in this way become victims."[22] If middle-class men returning from their assignations brought back the taint of disease—here clearly associated with the poor and working classes—into the very "bosom of families" (a metaphor that reminds us of the risk that married women faced from infection by their husbands), then the certainty of geopolitically defined class difference was belied by the susceptibility of middle-class bodies.[23] This somatic vulnerability was, in turn, metonymically associated with the urban geography itself such that, as Judith Walkowitz has noted, "for mid-century Victorians, prostitution constituted a distressing street disorder which threatened to infect 'healthy' neighborhoods. . . ."[24]

The coincidence of this middle-class fear of venereal contagion with an epidemic proportion of venereal cases among the British Army and Navy—not coincidentally perceived as a threat to the national defense and therefore to the "health" of the nation—provided the specific catalyst for the passage of the Contagious Diseases Acts. Following the disastrous losses of the Crimean War (1854–56) in which over twenty-two percent of the British forces perished, the vast majority from disease,[25] as well as the high number of British troops returning from tours of India during the 1860s who had contracted venereal infections,[26] a new attention was focused upon the health crises of the British military. In large part, military forces were comprised of poor and working-class men who enlisted in the Army or Navy only to find horrifying conditions consisting of poor pay, unsanitary living quarters, and intense periods of boredom. This situation, especially in the era after the 1848 revolutions on the continent, made military discipline so precarious that Brian Harrison has suggested: "At a time when the government could not rely on the loyalty of the socially underprivileged, it had to prevent troops and citizens from acquiring common interests and common ties. Instead of creating a national citizen militia, therefore, a bachelor professional army without family ties was assembled in large depots and moved regularly about the country."[27] Thus prevented from creating any sustained and sustaining ties outside of the military service and severely enjoined against forming any sexual liaisons within the service,[28] soldiers and sailors were left to spend their time and money on drinking and prostitution. One recent feminist historical account has described the situation as follows:

> It was a proverbial fact that brothels and drinking places sprang up in the vicinity of any army garrison town or camp. Soldiers' desire for prostitutes was seen to be based in men's involuntary sexual drive which made liaisons with prostitutes an inevitable, if unfortunate, necessity. The structure of military employment, with its delayed marriage and deliberate maintenance of a transient male population, was thought to exacerbate this need for sexual gratification. Soldiers were mere slaves to their passions and victims of the military life-style.[29]

Given the ideological justification for the "inevitability" of soldiers' and sailors' recourse to prostitutes as well as the lack of adequate sanitation facilities to inhibit the spread of infection, the incidence of venereal disease in the British army was indeed quite alarming. According to the Army Medical Department Report for 1859, of every 1000 men there were 422 reported admissions to the hospital for venereal disease.[30] As this figure indicates, venereal diseases caused an astounding loss of manpower which represented not only a significant monetary expenditure but also a serious depletion of those available for active duty.

It was in order to address these challenges to military efficiency and finance that the Contagious Diseases Acts were passed. Following upon the reports of the Royal Commission on the Health of the Army (1857) and the Committee to Inquire into the Prevalence of Venereal Disease in the Army and Navy (1862), which statistically documented the extent of venereal infections in the armed forces, a heightened awareness of the prevalence of venereal diseases among enlisted men led politicians to introduce legislation designed to control the contagion. The first of the Contagious Diseases Acts, passed in July of 1864, provided that in eleven named garrison and dock towns any woman identified as a diseased prostitute by a plainclothes member of the Metropolitan police could be compelled to undergo medical examination. An accused woman had the option of choosing to submit "voluntarily" to the examination or be brought up before a magistrate (thereby publicizing her accused status) and then bound over by his order. If found to be diseased she could be detained in a "lock hospital" for up to three months.[31] The first act remained ineffective in part due to a lack of financial and administrative resources, but perhaps more significantly due to a basic flaw in the concept, endemic to all of the C. D. Acts, *which sought to check diseased women while leaving their male clientele unexamined.* In an attempt to improve the legislation's efficacy, the first act was superseded in June of 1866 by a second act that extended the jurisdiction of the legislation to two additional military areas and instituted a system of compulsory periodic examination of all women who there was "good cause to believe . . . [were] common prostitute[s]" for a period of up to one year. While the earlier statute had required the examination of only those women thought to be diseased, the new act entailed the increased surveillance of all working-class women who lived in the environs of garrison and port towns for whom "good cause" (i.e., the testimony of a single undercover policeman) could be produced to verify their status as sex workers. An 1869 act amended the 1866 statute, extending its provisions to five additional districts, increasing the maximum period of detention from three to nine months, providing for moral and religious instruction of the women incarcerated under the act, and making the acts effective for an indefinite length of time.

Underlying all of the C. D. Acts were certain basic assumptions about the nature of male and female sexuality that characterized the larger Victorian middle-class understanding of prostitution. One of the most direct expression of these assumptions can be found in W. R. Greg's article "Prostitution" in the *Westminster Review* (1850), which eloquently expresses the prevailing sexual ideology of the Victorian middleclass for whom it was written:

> [T]here is a radical and essential difference between the sexes: the arrangements of nature and the customs of society would be even more unequal than they are, were it not so. In men, in general, the sexual desire is inherent and spontaneous, and belongs to the condition of puberty. In the other sex, the desire is dormant, if nonexistent, till excited; always till excited by undue familiarities; almost always till excited by actual intercourse.[32]

While the purpose of Greg's formulation was to establish the conditions under which women "fall" into prostitution, his assessment of the subtending sexual dichotomy transcends his immediate argument. For men, he declares, "sexual desire is inherent and spontaneous," that is, it results from the biological attributions of "maleness" which like all other secondary sex characteristics appear as a "condition of puberty." This biological explanation for the necessary "activity" of male sexual desire is presented in contrast to the "dormancy" of the "other sex" whose desire is only awakened as a function of male sexual "excitement." Thus, by grounding his claims in an assessment of male somatic necessity, Greg "scientifically" legitimates an ideological duality in which "natural" male desire "denatures" women by awakening in them that which is "naturally" dormant.

As an essential component of the "double standard," this sexual dualism allowed the assessment of legal culpability for sexual acts to fall most heavily upon women. Even for those, like Greg, who argued that prostitutes, and "fallen women" in general, were drawn into their sexualized identities by a variety of social and personal factors (with corruption by men, however, always necessarily serving as the efficient cause), the responsibility for their transgression ultimately lay with, or more appropriately "in," the woman. According to this argument, women who engaged in nonmarital sexual experiences—and especially, those who engaged in such encounters for money—always already violated the "nature" of their "sex" by acting upon the sexual possibilities of their bodies. Perhaps the most compelling example of this contradictory claim can be found in William Acton's *Prostitution,* which is remarkable not only because it so clearly illustrates the (il)logic at play in such assessments of male and female sexuality, but also because its author was a vociferous supporter of the C. D. Acts. Indeed, in the preface to the revised edition of the book that appeared in 1870, Acton lauds the "happy results" of the C. D. Acts and dedicates his text to arguing for the extension of the Acts to the "community at large." In a chapter succinctly entitled, "Causes of Prostitution," Acton produces a self-evidently confused account of his subject, one that characterizes his treatment of the issue. Beginning with his assessment of male desire (also discussed in the last chapter), Acton asserts: "Th[e] desire of the male is the want that produces the demand, of which prostitution is, in fact, the artificial supply of a natural demand, taking the place of a natural supply through the failure of the latter, or the vitiated character of the demand. It is impossible to exaggerate the force of [male] sexual desire. . . ."[33] Yet having initially established the "unnaturalness" of the "unmanly man" as the cause of prostitution since his lack of self-control leads him to seek "substitutes for, or imitations of the relationship resulting from love, and known as the married state" (163), Acton goes on to characterize the prostitute as follows:

She is a woman who gives for money that which she ought to give only for love; who ministers to passion and lust alone, to the exclusion of all the higher qualities, and nobler sources of enjoyment which combine with desire, to produce the happiness derived from the intercourse of the sexes. She is a woman with half the woman gone, and that half containing all that elevates her nature leaving her a mere instrument of impurity; degraded and fallen she extracts from the sin of others the means of living, corrupt and dependent on corruption, and therefore interested directly in the increase of immorality—a social pest, carrying contamination and foulness to every quarter to which she has access. . . . Such women, ministers of evil passions, not only gratify desire, but also arouse it. (166)

With this description, Acton attempts to cast the prostitute out of the sphere of the biologically female by foregrounding the ways she violates bourgeois gender expectations so that she becomes in his evocative characterization: "a woman with half the woman gone." Moreover, this half-woman is possessed of a powerful ability to produce the very desire that only two pages earlier Acton argued was part of men's essential "nature." Thus, Acton concludes that the prostitute constitutes "a sad burlesque of woman" and concomitantly that prostitution "is itself a cause of its own existence" (167), thereby legitimating the fundamental innocence of male sexual desire in the face of female culpability.

The effects engendered by this kind of dichotomous conceptualization of male and female sexuality are readily recognizable in the procedures enacted by the Contagious Diseases legislation. While the intent of the acts was to contain the spread of venereal disease throughout the military, the exclusive focus of their regulations was on the female population that sexually served enlisted men—even though it was widely recognized that men as well as women were instrumental in the transmission of venereal infections.[34] Indeed, while regular genital inspection of unmarried soldiers was general army practice until 1859, it was discontinued due to its unpopularity not only with the inspected soldiers but more especially with the inspecting medical officers.[35] However, these same medical officers, when called upon to conduct genital examinations of suspected prostitutes under the C. D. Acts, found little to object to in the exclusive examination of women, preferring instead to justify this exclusion of males by recourse to assumptions about the dichotomy between male and female "natures." As the *Report of the Royal Commission on the Administration and Operation of the Contagious Diseases Acts* (1871) clearly indicates, the asymmetrical relation between the female prostitute and her male client was unambiguously determined to be an essential factor in the enforcement of the legislation:

> Many witnesses have urged that as well on the grounds of justice as expediency, soldiers and sailors should be subjected to regular examination. We may at once dispose of this recommendation, so far as it is founded on the principle of putting both parties to the sin of fornication on the same footing by the obvious but not less conclusive reply that there is no comparison to be made between prostitutes and the men who consort with them. With the one sex the offense is committed as a matter of gain; with the other it is an irregular indulgence of a natural impulse.[36]

This formulation, which opposes the motives of female prostitutes ("gain") to those of their male clients ("natural impulse"), constructs an asymmetrical set of normative assumptions about the sexuality of the parties involved in "the offense." As Myna Trustram succinctly comments, "the method chosen to improve the [enlisted] men's health betrayed a basic belief that they were slaves to their animal passions and had to be protected against the worst consequences of this."[37] Hence, while men are described as involuntarily "indulging" a "natural impulse" inhering in the biological "nature" of their sex, women are perceived as willfully violating their "nature" in pursuit of more worldly ends. That these women were for the most part poor, under-paid, or unemployed "unskilled daughters of the unskilled classes,"[38] whose "gain" allowed them only to eke out the most meager of exis-tences seemed in no way to make them less culpable than their male procurers who had no choice but to yield to their "natural impulses."

It was in order to redress the oppressive consequences of this "double standard" that the movement to repeal the Contagious Diseases Acts coalesced during the late 1860s and early 1870s. Bringing together a variety of middle-class feminists, personal-rights advocates, working-class radicals, and evangelicals, the repeal movement grew from a small sectarian group into a large coalition of groups opposing state support what for they called "male vice."[39] Beginning with the organization of a successful intervention at a session of the Social Sciences Convention (held in Bristol in October of 1869) which otherwise supported the C. D. Acts, a group of activists opposed to the legislation convened to form "The Anti-Contagious Diseases Act Extension Association," which shortly thereafter changed its name to the "National Association for the Repeal of the Contagious Diseases Act." Since the National

Association initially excluded women, a parallel organization, the "La-
dies National Association for the Repeal of the Contagious Diseases
Acts" (L.N.A.), was established soon thereafter. Coming under the
charismatic leadership of Josephine Butler, a feminist activist whose
earlier experience in higher education and rescue work for women
provided her with ample resources for guiding repeal work, the L.N.A.
quickly moved into the forefront of the repeal efforts.

From the outset, the clearly feminist tenor of the L.N.A. shaped the
analysis of the repeal movement's attacks on the C. D. legislation. In
its first major public manifesto, the "Women's Protest," published in
the *Daily News* on 1 January 1870, the L.N.A. attacked the "double
standard" inherent in the C. D. Acts, noting that they entailed "a
momentous change in the the legal safeguards hitherto enjoyed by
women in common with men." The L.N.A.'s opposition to the acts
was further based on the observation that "it is unjust to punish the
sex who are the victims of vice, and leave unpunished the sex who are
the main cause, both of the vice and its dreaded consequences."[40] This
assignment of the "main cause" of prostitution to men—which became
the underpinning of all further repeal movement analysis—explicitly
challenged the assumptions about male sexuality asserted by the supporters of the acts. Rather than seeing men as the involuntary conduits
of their "natural impulses," the "abolitionists" depicted men as the
agents of women's degradation. This strategy of directly challenging
the prevailing, and in fact legislated, sex/gender ideology enabled the
repeal movement to articulate a counter ideology that situated male
and female sex roles in the context of contemporary sexual and class
relations.

The literature of the repeal movement, then, undertook to illustrate
the social conditions whereby working-class women were induced into
sexual relations with men for money. Challenging the notion that poor
women entered into the trade for "gain," abolitionists pointed to the
financial necessities that lead many women to seek to earn their income
in whole or in part from prostitution. Quoting Josephine Butler, Judith
Walkowitz notes: "Mid-Victorian feminists treated prostitution as the
result of the artificial constraints placed on women's social and economic activity: inadequate wages and restriction of women's industrial
employment forced some women onto the streets where they took up
the 'best paid industry'—prostitution."[41] The suggestion that prostitution might be a logical choice for women who had few other options
subverted the bio-moral argument, which sought to incriminate
"fallen" women, thereby shifting the responsibility for "vice" to those
men who took advantage of this female economic vulnerability. Shel-

don Amos in his 1877 survey of European legislation regulating prostitution makes the case succinctly: "The sole *cause* of prostitution,—in
the true sense of the word *cause*, that [is], if it alone were away, the
effect could not and would not follow,—is *the demand for it created
by the profligacy of men who are able to pay enough to tempt forth
the supply.*"[42]

By explicitly articulating the sexual asymmetry upon which the C. D.
Acts were predicated (i.e., "male profligacy"/female poverty), members
of the repeal movement challenged the assumption that male sexuality
"necessitated" the existence of prostitution. They foregrounded the
implicit equation of "masculinity" with the physical expression of
"male sex," and then undertook to separate these two components of
male gender ideology in order to argue that "maleness" was distinct
from male sexual activity and, indeed, that restraint of sexual expression ("continence") was the highest form of "masculinity." Thus, probably the most forceful argument marshaled against the acts, reiterated
in a multitude of forms, was that they tacitly—if not actually—legitimated a rampant form of male sexuality which overflowed the boundaries of the monogamous bourgeois family. For the sake of brevity,
one excellent example of this indictment of extramarital male sexual
activity produced jointly by the British, Continental, and General Federation for the Abolition of State Prostitution and the National Medical
Association (Great Britain and Ireland) for the Abolition of State Regulation of Prostitution provides the pattern that many repeal movement
texts followed:

> Men are practically taught that continence is no longer a duty, for
> the State has made provision, as far as possible, to enable them to
> sin with impunity; and the youth of every country where such
> legislation [regulating prostitution] exists, is also taught, as soon as
> old enough to comprehend it, that so far from this sin being consid-
> ered in them blamable or to be avoided, the State has entirely
> assumed that it will be practiced by youth, and so largely practiced,
> that it has gone out of its way, and made costly and elaborate
> arrangements, involving the grossest injustices upon women, in or-
> der, before-hand, to make this sin as free from danger for him as
> possible.[43]

In this passage the regulation of prostitution for the purposes of containing the spread of venereal disease is depicted as undermining a
definition of male sexuality for which "continence" is a "duty." However, the consequences of this male incontinence are not examined in

themselves (except in that they pave the way for "the grossest injustices upon women") but rather are indicted in so far as they suggest to young men that they may "sin with impunity." The focus, then, of the objection derives from the perception that the form of male sexuality that is legitimated by "the State" is not the "continent" familial ideal of the middle class but rather one that deems that "the sin," i.e., nonmarital sexual intercourse, will be "largely practiced" by "youth." The abolitionist case is, therefore, predicated on affirming the same normative definition of male sexual practice found in the antimasturbatory literature of the period (examined in the previous chapter) inasmuch as both sought to contain all legitimate expressions of male sexuality to the monogamous, reproductive, married couple. However, whereas the antimasturbatory texts focused primarily on defining deviations from this norm as "unhealthy," the writings emerging from within the campaign to repeal the C. D. Acts, even when produced by medical authorities, largely classified them as "sin."

The use of the language of "sin" as a part of the attack on the C. D. Acts reflects the both extensive religious involvement of many of the participants in the repeal campaigns and the larger religious underpinnings of familialist ideology. As Brian Harrison has demonstrated, religious affiliation provided a significant common denominator for a large number of the individuals prominent in nineteenth-century moral reform.[44] Within the repeal movements, a large number of participants were members of nonconformist congregations assuring that the enunciation of repeal positions would incorporate this Christian framework. Noting the coincidence of abolitionist and religious rhetorics, Paul McHugh comments:

> Religion represented a vital, urgent part of life for most middle-class reformers; their political rhetoric was often couched in devotional terms, and their insistence that "what is morally wrong can never be politically right" owed everything to religious conviction. The [anti-] Contagious Diseases Acts campaign was emphatically part of the underpinnings of politics with religious zeal in the late nineteenth century; Josephine Butler composed countless exhortatory prayers which were eagerly printed by repeal journals. Since they regarded religion as supremely important, repealers strove to demonstrate the full support of religious feelings—failure to have done so would have undermined the claim that their's was a moral crusade.[45]

Following the enthusiastic reception in Britain of revivalism during the 1860s,[46] the repeal movement drew upon this popular religious fervor both for its membership and for its style. Appealing to the ideology of "Christian marriage" as the legitimation for their pronouncements on male behavior, repeal campaigners adopted a revivalist strategy, stumping the country with emotion-filled speeches and meetings. Josephine Butler, in particular, was well known for her ability to hold her audiences' rapt attention and to use her emotional appeal to enlist supporters for the cause. However, perhaps even more important than these stylistic similarities, the abolitionists held the belief, in common with the other major mid-century political struggle marked by religious involvement, the Temperance Movement, that religious energy must be utilized widely throughout the nation, especially through movements for social reform.[47]

Within the repeal campaigns this notion of social reform expressed itself in two forms: through "rescue work" and through the advocacy of "social purity." The former concentrated on reclaiming "fallen" women, i.e., attempting to provide them both with skills to support themselves without recourse to prostitution and with the moral faculties to find a return to such "degradation" inconceivable; the latter focused on training men and boys to embody a continent, Christian ideal of "manliness" in defense of the sanctity of the Christian home. Both of these activities found adherents throughout the repeal campaign. Indeed, Josephine Butler herself, though an ardent feminist and an insightful analyst of the social conditions that led women into prostitution, had been involved in rescue work before she took on the leadership of the L.N.A. and was later the founder of one of the first purity organizations, the Social Purity Alliance, in 1873.[48] However, these religiously inspired activities also signaled deeper divisions within the repeal movement, divisions that would become increasingly apparent as the campaign to revoke the C. D. Acts progressed. The character of these divisions can be understood, in part, through a juxtaposition of two figureheads of the movement, Josephine Butler and her equally charismatic, if less well remembered, contemporary, Ellice Hopkins.[49] While Butler, whose prominent status often served to identify her as the movement's spokesperson, sought to make the repeal campaign a central feminist concern of the mid-nineteenth century, Hopkins was primarily concerned with using the repeal energies in order to reinforce a familialist ideology that located women's position in the home.

For Butler, who reflected the interests of both progressive Christians and secular "freethinkers," the primary arguments against the C. D. Acts were found in the blatant violation of both women's personal liberties and, more directly, women's bodies. Accordingly, in her denouncements of the C. D. legislation, she stressed the arbitrary nature of the accusations that could be laid against women, based solely on the testimony of a single male police officer, and decried the brutality of the required medical examination for which the speculum was specifically introduced into British medical technology. (Butler described these examinations as "instrumental rape.") These practices, in Butler's perspective, were symbolic of the larger inequities that all women suffered due to the asymmetrical distribution of power based on sex in British society.[50]

Ellice Hopkins, on the other hand, was an unabashed supporter of women's traditional roles, who, according to her biographer, believed that "home duties should take the first place in a woman's life," and that it was "the divine order that the man is the head of the woman."[51] Hence, rather than articulating a critique of the C. D. Acts' oppressive character, Hopkins focused primarily on promoting rescue work, instructing working-class mothers on how to avoid incest and immorality, and, most zealously, on founding men's chastity leagues. The last of these, which occupied a large portion of her energy throughout the 1880s, called upon Hopkins and her evangelical supporters to formulate a countervailing gender ideology that would replace those notions of masculinity that defined "maleness" as synonymous with physical expressions of male sexuality with a new concept that expressed masculinity in terms of "chastity." Thus, while Butler and the L.N.A. were able to crystallize a discourse which identified the oppression of prostitutes with the larger oppression of women in the culture, it was left to Hopkins and her cohorts to articulate a corresponding critique of male sexual ideology.

This split in the movement became increasingly apparent over time, such that after the repeal movement garnered what was virtually a total victory and the Acts were suspended in 1883 (they were finally fully repealed in 1886), most of the repeal momentum went, not into feminist or individual-rights struggles, but rather into campaigns against "male lust." Ironically, then, the legacy of the repeal movement, whose initial energies derived in large part from explicitly feminist motives to defend the integrity of women's bodies, was a popular reevaluation of the legal/licit limits for male sexual expression. Perhaps, the prime example of this focus on redefining male gender ideology can be found in the development of the "chastity leagues" in whose organization Ellice Hopkins played an instrumental role. Perceiving that her "rescue" work with prostitutes was an incomplete solution that failed to address the "cause" of prostitution (i.e., "male profligacy"), Hopkins called upon the Church of England Penitentiary Association in 1879 to establish an organization of men for the protection of women and children in order to give men "a more aggressive form of purity, something higher and more vivifying than taking care of their own virtue, that manly, militant virtue which grows strong in fighting the battles of God for the weak and defenseless."[52] In this seminal formulation Hopkins demonstrated the rhetorical strategy that became the hallmark of later prochastity literature: by pitting two elements of contemporary Victorian male ideology against one another, she suggested that the patriarchal power/responsibility that men held over/for women and children challenged them to extend their own personal struggles against sexual desire ("taking care of their own virtue") to a "higher" and "more vivifying" plane. Her use of a military metaphor ("fighting the battle of God") incorporated yet another aspect of male gender ideology (militarism being the state-sanctioned form of "male" aggression) as the "Christian" frame within which this new expression of male gender ideology could take place. Thus, Hopkins effectively rearticulated prominent elements of earlier definitions of masculinity in the legitimation of a new "continent," "manly" norm.[53] Using this analysis as the starting point for an effort to convince the Church of England to adopt a prochastity position, Hopkins emerged victoriously four years later in 1883 when the Church of England Purity Society (C.E.P.S.) was founded.

Along with the White Cross League which was initiated in the same year, C.E.P.S. set the stage for a nationwide series of diocesan conferences and local meetings that foregrounded the dissemination of the new male sexual ideology. Organized on the basis of a subscription membership, both the White Cross League and C.E.P.S. (which eventually merged in 1891 to form the White Cross League Church of England Purity Society, a.k.a. White Cross Society), quickly enrolled large memberships. Using a revivalist strategy that convened large gatherings around the country to espouse the new gospel of continence (often preached with great fervor and effect by Ellice Hopkins herself), chastity advocates addressed tens of thousands of men in the 1880s. In the first two years alone, over 15,000 men "pledged" themselves to chastity,[54] thereby affirming a code of five rules, inscribed on a pledge card (appropriately decorated with the paradigmatic symbol of medieval chivalry, St. George and the Dragon):

1. To treat all women with respect, and endeavor to protect them from wrong and degradation.
2. To use every possible means to fulfil the command, "keep THY-SELF pure."
3. To endeavor to put down all indecent language and coarse jests.

4. To maintain the law of purity as equally binding upon men and women.

5. To endeavor to spread these principles among my companions, and to try and help my younger brothers.[55]

With these five rules, local branches of the chastity leagues enunciated the doctrine of male continence. Simply put, men as well as women were now to be bound by the standards of premarital virginity and chastity within marriage. However, whereas men had heretofore been supposed to look to women as the guardians of moral rectitude, the pledge shifted the burden of moral responsibility to men themselves. Tying male continence to a patriarchal ideology that legitimated adult male ascendency over women and younger men, the social purity "pledge" authorized male chastity by appealing to the male prerogative implied in the notion of "protection." Thus, by "pledging" new members to the cause, local chapters of C.E.P.S. and the White Cross League effectively instigated men to affirm a new view of male gender identity which encouraged them to reject all nonreproductive, nonmarital sexual desires in order to reassert their larger patriarchal privilege.

The effects of local chastity league meetings were significant, then, both in terms of large-scale dissemination of the new norms for male behavior and in terms of the establishment of a new organizational basis for their implementation. As reported in a publication of the White Cross League, one country vicar noted significant changes in his community after forming a branch of the chastity organization: "What was the consequence? Information poured in on me. Mothers told me of their boys' temptations; the policemen put me on the track of dangers to my young women, and I was able to bring to book two men who were making themselves 'teachers of iniquity.' "[56] Even if the clergyman was exaggerating the effects of his efforts here in order to convince others of the efficacy of his actions, the implications of his claims are clear: not only did the local chapter of the chastity leagues serve to disseminate the normative ideology of male chastity, but they also established surveillance mechanisms whereby other local authorities (mothers and policemen, for example) could be enlisted to ensure its enforcement. Since with their hundreds of local chapters, chastity organizations provided a highly visible, widely dispersed network that undertook both the dissemination and collection of information on a vast range of male sexual practices, they could provide local support for the inculcation of new continent norms.

This penetration of the disciplinary strategies of chastity supporters into the daily lives of thousands of men and boys reiterated on a much

wider scale the contemporary concern with containing male sexual
activity found in the medical and pedagogical writings on masturbation
examined earlier. It should come as little surprise, then, that the very
extensive publications of the chastity leagues offered a wide selection
of antimasturbatory texts. In fact, much of the literature of the social-
purity movement was written by doctors, teachers, and clergy who
reworked the materials found in medical journals or in school sermons
for this wider "Christian" audience, as the titles listed in the *Catalogue
of Books and Papers on the Purity Question* (n.d.) suggest: the titles
include "Letter to a Lad," "Physical Consequences of Impurity," "Evil
Results of Impurity," "Testimony of Medical Men," "Plain Truth
about School," "Medical Opinions," and "Quacks and their Advertisements" among many others.[57] While most of these titles probably
circulated only in the thousands or perhaps tens of thousands, some
notable texts, such as Alfred Dyer's "Plain Words for Young Men on
Avoided Subjects" and "Safeguards against Immorality"were said to
have sold upwards of 150,000 copies each, and another White Cross
text, "True Manliness," is reputed to have sold over 1,000,000.[58] In
addition, the more popular tracts often were accompanied by (or derived from) lecture tours in which the author declaimed his or her
learned opinions before large audiences; for example, Henry Varley's
"Lecture to Men Only" was said to have been heard by over 250,000
men and in pamphlet form to have sold 90,000 copies.[59] Thus, the
social-purity organizations can be seen to have provided a wider context in which the antimasturbatory messages that had earlier circulated
primarily among professionals for dissemination through their institutional practices (medical, pedagogical, pastoral) could now be communicated directly to large public audiences either in person or in print.

While the social-purity version of the antimasturbatory message did
not differ significantly from its secular parallels in substance, it was
deployed in a markedly different rhetorical context. Since the medical
texts on/against masturbation were nominally written within a scientific discourse, they were constrained by the contemporary criteria for
"objectivity" and "truth" inherent to the genre; however, doctors
writing for "Christian" White Cross or C.E.P.S. publications had more
leeway to extrapolate on the moral and ethical implications of their
"scientific" findings. By eliding the differences among interpretations
of somatic experience defined by "scientific" and "Christian" frameworks, the social-purity texts were able to bridge these two social
paradigms, thereby providing an overreaching religious ideology
within which the medical assessment of the male body could be marshaled to social-purity ends. In general, the antimasturbatory writings

of social purity authors made an implicit and often explicit connection between the physical male body and spiritual (male) "body of Christ" in order to propose that individual males identify their somatic experience with "the Holiness of Him in whose Body we are baptized."[60] For example, the use of the epigraph "I keep under my body, and bring it into subjection" (I. Cor. IX. 27) as the frame for one pamphlet otherwise devoted to the development of a physical regime to control sexual desire (e.g., it suggests "plentiful use of cold water," "constant occupation," "moderation," "avoid[ing] unhealthy excitements," etc.) encourages readers to interpret their "subjection" of the body as part of a larger Christian way of life in which Christ's physical suffering provides the model for a proper relation to one's body (i.e., one gives up one's body for a greater good).[61] Within this Christian paradigm, men were to conceptualize their bodies in terms of the "Holy Body of Christ" so that they could interrupt their physical (sexual) desire with intellectual and spiritual understanding. This reinterpretation of the male body as "Christ's body" provided the mechanism whereby the social purity reformers sought to mark the individual with the stigmata of social belief in order to utilize the authority of Christian discourse to define a new "chaste" embodiment of masculinity.

The antimasturbatory literature of the chastity leagues reflected this larger Christian project by underscoring the need for self-mastery and self-control as the medical prescription for the continent norm. C. G. Wheelhouse, one-time president of the British Medical Association, clearly framed the issues in his pamphlet "The Special Temptation of Early Life. An Attempt to Solve the Difficulty of a Pure and Healthy Minded Child on the Subject of Solitary Sin": "so dreadful is the hold with which this terrible vice seizes its victim, that he soon loses all control over himself, and abandons himself without restraint or check to its vicious indulgence."[62] In this characterization, the masturbator is the male out of control: given over to the "vicious indulgence" of his "vice," the hypersexualized habitual onanist abjures the "restraint" that would characterize his "subjection" to a higher ideal. As he indulges in his "solitary sin," the masturbating youth becomes a "victim" to his young male body which through its focus on his "sex" perverts its own "manliness." F. Le Gros Clark, in his text, "The Perils of Impurity: A Few Words of Warning to Boys and Young Men," takes up precisely this connection between sexual expression and masculinity:

> Unfortunately there are many false notions about manliness among boys, and in trying to imitate those who are older than themselves, they are more disposed to follow bad than good examples. In a

certain class we see that this is the case in the use of disgusting oaths and filthy language. But my special object is to notice the common impression which boys have, that they become more manly by imitating, so far as they can, their elders, by the indulgence of the sexual passion in secret and alone.[63]

Writing for boys who are necessarily in the process of becoming men, Clark attempts to convey a crucial distinction between the attainment of the biological maturity and the achievement of "manliness." While the expression of sexual desire may have the appearance of denoting adult male status, Clark claims that "solitary vice leads to the very reverse of that which is manly."[64] In other words, the experience of what appears to be a biologically determined characteristic of maturation in the male sex, the physical development of sexual capacity, when experienced solely in relation to one's own person actually manifests the "reverse" of that which is "manly." In order to make this claim, Clark implicitly creates a separation and simultaneous rearticulation of physical sex and gender ideology: "manliness" must first be divorced from the male body per se and then reascribed to a certain limited range of somatic possibilities in order that the "manly" take on the quality of the continent.

This distinction between the "manly" and the "male," then, characterizes the conjunction of medical and social-purity literature. However, in the gap between the biologically "male" and the culturally "manly" arises the necessity for the establishment of a socially defined set of normative behaviors that assure the ascendency of the latter over the former. Within the literature of the chastity leagues this assurance derived from the male's self-mastery over his sexual impulses. In one C.E.P.S. publication, "The Testimony of Medical Men," a sampler of medical writings on masturbation, William Acton provides what can be seen as the quintessence of the social-purity position: "It is a solemn truth, that the sovereignty of the will, or, in other words, the command of the man over himself and his outward circumstances is a matter of habit. Every victory strengthens the victor."[65] Here Acton voices the opinion expressed by all the medical "experts" quoted in C.E.P.S. pamphlets who seek to redefine the *active* role of "manly" behavior (over and against feminine passivity) so that it is no longer understood in terms of the active expression of male sexual desire but rather in terms of *active self-control*. The new locus for "true" male experience becomes the personal struggle between "will" and "desire," "reason" and "passion," "mind" and "body," which is described as a contest against oneself that must be "won." The metaphor of "victory" over (nonmarital, nonreproductive) sexual expression literalizes the battle between two gender ideologies, one that defines "maleness" through the active expression of male sexual desire and another which defines "manliness" through its active suppression. It is precisely the prevalence (or defeat) of the new continent norm, then, that is manifest through each individual's contest with himself. Hence, by deploying the medical authorities discussed in the last chapter to legitimate this new ideology of "active" restraint, the chastity leagues effectively utilized the discourse of "health" characterized throughout this chapter in order to anchor their campaign against "male lust."

Having first established this culturally legitimated basis for articulating their chaste male norm, the social-purity activists were able in 1885 to translate this "pure" standard into a legal sanction with the passage of the Criminal Law Amendment Act. Although legislation of this kind had been on the social-purity agenda even before the C. D. Acts were suspended in 1883, they had been unable to marshal enough parliamentary support in favor of their attempts to raise the age of consent for young women, to prevent the "entrapment" of children into prostitution, and to interrupt the foreign "traffic in women" to be able get such legislation enacted. However, when a series of articles by William Stead entitled, "Maiden Tribute of Modern Babylon," appeared in the *Pall Mall Gazette* in the summer of 1885, the campaign against male vice turned into a national furor and the long-awaited legislation was passed with breathtaking alacrity.[66] Stead's articles were in themselves a scandal: based on the notion that young virgins were being sold into foreign prostitution, Stead instigated the "purchase" of a young working-class girl and then wrote about his escapade in lurid detail. Not surprisingly, the "Maiden Tribute" articles were incredibly popular—appearing almost immediately in a widely circulated pamphlet form—and catalyzed public opinion in favor of legislation restricting male sexual access to young women. The expression of public outrage at what was perceived to be the incursions of privileged men on the relatively vulnerable bodies of working-class women culminated in a massive public demonstration (estimated at over 250,000 people) in Hyde Park on 22 August. The result was the swift passage of the Criminal Law Amendment Act (48 & 49 Vic. cap. 69), "An Act to make further provision for the Protection of Women and Girls, the suppression of brothels, and other purposes."

While the main purpose of the bill was to raise the age of consent for girls from thirteen to sixteen, and to provide police enforcement for the regulation of brothels, it also included in the now infamous section 11, the first legal classification of sexual relations between men not predicated on earlier ecclesiastical and moral injunctions against specific sexual acts, stating:

> Any male person who, in public or private, commits, or is a party to the commission of, or procures the commission by any male person of, any act of gross indecency with another male person, shall be guilty of a misdemeanor, and being convicted thereof shall be liable at the discretion of the court to be imprisoned for any term not exceeding two years, with or without hard labor.

Prior to the passage of the Criminal Law Amendment Act, legislation regulating sexual acts between persons of the same sex derived from Henry VIII's statute of 1533 which made "Buggery committed with Mankind or with Beast" a capital offense (25 Henry VIII, c. 8). Although the death penalty was set aside in 1861, the essential definition of the crime continued unchanged, proscribing "sodomy" whether committed with (or by) a male or female.[67] This legal injunction, derived from canon law, against a particular type of "unnatural" act— not confined to a single sex or even a single species—was transformed by section 11 of the 1885 legislation which instead prohibited a variety of undetermined "acts of gross indecency with another male person," whose "indecency" derived not from the specific nature of the practice but rather from the fact that they were committed by two (or more) men.[68]

To some interpreters, this section has seemed so entirely inconsistent with the act's primary concern for controlling cross-sex practices that it appears to have been included by its author, Henry Labouchere, in order to discredit the act as a whole.[69] However, when we consider the bill's emergence from those larger transformations of the Victorian sex/gender system described above, the section seems entirely consistent with the ideology of male continence that initially inspired the campaigns from which the legislation emerged. If, as Jeffrey Weeks has suggested, prostitution and sexual activity between men were both understood to be "part of the continuum of undifferentiated male lust, products of men's sexual selfishness," then it is clear that they were construed by morality crusaders as different manifestations of the same problem.[70] Thus, as this interpretation of the "lustful" origins of both male sexual acts *and* sexual acts between men was inscribed in the 1885 legislation—the latter remaining in effect until 1967—it promulgated a concept of male sexuality that was intimately connected to the public redefinition of normative male sexual behavior that had surfaced throughout the 1870s and 1880s. Moreover, even though section 11 defined "acts of gross indecency" between men as a lesser crime than sodomy had previously been considered to be, it introduced into British jurisprudence a new category of malfeasance based solely on the (male) sex of sexual partners. The criminalization of same-sex practices between men generally, "in public or private," therefore superseded the earlier legal injunction against a specific kind of act ("sodomy"), creating a legal definition of individual *male* behavior that led to the specification of a "class" of offenders over and against previous notions that held "sodomy" to be a potential capacity (i.e., the capacity for "sin") inherent in all.[71] It is this legal definition, then, that will be sensationally embodied by Oscar Wilde ten years later when he is convicted on seven counts of committing "acts of gross indecency with another male person" and hence it is to his legal ordeals that we must now turn in order to understand the significance engendered by the new criminal category.

PART II

PART II

PRESSING ISSUES

In the opinion of some, English homosexuality has become much
more conspicuous during recent years, and this is sometimes attributed to the Oscar Wilde case. No doubt, the celebrity of Oscar Wilde
and the universal publicity given to the facts of the case by the
newspapers may have brought conviction of their perversion to
many inverts who were before only vaguely conscious of their abnormality, and, paradoxical though it may seem, have imparted greater
courage to others; but it can scarcely have sufficed to increase the
number of inverts.

Havelock Ellis

Following a paragraph that begins "as to the frequency of homosexuality in England and the United States there is much evidence," this
quotation from the introduction to Havelock Ellis's *Sexual Inversion*
addresses the implication that the number of "inverts" had grown
as a result of "numerous criminal cases and scandals . . . in which
homosexuality has come to the surface."[1] In formulating his response
to this suggestion and to the underlying fears that motivated it, Ellis—
nominally quoting a general, and hence unattributable, cultural voice—
underscores the links between the "Oscar Wilde case" and the emergence of a "conspicuous" form of "English homosexuality." For, while
ostensibly attempting to deny the validity of the contention that the
reporting on Wilde's case "increase[d] the number of inverts," Ellis's
text paraleptically portrays Wilde as the example that defines the
phenomenon and thereby represents Wilde as the paradigmatic case of
a behavior that the rest of the text will then elucidate.

Without question, Wilde's trials and conviction were the most widely
publicized events of their kind in the nineteenth century. As such
they were instrumental in disseminating new representations of sexual
behavior between men that were no longer predicated upon the evocation of a sexual crime that earlier in the same century was still named
(often in Latin) as unnameable: sodomy.[2] However, in playing upon

the word "conviction," Ellis's text also draws attention to the divergent and contradictory effects induced by the trials' newspaper coverage. Although the press reports may have given those men who had little knowledge about their feelings toward and sexual pleasures with other men a more concrete comprehension (a "conviction") of their sexual experience, it did so only by constituting this experience as a "perversion" or "abnormality" for which one could be convicted. Yet, since the conviction that sent Wilde to prison for two years could not entirely efface his eloquent courtroom defense of his conviction that same-sex pleasures were "beautiful," Ellis concludes by conceding that "paradoxical though it may seem, [the newspaper reports on the trials may] have imparted greater courage to others."

Not coincidentally, a similar passage occurs in the "Conclusion" of *Sexual Inversion,* so that the allusions to Wilde's trials effectively frame the first English text dedicated to the topic.[3] Here Ellis attributes the following remarks to "a well-informed American correspondent":

> The Oscar Wilde trial, with its wide publicity, and the fundamental nature of the questions it suggested, appears to have generally contributed to give definiteness and self-consciousness to the manifestations of homosexuality, and to have aroused inverts to take up a definite attitude. (352)

According to Ellis's informant, the trials—or more properly the knowledge effects produced by the "wide publicity" given to the trials—become the medium through which "homosexuality" comes into a new "definite" and "self-conscious" relation to itself. That is, "inverts," when, in the text's sexually charged language, "aroused" by the widely propagated representations of the legal events, come to be able to establish an "attitude" for themselves. This "attitude," then, denotes an epistemological shift whereby the interpretation of sexual relations between men is liberated from a specific link to a particular set of legally prohibited acts and begins to mark out a pattern of characteristic behaviors and relations to the world. The first correspondent then goes on to quote his own "correspondent"—one who had self-professedly "thought and experienced deeply in the matter"—as to the impact the trials had on the community of men who engaged in sexual acts with other men. This second informant remarks that while he had no qualms in breaking legal or moral injunctions for himself, "I now had to ask myself how far I was justified in not only breaking the law, but in causing a like breach in others, and others younger than myself. . . . I cannot say that the trial made me alter my course of life, of the rightness of which I was too convincingly persuaded, but it made me much more careful, and it probably sharpened my sense of responsibility for the young" (352). Wary of legal conviction, the writer notes that despite his personal conviction about the "rightness" of his behavior he will now anticipate the effects of increased surveillance on himself and his (primarily younger) partners by adopting a more vigilant outlook. However, he continues "but I also think it [the results of the trial as a whole] may have done some good in that it made those who, like myself, have thought and experienced deeply in the matter—and these must be no small few—ready to strike a blow, when the time comes, for what we deem to be right, honorable, and clean" (352–53). For Ellis's informants, then, it seems that the contradictory effects induced by the reporting on Wilde's trials not only made them highly conscious of the legal injunctions against the sexual practices that gave them pleasure but also catalyzed their own self-awareness by redefining and rearticulating their status as sexual subjects.[4]

As this brief analysis suggests, the story of Wilde's trials played no small part in crystallizing the concept of "male homosexuality" in the Victorian sexual imagination. Conversely, Wilde was and remains so central to late-nineteenth-century sexual iconography precisely because he became the figure around which new representations of male sexual behavior in England coalesced. Indeed, long after his death—and even today—Wilde continues to function as a powerful figure in popular narratives of sexuality. To cite just one notable example: In its front page coverage of the 1987 March on Washington for Gay and Lesbian Rights, the largest such gathering in the history of sexual liberation movements, the *Washington Post* characterized the convocation of over 500,000 people by saying: "Yesterday's rally would have astounded Oscar Wilde, the nineteenth-century author and playwright once jailed for engaging in what he called 'the love that dared not speak its name.'" This single, not-quite-accurate, historical allusion leaps out of an article otherwise devoted to reporting "the facts" about one of the most visible political actions in recent years. For, rather than being just superfluous detail, the reference to Wilde situates the march in a historical narrative that implicitly juxtaposes the supposed "repression" of the Victorian past—so graphically conjured up by Wilde's imprisonment—to the apparent sexual "freedom" of the contemporary American present. Thus, in the *Washington Post* story, Wilde's life, and especially his conviction, acts as an important historical reference for representing contemporary gay experience: It allows the paper to allude obliquely to the ongoing sexual oppression against which the march was mobilized, while simultaneously consigning such manifest discrimination to the seemingly distant past.

In the years since Wilde's imprisonment, his name has served both to evoke a general form of sexual activity between men and to characterize the kind of males who engage in such acts. Indeed, as the condensation of Wilde's "crimes" with his "character" became ubiquitous in the first decades of this century, his given name alone came to designate a standard deviation from normative male sexuality. For example, until the 1920s the word "Oscar" was popularly used as an epithet among British working-class youth, specifically to challenge the presumptive "masculinity" of individual men.[5] Since this usage was predicated on the journalistic practice of repeatedly investing the signifier "Oscar" with the underlying determinants of difference that were at play in the case (see chapter 5), it suggests the extent to which the public representations of Wilde's behavior provided the basis for (de)legitimating a range of gender-specific practices, both sexual and nonsexual. However, if the public disclosure of Wilde's erotic preferences and practices created new possibilities for articulating the difference between acceptable and unacceptable male gender identities, it also provided men who experienced similar feelings and attractions with a new way of expressing—both to themselves and to each other—the reality, if not the health or acceptability, of their experiences. When the eponymous character in E. M. Forster's (posthumously published) homoerotic novel *Maurice* remarks: "I am an unspeakable of the Oscar Wilde sort,"[6] he indicates that he participated in a form of behavior that "dared not speak its name" *precisely by speaking Wilde's.* Thus the character reiterates the representation of Wilde as a sign of illegitimate and unarticulable sexuality (i.e., "an unspeakable"), but in this case in order to interrupt the discursive exclusions engendered by the unnameablity of his own sexual practice.

It is important to remember, however, that these invocations of "Oscar Wilde" are always historically situated. Indeed, more often than not, they (re)produce a constellation of attributes that define "homosexuality" in opposition to and as the legitimation for shifting conceptions of normative sexuality. For instance, when the recollection of Wilde's convictions erupts into *Lark Rise to Candleford* (1945), Flora Thompson's novel trilogy depicting an English village's transformation from a preindustrial agrarian community to a modern suburb, the text rewrites this disturbance nostalgically in order to (re)produce its familialist ideology for postwar Britain where bourgeois domesticity was increasingly embattled.

> The tragedy of Oscar Wilde did nothing to lessen their natural distrust of intellect, but it did enlighten the younger generation in a

less desirable manner. There were vices, then, in the world which one had not hitherto heard of—vices which, even now, were only hinted at darkly, never described. Fathers for weeks and weeks kept the newspapers locked up with their account books. Mothers when appealed to for information shuddered and said in terrified accents: "Never let me hear that name pass your lips again."[7]

With this brief historical reference, the text shifts modes from a "realistic" depiction of Victorian family life to a moralistic assessment of the "tragedy of Oscar Wilde" that threatened to interrupt it. The description underscores the extent to which newspaper coverage of the legal proceedings served to create new, "less desirable" possibilities for constructing sexual meanings and then projects its disapprobation onto gender-specific, parental authorities who are reciprocally legitimated as sexual experts. By invoking the bipolar protective powers embodied by "fathers" (aligned with the public/political world of commerce) and "mothers" (identified with the domestic/private world of emotion) in defense of the "younger generation," *Lark Rise* reanimates the threat that Wilde's case seemed to pose to the familial ideal of the Victorian middle class in order to provide *retrospectively* an opportunity for reclaiming this very ideal. Hence, as his "name" is metonymically linked to his crimes, signifying "vices . . . one had not hitherto heard of" and providing a concrete way of evoking "vices which *even now*, were only hinted at darkly, never described" (my emphasis), "Oscar Wilde" comes to signify a particular form of male sexual transgression against nineteenth-century domesticity in order to (re)produce—in the mid-twentieth-century—a legitimation for the family itself.

What these various invocations of Wilde's name suggest is that, throughout the century since his conviction, the enduring knowledge effects initiated by his trials have continued to (re)produce "Oscar Wilde" as an index for a variety of "unspeakable" male homoerotic practices and desires. While this indexical usage was clearly predicated upon a variety of cultural meanings already attached to Wilde's person(a) prior to his 1895 legal ordeal, the "universal publicity given to the facts of the case by the newspapers"—as Havelock Ellis so felicitously phrased it—both embellished and expanded his notoriety as a public figure. Even as one of the first and, indeed, most successful nineteenth-century men to self-consciously market himself as cultural icon, without the trials Wilde would never have achieved (in the days before *People* magazine) the ubiquitous coverage that derived from his "downfall." Unquestionably, this textual explosion was connected to the titillating revelations about Wilde's sexual practices; to the high visibility of the cast of characters; and to the larger historical processes that inscribed modes of embodiment for middle-class males outlined in the last three chapters. Yet, in representing the events of the trials, the newspapers also produced narratives that organized this constellation into highly readable and highly entertaining stories in which Wilde was (as he usually liked to be) the center of attention. Moreover, since in these stories "the facts" of the case were necessarily mediated through the generic frameworks popularized by an emerging mass-market press, they organized meaningful patterns of information that privileged certain interpretations both of the legal proceedings per se and of the sexual activities they called into question.

It will be the project of the second half of *Talk on the Wilde Side* to explore the interplay between these structures of meaning and to indicate how they helped to transform the possibilities for conceptualizing male sexual practices. By examining the shift from "sodomy," a cultural/legal proscription derived from ecclesiastical law against specific, transgressive sexual *acts*, to the creation of a new secular, criminal injunction against specific sexual *relations* between men, now labeled "acts of gross indecency with another male person," the next chapter will explore the epistemological and legal frames that conditioned Wilde's emergence as a paradigmatic sexual figure. The following two chapters will then examine the specific representations of Wilde that appeared in both the daily and Sunday papers throughout the period of his trials in order to explore how these journalistic representations articulated a constellation of qualitative attributes as the signifiers of sexual difference. Chapter 5, "Typing Wilde," will focus on the accounts of *Wilde v. Queensberry* in which the legal contest to determine whether or not the Marquis of Queensberry was "justified" in claiming that Wilde "posed as a sodomite" provided the occasion for considering what it meant to be a "type" of man who had a "tendency" toward engaging in sexual acts with other men—without ever specifying that Wilde ever actually engaged in such acts. The last chapter, entitled "Disposing the Body," will then examine the newspaper narratives of Wilde's prosecution for committing "acts of gross indecency with another male person" in order to suggest that that these stories effectively mapped the gender implications about Wilde's "tendency" onto an unspecified/unreportable set of sexual practices by metonymically displacing them into Wilde's body itself. Thus, the concluding portion of the book will attempt to illustrate the representational processes and practices though which Wilde came to exemplify the "type" of sexualized person easily recognizable today—less than one hundred years later—as "the male homosexual."

4

LEGISLATING THE NORM
From "Sodomy" to "Gross Indecency"

In the old days men had the rack. Now they have the press. That is
an improvement certainly. But it is still very bad, and wrong, and
demoralizing.
> Oscar Wilde, "The Soul of Man under Socialism"

During its brief session in 1533, the English parliament took time
from its general preoccupation with Henry VIII's marriage disputes
and its specific concern with such major issues as "the submission of
the clergy to the king" and "the establishment of the succession of the
king's most royal majesty in the imperial crown of the realm" to pass
the first civil injunction against sodomy in British history.[1] Prior to this
secularization, sodomy had been defined in strictly ecclesiastical terms
as one of the gravest sins against divine law whose name alone proved
such an affront to God that it was often named only as the unnameable.[2] As one in a constellation of liminal offenses (such as blasphemy,
heresy, apostasy, witchcraft, prostitution, and usury) whose punishment merited religious execution, sodomy—or more precisely, the active exclusion of sodomy—provided an occasion for the Catholic
church to violently mark "God's law" on the bodies of its "flock" and
simultaneously to define the limits of its authority over Christian bodies
and souls.[3] As Michael Goodich points out: "In English law, it would
appear that sexual morality fell early under church authority, and
crimes against nature were identified with heresy."[4]

Since sodomy, like heresy, constituted a transgression against the
word/law of God, its punishment provided an occasion to reaffirm
religious "truth" and thereby to reiterate the material human relations
that "truth" organized.[5] In this context, "sodomy" did not refer exclusively or even primarily to sexual relations between members of the
same sex, but indicated a spectrum of nonprocreative sexual practices

ranging from use of a dildo or birth control to anal intercourse (between men, or between men and women) and bestiality.[6] When 25 Henry VIII, c. 8, made "the detestable and abominable vice of buggery committed with mankind or beast" a felony in 1533, it transformed the broader implications of the religious offense into a specific legal injunction against a set of non-procreative sexual practices.[7]

Although the ostensible justification for this new legislation was that "there is not yet sufficient and Condyne punishment apoynted and limited by the due course of the Lawes of this Realme," the transformation of sodomy from an ecclesiastical to a secular crime must also be seen as part of a large-scale renegotiation in the boundaries between the Catholic church and the British state. Indeed, as the first in a series of statutes that recodified crimes formerly falling under the jurisdiction of ecclesiastical courts as felonies, the creation of a legal injunction against sodomy provided a model strategy designed to curtail the power of the Catholic church by removing its right to try those offenses that directly reproduced its authority.[8] Yet, given that one of the primary conflicts in Henry VIII's struggle against papal authority concerned the church's right to insist that as a Christian subject the king was bound *body and soul* by the sacrament of marriage, the choice of sodomy as the first such state appropriation of canon law can hardly have been coincidental.[9] For, the criminalization of sodomy would seem to have effectively transferred the power to define and punish "unnatural" sexual practices to the state and conversely to have made the state— in this case coextensive with a king who sought to abrogate his wedding vows—the sole source for establishing the range of acceptable, legitimate, or "true" relationships.[10] In particular, by claiming for the sovereign the right to punish and hence execute those convicted for the "vice of buggery," parliament (here acting at the king's behest) not only claimed the right to define the legal culpability for "sinful" sexual practice but also negated the pope's authority over the bodies and the property—if not the souls—of the king's subjects. The criminalization of sodomy, then, can be seen both to have introduced a legal injunction that would remain a capital offense until 1861, and also to have consolidated the state's power to seize and control the bodies of its subjects.[11]

Less than a hundred years after the passage of 25 Henry VIII, c. 8, Sir Edward Coke's *Third Part of the Institutes of the Laws of England* (the legendary jurist's highly influential systematization of English penal law) included "sodomy" in a volume "concerning High Treason and other pleas of the crown." Coke's treatise testified to the successful

rearticulation of "the unnameable sin" as a "crime" and simultaneously reapplied much of the offense's earlier religious interpretation to
the civil code.[12] As the tenth entry in a list of over one hundred crimes
against the state, the section "On Buggery, or Sodomy" situated sodomy's first extensive legal explication in the (con)text of a major reorganization of British legal doctrine, thus providing one of the most effective means for recouping this category derived from canon law.[13] Since
the opening sentence of Coke's account ("If any person shall commit
buggery with mankind or beast; by the authority of parliament this
offense is adjudged a felony") foregrounds the state's jurisdiction over
the offending individual who undertakes the act rather than defining
the offense per se, it constructs this person's adjudication as the point
where civil procedures subsume ecclesiastical meanings. Hence, at the
moment of legal intervention, the sodomite becomes both the person
over whom the state's authority is made manifest and the text upon
which the act's legal and cultural significance is inscribed.

Significantly, then, the body is conspicuously absent from Coke's
ensuing definition of the crime: "Buggery is a detestable, and abominable sin, amongst Christians not to be named, committed by carnall
knowledge against the ordinance of the creator, and order of nature,
by mankind with mankind, or with brute beast, or by womankind with
brute beast." Using the traditional canonical appellation to equate the
"unnameable" "sin" (i.e., the "sodomy" already named in the chapter
heading) with the named act ("buggery"), Coke's text conjoins the
religiously execrable with the legally reprehensible.[14] Similarly, his
formulation seems to introduce a distinction between "the ordinance
of the Creator" and "the order of nature," only to reunite them as
the ultimate ground for legal statute; it thereby enlists them both to
legitimate the state's jurisdiction over the offense and to signify the
state's authority over these realms. That Coke's reinterpretation reiterates the ecclesiastical form of the objections against sodomy in order
to explain a law that does not manifestly depend upon them illustrates
the extent to which, by the early seventeenth century, legal thought had
redeployed both the rhetoric and the authority of the now increasingly
superseded ecclesiastical courts in legitimating its condemnation of
sexual offenses.

In turning from the transcendental/religious horror of the "abominable sin" to a historical digression on its philological and sociological
origins, Coke deploys what he defines as the essential foreignness of
the crime to inveigh against the very religious authority that first
enjoined it:

> *Bugeria* is an Italian word, and signifies so much, as is before de-
> scribed, *paederastes* or *paiderestes* is a Greek word, *amator puer-*
> *orum*, which is a species of buggery, and it was complained of in
> parliament, that the Lumbards brought into the realm the shamefull
> sin of sodomy, that is not to be named, as there it is said. (58)

The attribution of "buggery" to the Italians plays on the suggestion
current by Coke's time that the Roman church was the hotbed of
sodomy. As Louis Crompton has suggested, this characterization permitted the mapping of sexual transgression onto national/religious
differences and hence became an effective means of furthering the
crown's struggles against the Pope's authority.[15] Indeed, the strategy
was so successful that it engendered a metaphorical equivalence in
which "the Papacy itself [was] a 'second Sodom,' 'new Sodom,' 'Sodom
Fair,' nothing but 'a cistern full of sodomy.' "[16] Thus rerouted through
civil law, sodomy loses its earlier clerical affiliations with heresy in
order to be redeployed as a political charge against the very church
that first produced it. By the early seventeenth century, it seems that
sodomy had become an important element in the (ideological?) (re)pro-
duction of the British government's temporal and religious sovereignty,
reinforcing the state's right to adjudicate personal, social, and even
spiritual limitations on the human body.

Having first provided this legal, cultural, political, and religious
context for the crime, Coke's text finally moves on to consider what it
had ostensibly sought to address all along: the criteria for determining
legal culpability. In specifying the legal proof necessary for conviction
("So as there must be *penetratio* [penetration], that is *res in re* [the
thing in the thing], either with mankind or with beast, but the least
penetration maketh it carnall knowledge"), Coke's gloss on this criterion foregrounds the heretofore absent body as the site whereupon the
offense is written. Announcing a doctrine that would require judges
and juries to decide whether the body (of man, woman, or beast) bore
the marks of *"penetratio,"* Coke proposes a somatic hermeneutic that
provides specific guidelines for inducing the body to testify against
itself. Since those convicted of sodomy on the basis of this testimony
were liable to public execution, their deaths would transform their
corpses into physical signs of the crime, producing a spectacle that
reiterated the crown's absolute power to seize upon the bodies and the
lives of its subjects.[17] By linking the offense and its punishment to the
very life of the body, sodomy's status as a capital crime organized the
meanings attributed to it as a property of the very body itself and as
such situated it as "part of a universal potential for disorder which lay

alongside an equally universal order."[18] When the final lines of Coke's legal account return to "Holy Scripture" naming sodomy as a "detestable sin" that is at once a "crying sin," his classification comes full circle, making the sodomite's body the site for the reorganization of the relations between church (sin) and state (felony).[19]

This legal imbrication of sodomy's secular and religious significance provided a frame for its representations in Renaissance culture. In *Homosexuality in Renaissance England*, Alan Bray extrapolates the implications of these overlapping meanings and indicates that "sodomy" played a complex role in the religious, political, and literary texts of the period. Noting that "sodomy" continued to evoke religious connotations even after its criminalization in the sixteenth century, Bray suggests that it retained a "mythic" association which often placed it in the company of werewolfs, basilisks, sorcerers, and heretics.[20] However, these meanings were now overlaid with references to social and political behavior, so that they came to signify moral as well as religious transgressions. Coke once again provides an index for this constellation when he remarks: "The sodomites came to this abomination by four means, viz. by pride, excess of diet, idleness, and contempt of the poor." While this list of inducements to sodomy continues to play on the religious and sexual implications of the earlier ecclesiastical charge, it also marks them out as deviations from the virtuous self-government propounded by Protestant theology so that, Bray argues, they begin to refer to an essentially moral concept: debauchery.[21]

As this moral association became a salient element of sodomy's cultural specificity, it linked notions of sexual and personal excess to the particularity of a criminal charge. Analyzing numerous references to sodomy in the period and especially during the reign of James I, Bray concludes that, rather than providing evidence of actual sexual or religious transgressions, attributions of sodomy functioned as political accusations by underscoring implications of extravagance and irresponsibility:

> It was the Court—the extravagant, overblown, parasitic Renaissance court—not homosexuality which was the focus of their attention. What homosexuality provided was a powerfully damaging charge to lay against it; at what should have been the stronghold of the kingdom, there was only weakness, confusion, and disorder.[22]

That the theological meanings of the crime were subordinated to the political context illustrates their continuing disarticulation from a strictly ecclesiastical discourse and their rearticulation within an emerging secular frame. Bearing the accreted significance of its cultural history—first as sin and then as crime—sodomy became an index for a variety of "excessive" behaviors that were then referred back to the body as their source and their proof.

The accounts of the trial, conviction, and execution of the Earl of Castlehaven in 1631 are among the few extant examples of how this nexus of meanings was produced.[23] Mervyn Touchet, ninth Lord Audley and second Earl of Castlehaven in the peerage of Ireland was brought before an assize of his peers on 13 April 1631 to answer charges that he "abetted a rape upon his Countess," "committed sodomy with his servants," and "commanded and countenanced the Debauching of his Daughter." Instigated by his second wife who claimed that Lord Audley had impelled one of his servants to rape her in his presence (i.e., in his own bed) and then later encouraged the same servant to rape her daughter, the trial inspired several popular accounts over the next seventy years, detailing acts of aristocratic extravagance, sexual license, familial violence, and religious impiety that remain shocking even today.[24] Drawing on the sensational testimony presented in the case, the narratives indicate in abundant detail that the Earl's menage had been marked by great excesses: although sodomy was only one of a number of punishable transgressions that included rape upon his wife and daughter and the keeping of a household prostitute, it was the crime that merited his death sentence. The representation of the Lord High-Steward's address to the court concerning the severity of this charge makes its implications clear:

> As for the *Crimen Sodomiticum* . . . I shall not paraphrase upon it, since *it is of so abominable and Vile a Nature* (that as the Indictment truly expresses it, *Crimen inter Christanos non nominandum*) *it is a crime not to be named among Christians*; and by the Law of God, as well as the Ancient Laws of *England*, it was punished with Death. . . . As to this Indictment there is no other Question, but whether it be *Crimen Sodomiticum penetratione*, whether he penetrated the Body, or not; to which I answer, the Fifth of *Elizabeth*, sets it down in general Terms, and *ubi Lex non distinguit, ibi non distinguendum* [i.e., where the law does not distinguish, let there be no distinction made]; and I know you will be cautious how you give the least Mitigation to such abominable Sins; for when once a Man indulges his Lust, and Prevaricates with his Religion, as my Lord *Audley* had done, by being a Protestant in the Morning and a Papist in the Afternoon, no wonder he commits abominable Impieties; for when Men forsake their God, 'tis no wonder He leaves them to themselves.

Moving from a description of the indictment through a brief consideration of the legal proofs and then returning to religion, this passage
provides an excellent illustration of the shifting meanings engendered
by the charge of sodomy. Initially named only in Latin, sodomy enters
the text in a legal form that recasts its traditional Christian nomination
as "unnameable sin" in the language of "crime." Invoking the authority
of both divine and temporal law, the Lord High-Steward's speech then
legitimates the power of the court to pronounce the death sentence
upon the offender. However, since he indicates that the crime is to be
adjudged solely by the act of penetration and cites the appropriate
parliamentary act, he underscores that it is secular (il)legality that
places the body at stake and conversely mitigates any other religious
criteria for such a decision. Thus, when he returns to the "prevarica-
tion" of Lord Audley's religious practice, it is not in order to reiterate
Audley's violation of the "Law of God" but to use the political implications of Audley's "Papis[m] in the afternoon" to substantiate the sexual
charges against him. In narrating the announcement of the guilty verdict and death sentence, the text returns to the Lord High-Steward's
religious admonishment ("as your Crimes have been Abominable, so
let your Mortification for them be as remarkable. 'Tis not a flight and
formal Contrition can obliterate your Offenses, for you have not only
Sins against the Law of God and Nature, but against the Rage of man.
. . ."), demonstrating the overdetermined significance that the rhetoric
of "sin" plays upon and suggesting that the legal pronouncement
against "sodomy" was one of the moments at which these meaning
were transformed.

The rhetorical positioning of sodomy between sin and crime continued to shift during the last decades of the seventeenth century, as the
relationship between sin and crime itself was increasingly problematized by the emergence of popular "projects"[25] to supplement and/
or augment legal and religious injunctions against "immorality" and
"vice." Almost immediately after the abdication of the last Catholic
monarch, James II, in 1688 and the ensuing coronation of the Protestants, William and Mary, an increasing attention was brought to bear
on "licentious" behavior as an affront both to the precepts of religion
and to the security of the state. Drunkenness, prostitution, violation of
the Sabbath, gambling, swearing, and other "corruptions of manners,"
were believed to abound; their unchecked proliferation seemed to
testify to a loss of authority by the society's great institutions and
to undermine the culture's very foundations. As one tract succinctly
phrased it: "If there be no power in the Church sufficient to enforce a

regularity of life, and the civil magistrate be remiss and negligent, great confusions and disorder will need ensue in the state."[26] Whereas for centuries the Catholic church had maintained the confessional as a technology that linked the supplicant's necessity for self-knowledge to the priest's representation of God's omniscience, creating a dense epistemological nexus through which the minute details of individual experience (the "regularity of life") could be made known, the procedures of the Protestant church instead situated the individual in a more immediate epistemological and ontological relation to God, providing fewer such opportunities for the faithful to inform upon themselves. Consequently, unlike the Catholic church, the Church of England was never able to orchestrate a continuous authority over its subjects, especially as the institutions and rituals of the "Roman faith" came to be increasingly associated with religious and political oppression. As there appeared larger and larger gaps in what the Church of England could legitimately claim to know of each person's behavior, and as religious dissent challenged even this more restrained institutionalization, its ability to monitor and ultimately affect individual behavior was substantially limited. By the end of the seventeenth century, the radical negation of Catholicism in England had removed the sole authority for moral supervision from the church and stimulated the development of a uniquely English approach to moral enforcement.

During the 1690s, groups of men made anxious by what they perceived as the moral and religious degeneration of their nation banded together to form the Societies for the Reformation of Manners.[27] Originally initiated by "private men"—primarily skilled craft workers or merchants—in the Tower Hamlets of London's East End to address the transgressions of their own community, the idea for such societies quickly spread throughout London and beyond. These groups looked to each other for support and advice, so that by 1701 Josiah Woodward noted that there were "near twenty societies of various qualities and functions formed in subordination and correspondency with one another and engaged in this Christian design in and about this city and its suburbs."[28] Coinciding with Queen Mary's admonishment to the Middlesex justices (in July 1691) that the courts be especially vigilant in prosecuting offenders against moral law, the new Societies took advantage of the royal enthusiasm for their cause in order to press their complaints. Since they perceived that the legal process could do little without detailed information on specific infractions, they undertook to obtain and record such information; lists of their prosecutions included the name and address of the prosecuted, the offenses charged, the verdict and punishment, along with the names of court officials who participated in the case. In addition, and perhaps most strikingly, the Societies actively encouraged individuals to watch for and report violations among their neighbors and friends. As Dudley Bahlman observes:

> [T]he members [of the Societies for the Reformation of Manners] concluded that even if the justices were willing to issue warrants as readily as they issued their order against vice, they could do little without information. Therefore they resolved to enlist as many informers as they could; and to make the work of informing as easy as possible, they had blank warrants printed at their own expense. A member of the society, upon the word of an informer, could fill out one of these warrants and take it to a justice, who, after examining the member under oath, would sign it and seal it.[29]

Mediating between the Church, the Law, and the public sphere, the Societies were instrumental both in propagating a new technology for moral enforcement and in attaching this technology to the exercise of the state. If, as Foucault has suggested, the rationality of modern state power was formulated along two axes, which he labels "the doctrine of reason of state" and the "doctrine of police,"[30] the Societies can be seen to have significantly developed this rationality as a consequence of their efforts. Since their organizational procedures necessarily led them to inspect individual behavior in its most mundane detail in order to produce and record information that could lead to public prosecutions, they undertook the function of policing the populace and thereby extending the range of experience that was visible to legal enforcement. Simultaneously, they legitimated their actions (often in the face of extremely hostile public condemnation and/or violence against informers) by claiming—in the words of John Disney—"it deserves to be somewhat more largely considered how far the public Interests of *Society* and *Civil Government* are embarqued in the Execution of those [moral] Laws; what fatal *Mischiefs* issue from the *Neglect* of this part of our Duty; and what *Advantages* both to the Prince and People from the *faithful Discharge* of it."[31] The prosecutions by the Societies for the Reformation of Manners provided occasions for recasting the legal instantiations of religious ordinance—from Sabbath breaking to sodomy—in the language of "public interest" and thereby coordinating the extirpation of "sin" with the establishment policing techniques in behalf of a moral code for "*Society* and *Civil Government*."

The effect of this coordination on the popular representations of sodomy is graphically demonstrated in documents describing a series of trials that resulted from raids on London's "molly houses"—raids quite likely initiated by the Societies for the Reformation of Manners whose agents also testified in the prosecutions—in the spring of 1726. Appearing in *Select Trials for Murders, Robberies, Rapes, Sodomy, Frauds, and Other Offenses at the Sessions House in the Old Bailey*,[32] the representations of these cases both reveal the existence of a highly developed London subculture within which men engaged in physical and emotional intimacies with each other and illustrate the means by which the public attacks on this subculture consolidated a moralistic interpretation of sodomy.[33] While the information about these trials and their contexts is necessarily sketchy, the reports in the *Select Trials* indicate that several informers went regularly to the London pubs where these men congregated and passed themselves off as sympathetic to their activities.[34] In so doing, the informers obtained not only the names of individual men who engaged in same-sex practices but also documented the elaborate rituals that accompanied these practices.[35] For example, the *Select Trials* version of the proceedings against Gabriel Lawrence for sodomy indicates that Samuel Stevens (who appears to have been one of the informers for the Societies for the Reformation of Manners) testified:

> Mother Clap's house was in Field-Lane, Holbourn. . . . It was notorious for being a Molly-House. I have been there several Times in order to detect those who frequented it: I have seen 20 or 30 of them hugging and making love (as they call'd it) in a very indecent Manner. Then they used to go out by Couples into another Room, and when they had come back they would tell what they had been doing, which in their Dialect they call'd marrying. (193)

While this account depicts the activities of the molly house as a parodic reenactment of the sacramental *and* legal affirmation of reproductive monogamy—and other accounts go even further, referring to the inner room where sexual encounters took place as "the chapel," indicating that sexual partners were designated as "husbands," and suggesting that after intercourse some men enacted false childbirth, sometimes even going so far as to baptize their "offspring"[36]—the attempt to characterize these practices as blasphemous or heretical is conspicuously absent. Indeed, even the legitimating invocation of the offense's ecclesiastical formulation, which appeared so conspicuously a hundred years earlier in the Lord High-Steward's indictment and summation at Lord Audley's trial, is largely missing from the text.

Instead, *Select Trials* focuses on representing in detail the activities of which the men named were accused and on recounting their responses to these charges.[37] The one exception to this pattern occurs in the cases of men found guilty and sentenced to death; here, as a supplement to the court proceeding, a narrative by the clergyman who attended the condemned man in his final days in prison is appended. Called "the Ordinary's Account" and entirely set off by quotation marks, the appendix provides a short biographical sketch and then indicates whether or not the man executed made a public confession of his crime;[38] however, while this brief narrative often underscores the dead man's love for the Church of England, it rarely enters into a full-blown religious reinterpretation of the crimes for which he was killed.[39] Thus, by the time the *Select Trials* were published during the second third of the eighteenth century, the emergent focus on sodomy's legal prosecution as represented in the narrative accounts of the courtroom proceedings seems to have largely displaced a residual focus on the charge's religious significance, rendering its popular descriptions primarily as transgressions against the "laws of man" or, perhaps more accurately, against the "laws of manners."

In this context, it is interesting to contrast the representations provided by the *Select Trials* to a contemporaneous pamphlet entitled *Plain Reasons for the Growth of Sodomy in England.*[40] While the accounts of the trials indicate that those who participated in London's molly houses were drawn from a variety of occupations (woolcombers, ale-house keepers, tradesmen, cabinetmakers, fruitsellers, teachers, etc.) the anonymous author of *Plain Reasons* addresses his text to the social transgressions of "fine gentlemen" and abjures the discussion of legal proceedings. Instead his text frames "sodomy" as a description of the degraded manhood that he attributes to certain members of the wealthy classes and seeks to imbricate "unnatural vices" with "unmanly" behavior. To this end, the pamphlet begins by nostalgically lauding the ideal from which his contemporaries had fallen away ("Our Forefathers were trained up to Art and Arms; The Scholar embellish'd the Hero; and the fine Gentleman, of former days, was equally fit for the Council and the Camp") and blaming the education that young men of wealth receive for the demise of this former grandeur ("he was brought up in all respects like a *girl* . . ."). The consequences of this fall are unequivocal for the author:

> Unfit to serve his King, his Country, or his Family, this Man of Clouts dwindles into nothing and leaves a Race as effeminate as himself; who, unable to please the Women, chuse rather to run into

unnatural Vices one with another, than to attempt what they are
sensible they cannot perform.

Here the sequence of decay begins with the "Man of Clout's" inability
to perform his socially designated functions and then degenerates into
the "effeminacy" of his progeny, resulting only in "unnatural Vices
one with another" when, at a tertiary level, the degraded offspring
finds himself unable to satisfy a woman sexually. Thus, rather than
being seen as the cause of social decay—as will be the case for "the
homosexual" whose social pathology derives specifically from his
choice of sexual object—"sodomy" here is merely the rhetorical designation for an extreme form of social dissolution predicated on the
negation of the "manly" ideal, "anything of *Manliness* being diametri-
cally opposed to such unnatural Practices." Concomitantly, as the
chapter titles indicate, the text addresses "sodomy" only as a symptom
of behavioral deviations: "The Effeminacy of Men's Dress and Manners, Particularly Their Kissing Each Other" and "The Evils of the
Italian Opera," suggesting that the specific sexual/sinful significance
formerly attributed to the charge has been (re)articulated in the legitimation of an emerging masculine norm.[41]

When during the second half of the eighteenth century, Blackstone's
Commentaries on the Laws of England (1769) recategorized sodomy
among "Offenses against the Persons of Individuals," sodomy's relation to increasingly normative cultural meanings was recouped by legal
discourse.[42] Included in a chapter devoted to such crimes as mayhem,
forcible abduction ("vulgarly called stealing an heiress"), and rape,
sodomy—which Blackstone's delicacy forbade him from ever actually
naming—at first appears somewhat anomalous. Unlike the other offenses listed under this rubric, which refer to acts of grave bodily harm,
it is not readily apparent why "the infamous crime against nature"
constitutes an assault "against the security of [the] person." In his
analysis of the *Commentaries*, legal historian Alex Gigeroff suggests
that Blackstone may have been drawing upon "the spiritual concept
of a person" in determining sodomy's classification suggesting that
"participation in this kind of act is an offense or an affront to the
spiritual aspect of man."[43] Yet while Blackstone's brief section does
use the quasi-religious euphemism *peccatum illude horrible, inter
christanos non nominandum* and attributes the legitimacy of capital
punishment against the crime to "the express law of God," his—albeit
elliptical—analysis is not manifestly religious. Indeed, Blackstone's
inclusion of sodomy among "offenses against the person" instead of
among "offenses against God and Religion"—where he placed, for

example, "open and notorious *lewdness,* either by frequenting houses of ill fame . . . or by some grossly scandalous and public indecency"—would seem to militate against interpreting his classification of the crime on a strictly spiritual basis. Rather, it seems more plausible to attribute Blackstone's categorization, at least in part, to a normative conception of legal culpability, so that the violation "against the person" can be seen as a violation against the specific cultural identification of what a *male person* should be. This interpretation would seem to be further corroborated by the fact that unlike Coke and the jurists following him, who defined sodomy as a crime applicable to both men and women, Blackstone specified that "the infamous crime against nature" was "committed either with mankind or beast." The narrowing of sodomy's purview to specifically male practices transforms the crime from a generalized injunction against a range of transgressive behaviors formerly labeled as "sin" into a particular "offense against the person" whose "offensiveness" derives from the cultural meanings ascribed to the male sex of the person(s) involved.

While it is well beyond the scope of this discussion to address the larger transformations in legal standards framing such a redefinition of "the person," it is important to note that Sir Leon Radzinowicz, in his compendious study of English legal development, *A History of English Criminal Law,* describes the second half of the eighteenth century as the period during which the moral-reform movements of the preceding hundred years were able to consolidate their impact on legal doctrine.[44] Stressing that the arguments for legislating and policing morals took on an overt middle-class bias during the period and that increasing numbers of middle-class officials (especially clerics, lawyers, and politicians) participated in "reform" activities, Radzinowicz suggests that by the end of the century it had been accepted that certain acts were "so unusually dangerous and grievous to individuals, and from their frequency so injurious to the whole public, that they were lifted up into scale, and became criminal offenses."[45] The normative notion of "unusual danger to the individual" provides a relevant gloss on Blackstone's interpretation of sodomy as an "offense against the person," especially when this interpretation coincided with a marked increase in prosecutions against sodomy. As A. D. Harvey has shown, the number of arrests and the number of executions for sodomy rose dramatically in the first three decades of the nineteenth century.[46] Using the statistics from Middlesex as an indicator, Harvey states: "from less than one a decade in the second half of the eighteenth century, after 1804 executions for sodomy in Middlesex came to an average of one a year."[47] While the specific causes of this increase

remain elusive, it appears that the coincidence of emerging definitions
of normative sexual behavior (what Harvey calls "the massive reinforcement of sexual stereotyping") with aggressive private policing
and prosecution by the reform societies (in an era before the state
consolidated these activities under its jurisdiction) was instrumental in
fomenting the legal and public execration of sodomy.[48]

The newspaper accounts of the arrest of thirty men at the White
Swan in Vere Street, London, in 1810 prove excellent—and tragic—
examples of this coincidence.[49] Apparently the result of a long period
of surveillance and a carefully coordinated series of raids, the arrests
of the "Vere Street Club" provided the occasion for massive public
demonstrations against the offenders. If the press versions are to be
believed, those men found guilty were subjected to violent abuse—
both verbal and physical—as they were conveyed to and from the
pillory and even those men who were released because there was
insufficient evidence to prosecute them were often lucky to escape
without serious harm from the crowds that surrounded the police
courts.[50] Unlike the accounts provided in the *Select Trials* eighty years
earlier, however, the newspaper texts focus almost exclusively on the
public demonstrations against and harassment of the men convicted
of committing sexual offenses while censoring precisely those details
that would have formerly generated interest in such cases. In explaining
this textual silence, the newspapers profess their advocacy of standards
of public decency; for example, one paper notes: "The evidence adduced against these prisoners was of so black a hue, of so abominable
a nature, that we cannot pretend to give any report of it," and another
opines: "The existence of a Club, or Society, for a purpose so detestable
and repugnant to the common feeling of our nature that by no word
can it be described without committing an outrage against decency."
Constituting the crimes as beyond "decent" representation, the terms
that the press used to castigate the offenders indicate that the basis for
the crime's nonnomination was no longer predicated entirely on its
"sinful" nature but also on its violation of certain standards of "decency." Invoking "the name of decency and of morality, for the sake
of offended Heaven," one newspaper exhorted Parliament to quickly
legislate further punishments in order to deter future violations. Another publicly named those found guilty, calling them "the execrable
miscreants convicted of forming a club at the White Swan, in Vere
Street, to commit a vile offense" and applauded "the disgust felt by all
ranks in society at the detestable conduct of these wretches." As these
phrases suggest, while the penumbra of religious condemnation continued to adhere to the popular representations of sodomy, the force of

public condemnation was directed as much against "detestable conduct" as against "a most diabolical offense."

Throughout the nineteenth century, as religious dogma continued to lose its exclusive power to organize public knowledge and as the normative standards for male behavior were rapidly consolidated, sodomy's prosecution provided new opportunities to legislate normative behavior. In 1828, Parliament passed an omnibus bill, entitled "Offenses Against the Person" (9 George IV, c. 31), designed to repeal fifty-seven separate pieces of criminal legislation and reenact them under a single rubric in order, in the words of the Home Secretary Robert Peel, to "simplify them and make them clear."[51] This act reorganized the statutory basis for many serious crimes including "the abominable crime of buggery," which was (re)criminalized as a capital offense along the line of Blackstone's earlier classification. Sandwiched between the definition of "a woman secreting the dead Body of her Child" as a misdemeanor and the specification of rape as a felony, paragraph 15 states succinctly: "every Person convicted of the abominable Crime of Buggery, committed either with Mankind or with any animal, shall suffer Death as a Felon." Yet beyond simply recodifying "buggery," the bill also overrode earlier legal precedent which required (in cases of buggery, rape, and "carnally abusing Girls under the Age of Ten Years") two proofs—of penetration and emission—for conviction. Under the provisions of 9 George IV, c. 31, the requirement "to prove the actual Emission of Seed in order to constitute carnal Knowledge" was suspended so that "carnal Knowledge shall be deemed complete upon the Proof of Penetration only." While arguing for this proposed change in the standard of proof, Peel focused primarily on alleviating "the suffering of the unfortunate female who was the victim of the offense," indicating that his inclusion of buggery with the other two offenses was part of a more general containment of male sexual violence against women. However, this (re)articulation of the legal criteria necessary for conviction not only changed the specific standards of evidence that defined the crimes but also shifted the doctrinal basis for criminalizing the acts themselves. As Peel's speech for the bill indicates: "It was his strong opinion that one of those descriptions of proof was unnecessary and that it was not necessary to a capital conviction to prove more than that which constituted *the moral offense* as far as the offending party was concerned."[52] No longer, then, was sodomy's criminalization as a capital offense designed to enforce a biblical injunction against nonprocreative sexual behavior (which was the motivation for the required dual proof), but instead to maintain a certain "moral" standard for individual behavior. By specifically linking the death penalty to the "immorality" of the charge—in the absence of any reference to earlier "sinful" connotations—Peel both privileged socially determinant behavioral standards (norms) as legitimating state intervention on the bodies and lives of the citizenry and simultaneously characterized sodomy as such a normative transgression.

As the first half of this book attempts to demonstrate, development of normative standards for male (sexual) behavior was a critical element in the self-definition of British middle-class throughout the nineteenth century. The increasingly energetic activities by numerous organic intellectuals of the bourgeoisie (doctors, educators, clerics, alienists, parents, feminists, evangelicals, etc.) not only to define but also to watch for and to enforce new ideological articulations of sex, age, and class foregrounded the transformations in these elements of the sex/gender system.[53] Since sodomy's legal definition necessarily mediated between an earlier organization of sexual practices predicated on the ecclesiastical affirmation of reproductive monogamy and a newer configuration that sought to enforce certain cultural limits on the deployment of the body, its status as a capital offense provided the point at which these two regimes overlapped. So long as sodomy continued to merit execution—even if only theoretically—its punishment still provided an occasion for the state to inscribe the offender's body with/as a hieroglyph that signified its power to use death in order to regulate the very basis of life, even while it was in the process of creating and organizing new technologies which (re)produced a more diffuse, yet more minute exercise of power over all aspects of that life. However after 1836, the year that the last execution for sodomy took place, the volatility of this semiotic/somatic juncture was attenuated, so that when sodomy was removed from the list of capital crimes in 1861, it signaled an effective shift in the legal basis for sodomy's criminality from an initial secularization of canon law to an essentially normative transgression.[54]

This transformation was further consolidated with the passage of section 11 of the Criminal Law Amendment Act of 1885 (see chapter 3) which created a new statutory category, "acts of gross indecency"— wholly independent of any ecclesiastical connotations—to define the legal injunction against sexual practices between men. Predicated on the need to legislate proprietary standards for male sexual behavior, the Criminal Law Amendment Act defined limitations on a range of male sexual behavior (primarily with prostitutes and adolescent girls) on behalf of the middle-class familial norm. In arguing for the bill before the House of Commons, Sir R. Assheton-Cross, the secretary of state for the Home Department, succinctly stated the aim of the legislation: "the purity of the households of this country shall be maintained and . . . those who wish to violate them shall be punished."[55] This defense of "household purity," then, provided the legislative context for rearticulating under the rubric of "gross indecency" the illegality of a diverse set of sexual activities that men could engage in with each other. For, unlike sodomy, which specified the illegality of a limited range of sexual activities ("buggery with mankind or beast") whose transgressive character derived from a Judeo-Christian affirmation of monogamous procreative sexuality, "acts of gross indecency" had no particular specificity save for the genital similarity of the sexual actors and were defined against a normative standard that deified the "purity" of the middle-class "household."

However, while this legal basis for prosecuting sexual acts between men was markedly shifting in relation to emerging sexual norms, the cultural significance ascribed to such legal shifts necessarily lagged behind their legislative transformations. If, as I have argued, the legal conceptualization of sexual behavior between men was increasingly predicated upon normative rather than religious or moral definitions of male sexuality, then the newspaper coverage of particular violations of these norms can be seen to have provided an excellent opportunity to consolidate these transformations in the public sphere. In particular, the extensive police and court reports appearing in the Victorian commercial press literally covered the newspaper page with representations of transgressive sexual practices (adultery, rape, prostitution, bestiality, pedophilia, homosexuality, transvestitism, etc.) ostensibly in order to represent the triumph of the norm and the rule of law. However, since the titillating content that these reports proffered was also relied upon to sell papers, their lurid details necessarily informed readers about the existence—if not the prevalence—of these counterhegemonic practices. That the press coverage of the state's attempts to regulate sexual behavior increasingly became a staple of the news throughout the century indicates the degree to which the normalization of sexual practice was a volatile and contested process.

As the courts and police undertook to define and enforce increasing numbers of sexual and marital offenses, they provided the press with the opportunity for rearticulating sexual practices across the spectrum of class differences. For example, when the passage of the 1857 Matrimonial Causes Act established secular courts and procedures for divorce, even the *non plus ultra* of bourgeois domesticity, marriage, came under increased scrutiny as reporting on divorce cases familiarized the reading public with both the failings of this institutionalized ("heterosexual") standard and the new possibility—at least for the middle and upper classes—of annulling it. Since the dissolution of marriage became available as news at exactly the same moment that the organic intellectuals of middle-class were going to great lengths to portray marriage as a "natural" human condition (see chapter 2 above), the popular journalistic representations of divorce proceedings represented resistance to this ideology as "newsworthy" and thereby implicitly reterritorialized it as an anomalous (hence nondeterminant?) deviation.

In a similar manner, trials involving other sexual practices can be seen to constitute what Victor Turner has called "social dramas," in so far as they bring into play certain contested elements of social behavior and through this conflict allow individuals "to take sides in terms of deeply entrenched moral imperatives and constraints, often against their own personal preferences."[56] This definition seems particularly appropriate for those cases that so catalyzed public interest that they transformed news into "scandal." While it is impossible to rigorously specify precisely what constitutes a scandal, perhaps the best way to define one is in terms of the reactions it evokes.[57] For clearly, a scandal differs from news per se inasmuch as it provokes readers "to take sides" usually in a highly emotional or affective manner. The volatility characterizing these processes of social division and judgment in turn suggests that a scandal's "content" must in some sense include behavior that confounds the very certainty of basic social distinctions and implies that there are no clear (moral, ethical, legal) boundaries for human action. By thematizing this sense of cultural indeterminacy, scandals open up a liminal period during which the normative values and practices of a culture are contested. Individuals and groups (including classes and class fractions) then align themselves according to their responses to the behaviors at issue, thereby reconstituting hegemonic configurations and ideologies in relation to the previously undefined or transitional activities. Scandals would appear, then, to crystallize new configurations of social difference by articulating heretofore marginal elements of a social formation in relation to those normative standards against which positions may be taken, judgments may be formed, and alliances may be created.

In one of the rare attempts to theorize this ubiquitous yet universally overlooked form of social transformation, Max Gluckman suggests that scandals perform a unifying function within a culture by "creating a past history for the members in relation to one another" and by "competitively aligning [individuals and cliques] against each other."[58] While Gluckman's conclusion is based on an analysis of precapitalist social formations, his suggestions seem adaptable to the context of nineteenth-century Britain with one major distinction: unlike the more contained cultures that both Turner and Gluckman consider, in which individual members have (more or less) immediate access to the actors in—or, at least, the context of—the "social drama," the national scandals occurring in Britain during the last half of the nineteenth century were necessarily mediated by the press. Indeed, the numerous "sexual scandals" played out in the press, at least from the 1870s on, constituted an increasingly common staple of the "new journalism's" attention. The widespread newspaper coverage of the arrest and trial of Ernest Boulton and Fredrick Park for conspiracy to commit sodomite acts (1870), the Besant-Bradlaugh trial for republishing pamphlets offering birth-control instruction (1876), the ongoing coverage of the campaign to repeal the C. D. Acts (see chapter 3), the homosexual scandal involving high officials at Dublin Castle (1884), the trial and acquittal of a notorious brothel keeper, Mrs. Jeffries (1884), and the "Maiden Tribute" affair (1885), among others, testify to the role that scandals played in consolidating popular understanding of a disparate set of sexual practices. To be sure, an analysis of the newspaper reporting on each of these particular incidents would undoubtedly reveal much about the emergence of popular discourses on sexuality in Victorian Britain; suffice it to say, here, that as an integral part of the emergence of mass journalism in the late nineteenth century, the coverage of sexual scandals was instrumental in articulating sexual behavior as an element of class and national identities and conversely in unifying class and national identities in relation to normative appraisals of sexual behavior.[59]

By way of concluding this increasingly lengthy narrative of (il)legalities and turning to the press accounts of Wilde's trials themselves, I'll consider one further legal proceeding, if only because it became (in 1889–1890) the first sensational prosecution under section 11 of the Criminal Law Amendment Act prior to Wilde's own.[60] Dubbed "the Cleveland Street Affair" after the small West End street where, at number 19, a male brothel proffering young postal employees to an upper-class and often titled male clientele became the center of a controversy that not only implicated several highly placed men (including Prince Albert Victor, second in line to the throne) in a web of—to use the Public Prosecutor's words—"unnatural lust," but also put both the state prosecution and the newspaper coverage themselves on trial. The circumstances of "the affair" are rather complex: on 4 July 1889, while pursuing an investigation of small theft from the Central Telegraph Office, the police interrogated a fifteen-year-old messenger boy named Charles Swinscow who appeared to have more money in his possession than his meager salary could account for. Under questioning

Swinscow revealed that he had earned the money by going to bed with "gentlemen" at the house in Cleveland Street run by a man called Charles Hammond. He also volunteered that he knew of at least two other telegraph boys who had pursued similar outside employment and noted that they had all been introduced to the practice by another messenger, Henry Newlove(!). These revelations led to a further investigation culminating in the prosecution of Newlove and an older man, George Veck, for procuring boys to "commit divers acts of gross indecency with another [male] person." The third man, Charles Hammond was also indicted but fled the country to avoid prosecution.

Although the indictments had received cursory treatment by both the *Times* and the *Star*, by and large the press had paid almost no attention to the case up until this point. However, when testimony given in both the investigation and the trials suggested the involvement of persons of rank and, in particular, that of, Lord Arthur Somerset (who upon learning of his implication in the case left for the Continent), journalistic interest was aroused. Fittingly, on 11 September 1889, the *Pall Mall Gazette* was the first to make the connection explicit:

> We are glad to see that Sir Augustus Stephenson, Solicitor to the treasury, was present at the Marlborough Street police court yesterday, when two prisoners were committed for trial in connection with a criminal charge of a very disgraceful nature. Mr Hannay refused bail for both the accused, and no doubt if found guilty by a jury they will receive exemplary punishment. But the question which Sir Augustus Stephenson will have to answer is whether the two noble lords and other notable person who were accused by the witnesses of having been the principles in the crime for which the man Veck was committed for trial are to be allowed to escape scot free. There has been too much of that kind of thing in the past. The wretched agents are run in and sent to penal servitude; the lords and gentlemen who employ them swagger at large and are even welcomed as valuable allies of the Administration of the day.

This account sketches out the terms within which the case was reported to the public. The specific criminal acts themselves were typically invoked euphemistically ("a criminal charge of a very disgraceful kind") if at all ("the crime for which the man . . ."), while the text elaborates with much gusto the inequities of the penal system. Thus, the sexual transgressions function here merely as a prelude to the political charges, metonymically infecting the latter with the immoralities generated by the former. When Veck and Newlove pled guilty on 18 September and received sentences of nine months and four months imprisonment respectively, the stage was set for the next act in the scandal.

While the state attempted to determine the legal and political feasibility of pursuing charges against Somerset and other named individuals, sectors of the press became impatient with what was deemed the sluggishness of the proceedings. On 16 November 1889, a newly founded Radical journal, the *North London Press*, published an article under the banner "THE WEST END SCANDALS," publicly naming Lord Arthur Somerset and the Earl of Euston as being "among the number of aristocrats who were mixed up in an indescribably loathsome scandal in Cleveland Street." The article then proceeded to claim that both men had been allowed to leave the country and "thus defeat the ends of justice, because their prosecution would disclose the fact that a far more distinguished personage [Prince Albert Victor] was inculpated in these disgusting crimes." Here again, as in the *Pall Mall Gazette* article quoted above, the nature of the sexual crimes seems only of interest insofar as it underscores the inequities of class privilege. The sexual practices are rendered as "indescribably loathsome"—itself a highly evocative description—and "disgusting crimes," but they take on significance not primarily in themselves but only as they become the opportunity for the "defeat of justice." Unfortunately for the editor of the paper, Ernest Parke, "justice" had not been quite so battered as he thought, and the Earl of Euston whom he had publicly described as having absconded to Peru to avoid prosecution was in fact still in the country and was not heavily implicated in the case. Taking umbrage at the inclusion of his name along with Somerset's as an unfair defamation of his character, Euston quickly brought charges against Parke for criminal libel.[61]

Parke's trial became the occasion for a flood of press coverage since it was the press itself that was now in the dock. The case juxtaposed Euston's claim that he had visited the house in Cleveland Street just once in the spring of 1889—as his counsel said, "prompted it might be by a prurient curiosity which did him no credit"—after having been given a card advertising *poses plastiques* (the Victorian equivalent of a strip joint) while walking in Picadilly. Upon learning that there were no *poses plastiques* but only young male prostitutes, the Earl claimed that he quickly left the house and never returned. The defense for its part attempted to prove both that Euston had visited Cleveland Street on several occasions and that he had willingly entered into the specialties of the house. The proof of this latter charge came in the testimony of a rather notorious male prostitute, John Saul,[62] who offered details of alleged sexual acts he had committed with Euston. Since the defense focus was on proving the justification for the statements about Euston published in the *North London Press*, the accounts of the trial foregrounded the question of the credibility of the testimony while rendering the particular claims made about sexual activities in very obscure language. Thus, the *Times* could report Saul's account of the activities that took place between him and Lord Euston only by describing them as unfit for publication. When Parke was found guilty on 17 January 1890, and sentenced to a year in prison, the press almost unanimously abjured from referring to the substance of the charges and instead editorialized about the appropriateness of the conviction.[63]

While the press coverage of the Cleveland Street affair provided the first major coverage of prosecutions under the Criminal Law Amendment Act for "committing acts of gross indecency," it represented these acts only to the extent that they constituted the necessary backdrop for a libel case, itself predicated on a challenge to unequal execution of justice based on class. The sexual crimes, although very explicitly placed at the margins of the reporting (and indeed often represented only by their suggestive absences), provided indispensable atmospheric interest because they confirmed the "degeneracy" of the aristocracy who were perceived as getting away with them while those less well off were punished.[64] Yet the peripheral nature of this coverage does not mean that the sexual acts were not themselves at issue, for clearly what was thematized in the subsequent references to the incident was not the question of legal justice but the sexual underpinnings of the case. Thus, when Wilde's *The Picture of Dorian Gray* appeared shortly after Parke's conviction in 1890, the *Scots Observer* concludes its damning review with an unmistakable reference to the Cleveland Street scandal:

> Mr. Wilde has again been writing stuff that were better unwritten; and while "The Picture of Dorian Gray" . . . is ingenious, interesting, full of cleverness, and plainly the work of a man of letters, it is false art—for its interest is medico-legal; it is false to human nature—for its hero is a devil; it is false to morality—for it is not made sufficiently clear that the writer does not prefer a course of unnatural iniquity to a life of cleanliness, health, and sanity. The story—which deals with matters only fitted for the Criminal Investigation Department or a hearing *in camera*—is discredible alike to author and editor. Mr. Wilde has brains, and art, and style; but if he can write for none but outlawed noblemen and perverted telegraph boys, the sooner he takes to tailoring (or some other decent trade) the better for his own reputation and the public morals.[65]

This prescient alignment of the events of the Cleveland Street scandal with Wilde's novel—which as we will see in the next chapter itself became a metonym for the "unnatural iniquity" of his own sexual practices—five years before his own trials would entirely eclipse this earlier incident as a cultural marker of same-sex relations between men, indicates the importance that the press coverage of such proceedings had as a means of structuring public representations of nominally "unrepresentable" practices. To the extent that the press provided a context both for the dissemination of information about sexual relations between men and for the organizing of that information into legitimately "public" forms, it constituted an important nexus for the construction of popular concepts of male sexuality. Even though the press reports on the Cleveland Street scandal attempted to maintain the homoerotic activities of the actors at the margins of its coverage, the marginalized practices still effectively structured the historical interpretation of the events, making it possible for the author of this review to impugn Wilde by association without any explicit reference to excluded acts. In the case of Oscar Wilde himself, however, no such pretense of marginalization was possible, and thus, it is to the newspaper accounts of his trials that we must turn in order to analyze the changing popular conceptualizations of sexual relations between men.

5

TYPING WILDE
Construing the "Desire to Appear to Be a Person Inclined to the Commission of the Gravest of All Offenses"

That was the consequence of their being too bad to be talked about, and was the accompaniment, by the same token, of a deep conception of their badness.

Henry James, *The Ambassadors*

On 28 February 1895 Oscar Wilde arrived at his club, the Albemarle, after an absence of several weeks and was presented with an envelope containing the Marquis of Queensberry's calling card. On the back of the card were scrawled the words: "For Oscar Wilde Posing as a Somdomite [sic]."[1] As the culmination of months of harassment by the Scottish aristocrat—who objected to Wilde's intimacy with his youngest son, Lord Alfred Douglas—the short text so incensed Wilde that it incited him to instigate legal action against its author. Filing charges under the 1843 Criminal Libel Act (6 and 7 Vict. I, c. 96), Wilde's legal representatives asked the court to interpret the marquis's text as a verbal attack upon his person and to hold its author criminally responsible for the consequences of his writing. Unfortunately for Wilde, the statute invoked on his behalf allowed the accused party a unique form of rejoinder: the defendant could assert his innocence by placing a competing interpretation of the alleged libel before the court—in what was termed a "plea of justification"—which sought to prove that the offending statement was both "true" *and* "published for the public benefit." If the court verified that both these conditions obtained, then the defendant would be deemed innocent of the charge and the libel found to be legally substantiated. Needless to say, the Marquis of Queensberry's lawyers quickly countercharged that such was the case. This defense tactic effectively transformed the legal proceeding in *Wilde v. Queensberry* into an interpretive contest both for determining the text's "true" meaning and for assessing its social significance. Hence, what was at stake in the proceedings of *Wilde v. Queensberry* was not simply whether or not the writing on the Marquis of Queensberry's card constituted a libel against Wilde, but also what it meant "to pose as a sodomite," whether Wilde had done so, and if publishing the knowledge of such a "pose" was in the public interest.

Framed by the tenor of these questions, the trial necessarily foregrounded the specificity of the phrase "posing as a sodomite." Since the contested statement did not actually accuse Wilde of "sodomy"— or of *being a sodomite*—for which a strict standard of legal proof (i.e., proof of penetration, see chapter 4) would have been required, the defense sought instead to show that Wilde was the kind of person— or at least that he had (re)presented himself as the kind of person— who would be inclined to commit sodomy. In support of this personification, the plea of justification tried to shift the legal focus on sodomy away from its traditional status as a criminally punishable sexual *act* so that it became in the defense's construction a defining characteristic of a type of sexual *actor* (the "sodomite"). In order to provide a credible standard of proof for this characterological claim, the defense's plea of justification listed thirteen allegations that "Oscar Fingal O'Flahertie Wills Wilde . . . did solicit and incite . . . [another male person] to commit sodomy and other acts of gross indecency." Here, playing upon the indeterminacy introduced by the word "posing," the defense interpretation subsumed the specific cultural and legal history evoked by the word "sodomy" with the newer, relatively unknown category, "acts of gross indecency," metonymically subsuming the former within the behavioral penumbra of the latter. Thus, even as the defense plea displaces "sodomy's" historical privilege as the sole basis for criminalizing sexual acts between men and constitutes it as one of a number of "other acts of gross indecency," the earlier concept is simultaneously recouped by the defense plea as the legitimating criterion through which a much wider variety of "indecent" relationships between men can be brought within the legal purview.

Yet even if the court was inclined to agree that by incorporating the residual meanings ascribed to the older sexual offense within their indefinite use of emergent legal category the defense had legitimated the "truth" of the statement that Wilde had "pos[ed] as a sodomite," the Marquis of Queensberry was still required to demonstrate that the publication of the statement was for "the public benefit." In order to satisfy this condition, Queensberry's plea of justification shifted its concern from Wilde's sexual to his literary practice. Claiming that

"Oscar Fingal O'Flahertie Wills Wilde was a man of letters and a dramatist of prominence and notoriety and a person who exercised considerable influence over young men," the plea charged

> that the said Oscar . . . Wilde in the month of July in the year of Our Lord One thousand eight hundred and ninety did write and publish and cause and procure to be printed with his name upon the title page thereof a certain immoral and obscene work in the form of a narrative entitled "The Picture of Dorian Gray" which said work was designed and intended by said Oscar . . . Wilde and was understood by the readers thereof to describe the relations, intimacies, and passions of certain persons of sodomitical and unnatural habits, tastes, and practices.[2]

Here, Wilde's text becomes the pretext for the assertion that his sexual practices were relevant public knowledge. Interpreting the interactions between the male characters in *The Picture of Dorian Gray* as a reflection of the "sodomitical and unnatural" relations that Wilde was supposed to have engaged in in his life—a far from self evident interpretation, as the subsequent critical commentary on the novel makes clear[3]—the defense plea introduces a theory of representation that defines Wilde's text as a vehicle "calculated to subvert morality and to encourage unnatural vice." By proposing a hermeneutic that fixes the literary work as a form of (in this case, counterhegemonic) sexual didacticism, Queensberry's defense sought to hold the author morally and legally responsible for the implications of his writing. However, by linking the claim that Wilde was a particular type of sexual "character" (and not that he had committed certain sexual acts) to a suggestion that this characterization had larger social implications because he was a writer, the plea introduces the possibility of reading Wilde's sexual proclivities into his writing in order to confirm him as a "certain person of sodomitical and unnatural habits, tastes, and practices." In other words, by foregrounding the literary text as an indication of its author's (and perhaps also its readers') sexual characteristics, the plea attempts to construct a way of discerning and subsequently signifying sexual "tendencies" without reference to sexual acts. Throughout the two and a half days of the trial, then, the Marquis of Queensberry's barrister, Edward Carson, undertook to impress upon the court *not* that Wilde had engaged in any specific sexual acts with any of the men listed in the plea, but rather that Wilde—in both his life and in his writings—had demonstrated a "tendency" toward "indecent" (i.e., nonnormative) relationships with other men. Hence, when Wilde's barrister, Sir Edward Clarke, rose in the midst of the opening speech for the defense to ask the court's permission to withdraw the prosecution against Queensberry, he did so by referring only to the imputations made against Wilde's writing—albeit in order to circumvent the defense's introduction of evidence about his client's sexual practices. Unfortunately by interrupting their prosecution to protect Wilde from the incriminating testimony that the defense appeared to have gathered against him, Wilde and his legal representatives effectively forced the court to find in the Marquis of Queensberry's favor. The short text scrawled on the back of the marquis's calling card, therefore, precipitated a legal contest that ended not only by affirming that Queensberry's words, "For Oscar Wilde Posing as a Somdomite," were "true" and "for the public benefit," but also by culling enough evidence to indict and ultimately to convict Wilde for committing *acts of gross indecency.*

As this scenario suggests, the proceedings in *Wilde v. Queensberry* were framed by the transformations in legal discourse from "sodomy" to "gross indecency" outlined in the last chapter. However, since in this case the question before the court concerned only Queensberry's legal culpability for his accusation that Wilde had "posed as a sodomite" and not Wilde's legal culpability for the sexual act per se, the finding in the case was not a critical moment in crystallizing the shifting *legal* relationship between these categories. Yet beyond a small circle who were intimates of the prosecutor and the defendant themselves (and subsequently for legal historians), these specifically juridical issues were greatly overshadowed by the interpretive effects (re)produced in the journalistic accounts of the trial. For, when it was splashed across the pages of almost every London newspaper and in fact across the front pages of most newspapers throughout Europe and North America, the "story" of "OSCAR & MARQUIS" (as the banner of the *Evening News* declared it) transformed the courtroom's narrower questions of legal culpability into larger ones concerning social/sexual meanings. If, as literary critic Mikhail Bakhtin has suggested, trials have historically proved a critical element for narrative development by linking the knowledge effects of juridical authority to more diffuse cultural practices, then the narratives of Wilde's legal proceeding can be situated within a historical pattern of interpretation that privileged the trial as a site for the production of meaning.[4] Hence, unlike the courtroom proceedings themselves, whose "interpretations" were delimited by the (nonnarrative) logic of the legal contest, the journalistic representations of the trials produced narratives from which a range of social significance could be read off. As the impetus for such trial narratives, the libel's text therefore became a pretext for producing a series of second order (con)texts that not only communicated the "events" of the legal proceedings from the relative obscurity of a Central Criminal Court chamber to the ubiquity of a national reading audience, but also rendered these proceedings as meaningful social practices. Indeed, by constituting their representations as "newsworthy," the newspaper reports defined the trials as exemplary and thereby rearticulated the courtroom contest between the two interpreters of Queensberry's text as a struggle between moral, legal, sexual, political, and aesthetic ideologies.

Given the highly emotional resonance of the criminal charge and countercharge, it is hardly surprising that the form that this journalistic rearticulation took was often "dramatic"—or indeed, "melodramatic."[5] While the particular styles of (re)presentation varied greatly from paper to paper: ranging from the staid, microscopic, monologic prose of the *Times* to the bold, sensational, illustrated pages of the *Morning Leader*, these texts were almost universally constituted and sold as dramatic narratives. To some extent, this choice of narrative mode derived from the excitement of the courtroom itself, where Wilde's polished testimony under direct examination and his highly ironic and often devastatingly funny replies to the defense cross-examination enveloped the proceedings in the "drama" of his own self-(re)presentation. For example, the heated dialogue between Wilde and his cross-examiner, Edward Carson, so captured the public imagination that it became a set piece in all subsequent depictions of the case. Yet beyond the formidable influence of Wilde's person(a), the formal organization of the public knowledge about the trial was also constrained by the cultural nexus that constituted "the news."

At a functional level, news can be described as a mode of information that is sold as a commodity on a regular (daily/weekly) basis. As such, it is structured by two fundamental demands: currency and marketability. During the last third of the nineteenth century, the emerging British mass-market newspaper industry addressed these demands by introducing both new technologies (i.e., by developing new high speed means for information gathering, printing, and distribution) and new discursive strategies (i.e., by adapting the narrative modes developed in earlier forms of popular literature to the representation of "current events"). After the 1880s, when the rising capital expenses of newspaper production necessitated the development of increasingly popular styles of journalistic reporting, the emergence of a distinctly different kind of journalism—which Matthew Arnold named "the new journalism"—foregrounded the significance of "telling a story" in order to increase newspaper circulations. As epitomized by William Stead's editorship of the *Pall Mall Gazette,* the new styles sought to establish an emotional relationship to the audience by drawing upon personalized narration, vivid language, evocative detail, and, most important of all, sensational subjects. While not all newspapers took up the extreme versions of these strategies found in the pages of the *Pall Mall Gazette* or the popular Sunday papers, to some extent journalistic practice was itself transformed by the narrative expectations they engendered.

In their attempts to popularize the journalist text and thereby cultivate large and diverse readerships, the new journalism's strategies can be seen to have foregrounded the narrativity of its "stories." Embedded in newspaper (con)texts, the "facts" were necessarily mediated by the apparatus of representation so that their "truth" was intimately connected to their "significance" *and* their marketability. By focusing this chapter on the analysis of the press's representations of *Wilde v Queensberry,* therefore, I hope to explore both how particular alternatives for male sexual behavior were defined in Britain at the end of the nineteenth century and how meanings were popularly attributed to them. More specifically, by analyzing the ways in which the journalistic accounts portrayed Wilde's "character" and situated this character within the narrative of a libel proceeding that ultimately found the Marquis of Queensberry justified in stating that Wilde "posed as a sodomite," I hope to examine the process whereby a cultural concept signifying a particular type of male individual who had a "tendency" toward committing sexual acts with other men was constructed. For, in the course of representing the libel proceedings in *Wilde v. Queensberry,* the newspapers effectively (re)produced the possibility for designating Wilde as a kind of sexual actor without explicitly referring to the specificity of his sexual acts, and thereby crystallized a new constellation of sexual meanings predicated upon "personality" and not practices.[6]

In Character

The headlines that appeared after the first day of testimony in *Wilde v Queensberry* (see Figs. 1–4) announced the spectacular nature of the events that were unfolding inside the chambers at the Old Bailey. Like the playbills of a West End theater or the chapter summaries of a sensation novel, the banners that heralded the news reports of the trial on the evening of 3 April and the morning of 4 April 1895 sought to

OSCAR & MARQUIS

The Strange Libel Case Opened.

SCENE IN COURT.

A Remarkable Letter to Lord Alfred Douglas.

Figure 1. *The Evening News,* 3 April 1895.

arouse—and then capitalize upon—the expectations of the prospective audience. With Wilde and the Marquis of Queensberry vying for top billing among a remarkable cast of characters (including several legal luminaries and a potential parade of young working-class men), and with much of the dialogue provided by one of the West End's most popular playwrights himself, the drama promised to be highly entertaining.

To belabor the theatrical metaphor a bit, like the borders of the proscenium these headlines quite literally "frame" Wilde: i.e, they use his name to mark the text out both spatially and interpretively, defining the epistemological stage upon which the action unfolds. Designed to attract the eye's attention from a page of otherwise minute print, the words "OSCAR WILDE" in enlarged typeface, often in a different font, not only denote the text's point of origin, both typographically and narratively, but also provide an organizing principle for the "copy"

OSCAR WILDE

DEFENDS HIMSELF AT THE OLD BAILEY.

CHARGES BROUGHT AGAINST HIM BY LORD QUEENSBERRY.

The Æsthete Gives Characteristically
Cynical Evidence, Replete with Pointed
Epigram and Startling Paradox, and
Explains His Views on Morality in Art.

Figure 2. *The Star*, 3 April 1895.

that follows. Since, as this journalistic jargon suggests, the newspaper texts largely reiterate their headline in various forms, returning again and again to the signifiers emblazoned there, they continually reconstitute and reinscribe the signs that designate their origin. Thus, the words "Oscar Wilde" appearing in bold-faced, large print at the top of a page of newsprint "frame" Wilde not only in the sense of putting a frame around "his story" (textually) or marking it out from a background (spatially), but also in the colloquial sense that they "frame" him for a crime. For, although Wilde is nominally and legally the prosecutor in the case, the headlines make it clear that he is the one who is in the public spotlight. To take the *Morning Leader* (figure 3) as a paradigmatic instance, the paper made "OSCAR IN THE BOX" the origin—if not the meaning—of the story, turning Wilde into the subject of both

OSCAR IN THE BOX.

THE MARQUESS IN THE DOCK.

MOST SERIOUS CHARGES FOR-MULATED AGAINST MR. WILDE.

OSCAR ANSWERS THEM BY AN ABSOLUTE DENIAL—HE TURNS EXTEMPORANEOUS EPI-GRAMS, AND EXCHANGES VIEWS OF META-PHYSICS, ETHICS AND ART WITH MR. CARSON, Q.C., WHO OPPOSES THE PLAY OF OSCARISM WITH DIRECT SUGGESTIONS OF IMMORALITY.

Figure 3. *The Morning Leader,* 4 April 1895.

legal and journalistic examination and therefore mitigating the case's legal and historical context. In the *Star's* version (figure 2), "OSCAR WILDE • Defends Himself at the Old Bailey • Charges Brought Against Him by Lord Queensberry," the Tory paper actually inverts the legal position of the two litigants, literally depicting Wilde as the accused and Queensberry as the accuser. By connecting the newspaper text to a larger cultural context in which "Oscar" or "Oscar Wilde" (re)pro-duced certain aesthetic/sexual meanings and by simultaneously focus-ing the ensuing narrative on Wilde himself, these headlines structure their signifying processes around the construction of a "character" whose idiosyncrasies will come to define a "type" of individual.

To some extent this characterological orientation reflects the fact that the extensive press coverage given to this particular litigation undoubtedly derived—at least initially—from Wilde's public status as

OSCAR WILDE LIBEL CASE.

TRIAL AT THE OLD BAILEY.

LORD QUEENSBERRY IN THE DOCK.

PLEA OF JUSTIFICATION.

Figure 4. *The Pall Mall Gazette,* 3 April 1895.

a popular playwright and as a (self-marketed) cultural icon. Indeed, at the time of the trial, Wilde was unquestionably at the height of his commercial and literary success: two of his comedies, *An Ideal Husband* and *The Importance of Being Earnest*, were simultaneously playing to the delight of West End audiences and his earlier dramatic works, *A Woman of No Importance* (1893) and *Lady Windermere's Fan* (1892), had garnered him much critical acclaim and financial remuneration in the preceding two years. In addition, the scandal that Wilde's novel *The Picture of Dorian Gray* caused on its initial appearance in *Lippincott's Monthly Magazine* (when the newsagent W. H. Smith refused to sell the issue) and then again a year later when it appeared in an expanded bound edition, contributed to his reputation both as a litterateur and as a *provocateur*.[7]

Yet even more than his status as a successful contemporary author, it was Wilde's self-produced image as a unique (if not *outré*) cultural figure that catalyzed the public interest in the trial. From the moment he left Oxford (in 1879) and went down to London, where due to his father's death and the ensuing familial insolvency he was forced for the first time to earn his income, Wilde had self-consciously marketed himself as a liminal figure within British society. His highly publicized tour of America in 1881 as the front man for Richard D'Oyly Carte's U.S. production of Gilbert and Sullivan's *Patience* not only established him as an iconic embodiment of the "aesthetic" type that the operetta parodied, but also demonstrated his ability to sell his association with this stylistic critique of bourgeois respectability—and especially male respectability—as a cultural commodity in its own right.[8] In her book, *Idylls of the Marketplace: Oscar Wilde and the Victorian Public*, Regenia Gagnier forcefully argues that Wilde's self-positioning as a "dandy" represented a highly developed criticism of middle-class ideologies and particularly those for male gender identity. She counterposes the figure of "the dandy" to that of "the gentleman," and his prototype "the public school boy," in order to illustrate that Wilde's personal aesthetic constituted an embodied challenge to the social and cultural—if not the economic—hegemony of the Victorian bourgeoisie.[9]

Given this counterhegemonic positioning, it is hardly surprising that during the 1880s Wilde's sartorial and aesthetic statements became the object of much disapprobation and satire. He was often caricatured in contemporary journals as a languorous, long-haired lover of sunflowers or as an "utterly" aestheticized utterer of epigrams, so that the representation of his large, lounging frame became an iconic disparagement of what was deemed to be male "effeminacy." It is important to note here that the "effeminacy" popularly attributed to the "aesthetic" or "decadent" movement had not yet produced an immediate corollary association with sexual relations between men. In fact, as the representation of Bunthorne in *Patience* illustrates, this effeminacy was often seen to align the "aesthetic" male with the domestic realm of the female, making him a more sought after object of female desire, if only because of a perceived commonalty of interests.[10] The supplementing of "aesthetic" effeminacy with connotations of male sexual desire for other men is, I would argue, one of the consequences of the newspaper representations of the Wilde trials. Hence, instead of marginalizing Wilde by depriving him of the legitimacy accorded to middle-class male "authority," these characterizations of Wilde as "aesthetic" or "effeminate" ironically served to publicize his style even more widely—as Ellen Moers writes, "in the *fin de siècle*, caricature, however insulting, was counted good publicity"[11]—and were thus instrumental in producing "Oscar" as one of the best-known "personalities" of the late-Victorian period.

By playing upon these indexical connotations of Wilde's commoditized self-image, the newspaper headlines testify that the semiotic shift from proper name to cultural category is predicated on the unarticulated nexus of difference (or "ideology") that overdetermines "Oscar" as a meaningful signifier. The *Evening News'* banner "OSCAR & MARQUIS" (figure 1) provides an explicit example of the strategy whereby the overly and overtly familiar "Oscar" is opposed to and conjoined with the aristocratic tag "Marquis" to denote not only the two sides of a "strange libel case" or two distinct class positions but, as the ensuing text will reveal, two poles of male behavior. Referring to Wilde paradigmatically as "The Aesthete," the *Star* (figure 2) prefaces its coverage by suggesting that Wilde embodied a cultural category for which definite "characteristics" can be isolated. Since the

specifics of this characterological typology situate Wilde in a duplici-
tous relation to language—marked by "cynical evidence," "painted
epigram," and "startling paradox"—the headline positions the reader
to confirm (or possibly to negate) this interpretation in the following
representations of his testimony and thereby engages the reader in
the (re)production of this category. Similarly, the *Morning Leader's*
subhead (figure 3) transforms Wilde's name into a noun phrase, "The
Play of Oscarism," denoting a certain "characteristic" relation to language that it then juxtaposes to "The Direct Suggestions of Immorality" articulated by Queensberry's barrister. This opposition serves to
reinforce the implication that Wilde's linguistic "indirection" hides the
actual "immorality" that Edward Carson's "direct" speech reveals and
thus it organizes the text around articulating the relation between the
"unrepresented" and the "unrepresentable": i.e., between language
and sexual relations between men.

By foregrounding the role that language plays in the representation
of Wilde's (sexual) experience—both by Wilde himself and subsequently by the press—the newspapers call attention to the explicitly
interpretive, or even "fictional," quality of their accounts and thereby
underscore the narratives' production of meanings. Indeed, this productive process is implicitly evoked by several of the opening paragraphs which, in their devotion to describing the crowded courtroom
"scene" on the morning of 3 April, interpellate readers as an active
"audience" whose attendance is deemed semantically critical to the
story.

> The Importance of Being Early was never better illustrated than at
> the Old Bailey this morning when long before 10 o'clock every seat
> where a pressman could sit had a couple of competitors for it. . . .
> *(Evening News)*

> Not for years has the Central Criminal Court at the Old Bailey been
> so densely crowded as it was this morning. People begged, bullied,
> and bribed for admission. . . . *(Star)*

> Quite an hour before the day's business opened at the Old Bailey
> this morning people were using every effort to gain admission to the
> old court. *(Echo)*

> Never, perhaps in the history of the old court has there been such
> organized demand for admission on the part of persons of apparent
> position; never, perhaps, have so many prominent persons been
> disappointed to find their prominence would not serve to gain them
> entrance to a criminal court. *(Morning Leader)*

Almost as if evoking an oversold opening night on which avid theater goers "beg, bully, and bribe for admission" to the latest Wilde production—and in the *Morning Leader's* version, on which even "prominent persons" are turned away—these passages underscore the "drama" of the case while simultaneously transforming the image of the packed chambers into a metaphor for the uniqueness, the "newsworthiness," the overwhelming significance of the events. This is not just any court proceeding, the papers seem to suggest, it is a proceeding about which important people very much want to know. The tiny, crammed court-room, thus, comes to signify not just those men who managed to squeeze into a particularly small and highly charged geopolitical space—and they were exclusively men in the restricted chambers of the Old Bailey, as the *Morning* notes—but also metonymically becomes the textual mark of a larger (reading) audience who can only "know" through the press. By infusing the metaphor of the courtroom as theatrical extravaganza with the textual markings of epistemological desire, the newspapers structure their texts as "spectacular," (re)producing what Roland Barthes called "myth": they imbue their first-order representations of the "facts" and "events" (denotation) with a second order of significance that naturalizes the social (con)texts within which these meanings emerge (connotation).[12] Yet as Barthes would later comment, the supposed "first order" is itself ideologically constructed such that "denotation is not the first meaning, but pretends to be so; under this illusion it is ultimately no more only than the *last* of the connotations."[13] Thus, the dynamic interplay between these levels of meaning in the newspaper accounts serves to legitimate both the facticity of "the events" and the authority of their narrative interpretations.

In the ensuing descriptions of the litigants, the juxtaposition of Wilde to the Marquis of Queensberry as two distinct—if not antithetical—icons of masculinity inscribes this mythic economy at *and as* the inception of the newspaper narratives. For, as each of the men comes not only to represent "himself" but also to signify a particular male "type" (e.g., the profligate and somewhat degenerate aristocrat v. the effusive and somewhat effeminate dandy), the story of their legal conflict also becomes the symbolic renegotiation of the categories of difference that motivate these typologies. The *Morning Leader* provides the most florid version of this pattern:

> Bound to recur and startle the world, whether it be with sunflowers or sonnets, plush or paradox, whether in the domain of art or in society, Oscar Wilde is again what he has before made himself, the

talk of every tongue and the cynosure of fame or notoriety or
ridicule—he does not pretend to care which, not being an ordinary
person. John Sholto Douglas, Marquis of Queensberry, has also
been, on another plane, a public person seen in many kaleidoscopic
lights, and when these two meet at such issues as are involved in the
Wilde-Queensberry case, opened yesterday at the Old Bailey, the
intensity of public interest is phenomenal. (4 April)

Accompanied by line drawings of the two men, a slightly smiling,
affable profile of the Marquis of Queensberry and an enlarged grotesque of Wilde's head, replete with ponderous lips, monstrous nose,
and bloated cheeks (see figures 5 and 6), this paragraph underscores
the "extraordinary" character of the both legal contest and the legal
contestants. Here Wilde is identified with the effects of his "persona,"
associated with "sunflowers or sonnets," "plush or paradox," details
that evoke both the extravagance and decadence of his dandiacal self-
production ("[being] again what he has made himself before"). Moreover, in conjunction with the grotesqueness of the accompanying drawing, they body forth the physical degeneration that such nonnormative,
non-"manly" practices portend. The Marquis, on the other hand, while
also described as a "public person," is not similarly associated with
the details of his personal history (which included a much-publicized
disruption of Tennyson's *Promise of the May*, a bitter divorce followed
by public cohabitations with his mistresses, and a series of vituperative
attacks on both the queen and the prime minister, Lord Roseberry, for
proffering his son a peerage);[14] instead Queensberry is portrayed both
verbally and graphically as incarnating "neutral" masculinity.

The *Evening News* in its juxtaposition of the two men makes the
implications of these two visions of maleness even more explicit:

> Lord Queensberry, who disdained a seat, stood in front of the dock
> with his arms folded, occasionally changing his attitude to make
> note of something that occurred to him. While Wilde was in the box
> the peer looked implacably across the court to where the poet, with
> his hyacinthine locks and air of easy abandon, almost lolled in the
> witness box. (3 April)

Queensberry, the erect, stalwart, "peer" "who disdained a seat," here
personifies the attitude of masculinity rampant: arms crossed, un-
breachable, an image befitting his own heraldic crest, a virtual icon of
outraged masculinity. The narrative voice identifies with Queensberry's
positioning and reports, as if through the marquis's "implacable" gaze,
the contrasting portrait of "the poet": soft, floral, unrestrained, Wilde

A SIDE VIEW OF MR. WILDE.

Figure 5. *The Morning Leader,* 4 April 1895.

OSCAR INDULGENTLY ANSWERS QUERIES FROM A JURY OF INTELLIGENT PHILISTINES.

Figure 6. *The Morning Leader,* 5 April 1895.

seems to recline in the witness box: i.e., he disdains the importance of his surroundings and appears without respect for the laws of realm or man (see figure 7). The images of the two men provide a studied contrast, almost as if they represented the "do" and "don't" panels in a Victorian etiquette book.[15] This tableau, in turn, became a set piece in the descriptions of the trials so that, for example, when the *Star* reported the opening of the second day of the trial, it reiterated these postures exactly:

> [T]he noble defendant, clad in a dark blue overcoat with a velvet collar, in place of the rusty black garment of yesterday was admitted to the dock and sat there quietly until Mr. Justice Collins arrived when he resumed his old pose with arms folded on the dock front.
>   Punctually at half past ten, Oscar was recalled to the witness box. Bland and attentive, his hands limply crossed and drooping or clasped around his brown suede gloves, he awaited the resumption of Mr. Carson's cross-examination. (4 April)

Here the contrasting descriptions of the litigants' body postures evince both a detailed presentation of the courtroom "scene" and a qualitative

OSCAR WILDE.

Figure 7. *News of the World*, 7 April 1895.

statement about the "characters." The gestural significance attributed to Queensberry's "arms folded" is defined over and against Wilde's "hands limply crossed," so that the latter can be read as a negation of the male propriety that impels the former. By stylizing the opposition between "Oscar" and "the noble defendant," the newspapers map the underlying determinations of difference that generate such normative assessments of male behavior onto their representations of these figures, thereby constituting these representations as confirmations of the "naturalness" of such difference.

As they embed the characterological opposition between the Marquis of Queensberry and Oscar Wilde in their narrative accounts of the trial, the newspapers inscribe this opposition in the determining action from which the journalistic "stories" ensue. Hence, the various depictions of the two men come both to personify the structures of difference through which the newspapers articulated their narratives and to represent the differences in question as the negation of the middle-class male norms outlined in the first half of this book. Political theorist Ernesto Laclau has suggested that the construction of such dialectal contradictions, i.e., binary pairings taking the form "A/non-A" or here "norm/not-norm," provides one of the primary strategies through which hegemonic discourses recoup "real opposition" within the terms of dominance and therefore (re)produce hegemony itself.[16] As such, he argues, this putative "oppositional" structure inheres in most of the cultural forms used to give shape to and engender meanings from the worlds in which we live. While at a general level this analysis offers an important insight into how certain values and practices are systematically privileged over and against all others, in the reporting on *Wilde v. Queensberry* such a strategy took on a unique importance which made it pragmatically even more critical. Since the allegations made against Wilde both in the libel itself and in the subsequent "justification" were defined in the dominant representational codes of the period as being literally "unrepresentable," *they therefore could not actually appear in print on the pages of the newspapers that purported to tell their story.* Hence the possibility of signifying these allegations *negatively* as the *absence* of what was precisely most representable, i.e., the dominant norms, allowed the newspapers to circumvent those very representational strictures that would have otherwise rendered their coverage of the trial both unintelligible and unmarketable.

The need for this representational strategy necessarily emerged even as the newspapers sought to represent the case's opening, since the moment Sir Edward Clarke rose to indicate the grounds for the prosecution, he immediately introduced the journalistically forbidden word "sodomy" into the courtroom. Moreover, because the defense's plea of justification was constrained by the alleged libel to name "sodomy" *repeatedly* even while it simultaneously sought to abjure this increasingly anachronistic term in order to define a more diffuse sense of the sexual possibilities between men, it made sodomy's legal (re)articulation a central issue in the proceedings. The appearance of this unprintable word as the crux of the case confounded the unmediated movement between legal context and public (con)texts, forcing the newspapers to attempt to circumvent their representational limits by translating the legal utterance into printable terms. Indeed, as the trial unfolded and the defense assiduously sought to undermine Wilde's prosecution by alluding to supposed evidence of his intimate relations with young working-class men, the stakes in the gamble for linguistic respectability were markedly increased. So while the courtroom proceedings circled around the unarticulated implication that Wilde had sought the sexual services of the men named in the plea of justification, the newspapers were challenged to report this testimony without actually revealing any of its very titillating substance.

In struggling to negotiate this edge of social acceptability and yet retain the sexual implications that made the trial newsworthy—*and indeed highly marketable*—the newspapers necessarily developed a compensatory set of signifying practices to invoke the unprintable signifier without naming it directly. They thereby opened up an interpretive space outside the legal purview within which a new sense of male sexual behavior could emerge.[17] For, in order to mitigate the semantic and commercial consequences that the exclusion of the word "sodomy" threatened to produce, the journalistic texts constructed a complex web of signifiers that endlessly deferred specifying the unnamed and unnameable accusations while explicitly denoting them as an absent site of signification that made their stories meaningful. In other words, they negatively characterized Wilde's behavior as "*im*moral," "*im*modest," "*un*natural," "*im*proper," "*in*decent," "*un*respectable," "*dis*reputable," etc., in order to avoid having to specify positively the actual sexual acts named in Queensberry's defense. Instead they portrayed Wilde's acts, and ultimately his "person," in terms of the overdetermined absence of those qualities that ideologically defined normative middle-class male behavior (e.g., "morality," "modesty," "nature," "propriety," "decency," "respectability," etc.). This representational configuration organized these highly evocative affirmations of bourgeois hegemony into an effective, gendered unity whose absence then indicated the presence of "unnameable" sexual acts. Hence, the newspapers represented the defense's suggestion that Wilde engaged in sexual relations with other men through a chain of signifiers that transformed these relations into the antithesis of the middle-class sexual norms for men and simultaneously produced "Oscar Wilde" as the metonymic embodiment of this chain.

The journalistic limits of enunciation, then, both excluded the mention of a signifier whose play had heretofore (re)produced the cultural/legal significance of sexual acts between men and simultaneously engendered a new configuration of signifying practices that would reorganize this (sexual) significance around that signifier's visible absence. Since the defense had similarly oriented its legal strategy around a verbal gesture that moved away from an actual invocation of "sodomy" while deploying its absence to motivate the notion of a type of individual who might be inclined to commit the "unnameable" act, the newspapers could both explicitly and implicitly incorporate the terms of this strategy into their representations of the case. By mediating between the defense interpretation and the popular limits for (sexual) representation, the newspapers reiterated the defense's attempts to construct a new category of sexual transgression that could be signified not by reference to specific "unnameable" sexual acts but by the depiction of a certain type of sexual actor.

Given this conjuncture of interpretive interests, it is not surprising that the inception of the newspaper narratives almost universally coincided with the textual shift from act to actor. Perhaps the most instructive example can be found in the *Evening Standard* which along with the *Daily Telegraph* and the *Morning* provided extensive daily coverage of the case. Beginning its story on 3 April with a detailed paraphrase of the prosecution's opening statement, the *Standard* represented both the libel's "unrepresentable" word and the fact of its unrepresentability by foregrounding the word's absence in the text.

> The libel was published in the form of a card which was left by Lord Queensberry at a club to which Mr. Oscar Wilde belongs. It was a visiting card with the Marquess of Queensberry's name printed upon it, and also had written upon it the words, "Oscar Wilde posing as ———."

As the paper mimics the publication of Queensberry's statement, it simultaneously censures the libel's proper name leaving only a blank as the mark of its excisement. Therefore the blank enters the journalistic text as the organizing principle of the narrative: it is the space occupied by the offensive signifier that motivates Wilde's legal action, the ostensible "subject" of the story, and yet it remains mute. Instead, Wilde's name alone serves as the site of meaning here so that it is invested with the trace of something that has been suppressed; something potentially libelous; indeed, something so potentially libelous as to warrant an article comprising five columns of a special edition's front page. The article then goes on to report Clarke's characterization of the suppressed word directly:

> Of course, it is a matter of serious moment that such a word as Lord Queensberry had written should be in any way connected with the name of a gentleman who has borne a high reputation in this country.

Pointing to the blank as a particular type of utterance ("such a word"), the paraphrase indicates that the missing word is not just any word, but a word with power: the power to threaten "a gentleman," even one "who has borne a high reputation in this country." This gloss reveals the word-not-written as a nexus for language, class, nationality, sexuality, and social status—if only through its ability to radically disrupt these connections. Now, however, since the blank space's indeterminacy threatens to rend the textual/sexual fabric entirely, the newspaper account attempts to contain the damage by suturing the gap paraleptically:

> It is not an accusation of the gravest offense. "Posing as ————" indeed appears to suggest that there was not guilt of the actual offense, but that in some way or other the person of whom the words are written has appeared to be, indeed desired to appear to be, a person guilty of or inclined to the commission of that gravest of all offenses.

The text's negative construction, "not . . . the gravest offense," indicates that indeed the "gravest offense" is precisely at issue. Displaced from the literal statement of the libel, the phrases "gravest offense" and "actual offense" become paradigmatic equivalents for the suppressed signifier, even as the "————" qualifies this relationship. No longer a strict negation or suppression, the quotation shifts the text's focus from the "offense" to a "person . . . [who] appeared to be, indeed desired to appear to be, a person guilty of or inclined to the commission of that gravest of all offenses." That is, it shifts the concern from the act to the actor.

This shift is even more marked in the reports provided by the *Echo*, the *Times*, the *Star,* the *Morning Leader,* the *Evening News* and the *Daily Telegraph,* where the entire phrasing of the libel is effaced from the text, so that Wilde as sexual actor becomes the only concrete referent for the alleged act.

> The libel was published in the form of a card that was left by Lord Queensberry at a club to which Mr. Oscar Wilde belongs. It was a visiting card with the Marquis of Queensberry's name printed upon it. Of course, it is a matter of serious moment that such a word as Lord Queensberry had written should be in any way connected with the name of a gentleman who has borne a high reputation in this country. *(Daily Telegraph)*

> In opening the case for the prosecution, Sir Edward Clarke pointed out the enormous gravity of the accusation leveled against Mr. Wilde

by the Marquis of Queensberry. But the defendant's plea raised a much graver issue, for in that plea it was alleged that the complainant had solicited various persons to commit an offense. *(Echo)*

It was a visiting card of Lord Queensberry with his name printed upon it, and it had written upon it certain words which formed the libel complained of. In respect of that libel so published, this charge was brought against the defendant. Of course it was a matter of serious moment that such a libel as Lord Queensberry had written upon that card should be in any way connected with the name of a gentleman who had borne a high reputation in this country. The words of the libel were not directly an accusation of the gravest of all offenses—the suggestion was that there was no guilt of the actual offense, but that in some way or other the person of whom the words were written did appear—nay, desired to appear and pose to be a person inclined to the commission of that gravest of all offenses. *(Times)*

Sir Edward Clarke at once rose and began the case. He told how the Marquis called at the Albemarle Club and left a card "To Oscar Wilde," which contained words that were gross and libelous. The accusation against Mr. Wilde was one of the gravest that could be made. But the card was not the only matter with which they would have to deal. By the plea put before the court a much graver issue was raised. There was no accusation in the plea that Mr. Oscar Wilde had been guilty of a criminal offense, but there were given the names of a number of persons whom he was accused of inciting to commit such offenses and with whom he was charged with improper conduct. *(Evening News)*

Sir Edward Clarke plunged at once in medias res. He first read to the jury the card which Lord Queensberry left open with the porter of the Albemarle Club for the plaintiff—containing a very grave allegation against Mr. Wilde's character—and pointed out that it seemed to stop short of actually charging the plaintiff with the commission of one of the most serious offenses. By the plea which the defendant had put before the court a much graver issue was raised. *(Star;* the *Morning Leader* copied this account verbatim in its report the next morning)

Here the texts both signal that the card was read into testimony and that this reading was beyond the scope of journalistic representability. However, unlike the *Evening Standard,* the *Morning,* and *Lloyd's Weekly Newspaper* where the libel's "unrepresentability" was represented by the marked absence of a single, specific word, these papers instead euphemistically render the contested statement by underscor-

ing—in the *Echo's* phrase—"the enormous gravity of the accusation."
Indeed, the *Star* and the *Morning Leader* graphically highlight the
suggestion that Queensberry's allegation was beyond the limits of
public discourse by confining even their incredibly vague paraphrase
of the libel, "a very grave allegation against Mr. Wilde's character,"
within the textual quarantine of hyphens. Thus, these texts symbolically presented the "allegation" as "unrepresentable," while simultaneously juxtaposing the unarticulated statement to what the *Times* refers
to as "the gravest of all offenses," or as the *Star's* less superlative
diction names it, "one of the most serious offenses." That the texts
turn around the "gravity" of the unnamed "offense" illustrates the
way in which the newspapers actively thematize the Marquis of Queensberry's imputations against Wilde as the case's pivotal (signifying)
moment, constituting them as of more importance than Wilde's contention that he had been maligned which (almost ironically) formed
the actual *legal* basis for the case. This journalistic identification with
Queensberry's interpretive position, reiterated in the *Echo,* the *Morning Leader,* and the *Star,* which all emphatically insist that the charges
made in the plea of justification constituted a "much graver issue,"
signals these newspapers' concern not simply with the unnamed offense
(sodomy) but with the suggestion that Wilde, in the *Times* rhetoric,
"desired to appear and pose to be a person inclined to the commission
of that gravest of all offenses."

By constituting Wilde's "pose" as the crux of the narrative, the
ensuing descriptions of Sir Edward Clarke's opening statement foreground the interpretation of Wilde's words—and not Queensberry's—
as the site of contested meaning. Although in his statement to the
court Clarke undoubtedly attempted to provide an account of Wilde's
background and to develop a story that could explain his relationship
with Alfred Douglas in nonincriminating terms, the newspapers represented this attempt by focusing on those aspects of the statement that
were most evocative and hence most incriminating. Thus, while the
actual specifics of the statement that appeared in any particular paper
varied widely—ranging from the *Evening Standard's* obsessively detailed paraphrases to the *Times's* summary sentences—all the dailies
were consistent in their emphasis on reporting an attempt to blackmail
Wilde for a letter he wrote to Douglas. In part, this emphasis can be
seen to derive from the cultural connotations already associated with
the criminalization of sexual relations between men: as H. Montgomery Hyde has suggested, by the time of the trial, and indeed even at the
moment of its passage, section 11 of the Criminal Law Amendment
Act had been dubbed "the Blackmailers' Charter."[18] Yet even more

important than the general implications ascribed to blackmail were the particular meanings attributed to the text that was the subject of the blackmail attempt: a "letter" from Wilde to Alfred Douglas, according the defense; a "prose poem," from an established author to an acolyte, according to the prosecution.

The story of the blackmail was first introduced to the court by Wilde's counsel who apparently sought to preempt the defense's ability to interpret the suggestive correspondence as sexually incriminating. His statement thus carefully situates the text itself within a narrative frame that tries to undermine the assumption that because Wilde was being blackmailed he had something to hide and simultaneously to introduce a competing *literary as opposed to sexual* standard for interpreting the writing in question. Since the *Evening Standard* (3 April) provides the most meticulously detailed reporting of this prosecution tactic, it is worth quoting here at length both in order to present the outlines of Clarke's narration and to illustrate the way in which it was taken up by the press:

> In the early part of 1894 [sic] Mr. Wilde became aware that certain statements were being made against his character. He became aware in this way. There was a man named Wood, who having been given some clothes by Lord Alfred Douglas, and who said that he had found in the pocket of a coat four letters written by Mr. Wilde to Lord Alfred. Wood came to Wilde early in 1893, and wanted him to give him something for the letters, representing that he was in great distress and wanted to go to America, and Mr. Wilde gave him £15 or £20 in order to pay his passage. Wood thereupon handed over to him the somewhat ordinary letters that had been written by him to Lord Alfred, but, as generally happens when people think they have letters of some importance, the letters of no importance are given up, and that which is supposed to be of importance is retained. That was the case in this instance. In 1893 Mr. Wilde's play *A Woman of No Importance* was being prepared for production at the Haymarket Theatre, and there came into the hands of Mr. Beerbohm Tree, the actor and manager, a piece of paper which purported to be, and to some extent was, a copy of the letter which had been retained by Wood and two men named Allen and Clyburn. On it was written, "Kindly give this to Mr. Oscar Wilde and oblige." Shortly afterwards Allen called on Mr. Wilde and said that he had the original letter and wanted him to give him something for it. Mr. Wilde absolutely and peremptorily refused, saying, "I have a copy of that letter and the original is of no use to me. I look upon it as a work of art. I should have desired to possess a copy; now you have been good enough to send me a copy, I do not want the original."

He sent Allen away, giving him a sovereign for himself, and almost immediately afterwards Clyburn came and said that Allen so appreciated his kindness that he sent back the letter. He handed over the letter, and Mr. Wilde gave him a sovereign for his trouble. Having once got the original letter in his possession, Mr. Wilde kept it, and it is in my hands now. He said then, and he says now, that he looks upon it as a sort of prose sonnet. He told Allen that it would probably appear in sonnet form, and on May 4, 1893, a publication was issued, called the *Spirit Lamp*, an aesthetic, literary and critical magazine edited by Lord Alfred Douglas, and on the first page was a sonnet in French described as "A letter written in prose poetry by Oscar Wilde to a friend, and translated into rhymed poetry by a poet of no importance." It was not an exact reproduction but a paraphrase of the letter. Here is the letter:—"My own boy. Your sonnet is quite lovely, and it is a marvel that those red rose-leaf lips of yours should have been made no less for music of song than for madness of kisses. Your slim gilt soul walks between passion and poetry. I know Hyacinthus, whom Apollo loved so madly, was you in Greek days. Why are you alone in London, and when do you go to Salisbury? Do go there to cool your hands in the gray twilight of Gothic things, and come here whenever you like. It is a lovely place—it only lacks you; but go to Salisbury first.—Always with undying love, Yours, OSCAR."

While it is no longer possible to ascertain the "factual accuracy" of this reported version, in the context of the courtroom this story (however it was first spoken) obviously had significantly different rhetorical and semantic effects than its journalistic counterpart. There the tale appeared in the flow of an opening statement designed to establish the legal grounds for the prosecution and at the same time to mitigate any foreseeable objections portended by the defense's plea of justification; here, bereft of both its persuasive intention and effect, the story merely provides anecdotal detail that underscores the representation of Wilde as a character who exists at and is familiar with the margins of respectable society. Shifting abruptly from a focus on Wilde's relations with the Douglas family (rendered in indirect discourse) to what is obviously meant to be taken as a verbatim account of Clarke's speech, the newspaper text rhetorically distinguishes the blackmail story from what precedes it: a change in narrative mode foregrounds the "significance" of the reported material, while the heightened sense of "realism"— produced in part by an embedded quotation appearing in Wilde's own "voice" as well as by the distinctive style of the letter itself— concomitantly evokes the "fictional" expectation that these bits of dialogue can be read as character development. By revealing Wilde as a social actor who not only repeatedly engaged with and ultimately paid off Wood, Allen and Clyburn but who was also prepared to legitimate his writing to them as "a work of art," the *Standard's* account implicitly juxtaposes the incriminating interpretations presupposed by the blackmail scene to their subsequent justification in the courtroom. Thus inserted in the "diagesis" of the courtroom narrative, the quotation of Wilde's letter constitutes his writing as a critical site for the trial's struggle over meanings even as it illustrates the symbolic function of the latter as an index of Wilde's character.

In reporting Clarke's gloss on Wilde's "prose poem," then, the newspapers establish a homology between textual interpretation and characterological assessment. For as Wilde's words are subjected to rigorous scrutiny by both the prosecution and the defense, they form the basis for a slippage between textual meaning and authorial intention so that the imputations made against the former (in the courtroom) will become (in the press) evidence against the latter. Thus, although the prosecution sought to introduce the question of "literary" meaning(s) in order to circumvent the monologic effects of legal interpretation and thereby interrupt the defense's ascription of "unnatural and sodomitical" significance to Wilde's texts, the representation of this strategy in a journalistic (con)text provided the opportunity for underscoring these writings as inherently sexualized. Since the blackmail letter was the first such text introduced in the case, it provides the initial occasion for articulating this connection.

> The words of that letter appear extravagant to those who are in the habit of writing commercial correspondence (laughter), or those ordinary things which the necessities of life force upon one every day, but Mr. Wilde says that it is a prose sonnet, and one that he is in no way ashamed of, is prepared to produce anywhere as the expression of a poetical feeling, and with no relation whatever to the hateful suggestions put to it in the plea in this case. *(Evening Standard,* 3 April)

> The words of that communication, Sir Edward Clarke continued, might seem extravagant to their more prosaic and commercial experiences, but Mr. Wilde was a poet, and the letter was considered by him as a prose sonnet, and as an expression of true poetic feeling, and had no relation to the hateful and repulsive suggestions incorporated in the plea in this case. *(Times,* 4 April)

> This [letter], said Sir Edward, might seem extravagant to those who were in the habit of commercial correspondence —(Great laughter in which Mr. Oscar Wilde joined)— but it was merely poetry, not

indicative of crime, maintained Sir Edward in effect. *(Pall Mall Gazette,* 3 April)

When Sir Edward Clarke read this letter there was a momentary and involuntary outburst of merriment. Sir Edward said it might provoke mirth in those used only to commercial correspondence, but Mr. Wilde denied that it was open to any unclean interpretation, or was more than the letter of one poet to another. *(Star,* 3 April; repeated verbatim in *Reynolds's,* 7 April)

By juxtaposing the "prosaic" realm of "commercial" correspondence to the "poetical feeling" evoked by Wilde's letter, these quotations signal the prosecution's attempt to define the "poetic" as a privileged source of significance that transcends "everyday" meaning. Yet since the newspapers are the medium of "commercial correspondence" par excellence, selling precisely those "ordinary things which the necessities of life force upon one every day" as "news," the narrative apparatus's epistemological and financial interests immediately undermine the claims to legitimacy that this "aesthetic" ideology propounds. Here the attempts to interpolate "courtroom" laughter into the otherwise strictly verbal accounts foreground the friction created when the prosecution's utterance appears in different (con)texts: what appears in the Old Bailey chambers as a joke about the insufficiency of a restrictive hermeneutic, provoking according to the *Pall Mall Gazette* "Great laughter in which Mr. Oscar Wilde joined," becomes in the other journalistic transcriptions an indication of the absurdity of such an interpretation. (Note how the *Star* makes the letter itself and not Clarke's comment the catalyst for the mirthful moment.) In other words, through the dual journalistic processes of de- and recontextualization, Wilde comes to be identified as the "poet" whose language moves athwart those mundane linguistic conventions that delimit the standard idiom (here variously opposed to "unclean," "hateful," "repulsive," or "criminal" usage) in which the newspaper reader is immediately engaged. Thus, while what is legally at stake in the letter's interpretation is whether or not it corroborated the Marquis of Queensberry's statement that Wilde was "posing as a sodomite," the journalistic (con)texts transform this interpretation by situating it in a narrative that identifies Wilde—both as writer and as sexual actor—as the sole locus of meaning.

The newspapers reiterate this identification on a more generic level when they take up Clarke's response to the defense allegations made against Wilde's published works in the plea of justification, allegations that in turn become the crux for the defense's vituperative cross-examination of Wilde. For, as they report Clarke's attempt to deny the sexual interpretations attributed to Wilde's writings, the journalistic accounts actually underscore the equation that Queensberry's solicitors sought to effect between Wilde's writing and his "character."

> There are two counts at the end of this plea that are extremely curious. It is said that in the month of July 1890, Mr. Wilde published, or caused to be published with his name upon the title page, a certain immoral and indecent work, with the title "The Picture of Dorian Gray" which is intended to be understood by the readers to describe the relations, intimacies, and passions of certain persons guilty of unnatural practices, and that in December 1894, was published a certain immoral work in the form of *The Chameleon*, relating to practices and passions of persons of unnatural habits. . . . These are two very gross allegations. Why they are added I can hardly imagine unless my learned friends . . . intend to suggest to you that if all the other evidence fails Mr. Wilde should be treated by you as a person inclined to certain practices because he published *The Chameleon* and "The Picture of Dorian Gray." . . . [B]ut I shall be amazed if my my learned friend can get from this anything that in the remotest degree suggests anything hostile to the character of Mr. Wilde. *(Evening Standard,* 3 April)

> There are two allegations at the end of this plea that are extremely curious. It is said that in the month of July 1890, Mr. Wilde published, or caused to be published with his name upon the title page, a certain immoral and indecent work, with the title "The Picture of Dorian Gray" which is intended to be understood by the readers to describe the relations, intimacies, and passions of certain persons guilty of vice and that in December 1894 was published a certain immoral work in the form of a magazine called "The Chameleon." . . . These are two curious allegations. Why they are added I can hardly imagine unless my learned friends . . . intend to suggest that if all the other evidence fails Mr. Wilde should be treated by you as a person inclined to certain practices because he published "The Chameleon" and 'The Picture of Dorian Gray' . . . but I shall be amazed if my my learned friend can get from this anything that in the remotest degree suggests anything hostile to the moral character of Mr. Wilde. *(Daily Telegraph,* 4 April)

> He [Sir Edward Clarke] would do nothing to extend the range of the case beyond the radius which was inevitable. But two of the allegations were so strange that he was bound to notice them. The first was that in July 1890, Mr. Wilde published a "certain immoral and obscene work entitled 'The Picture of Dorian Gray,' designed and intended to describe the relations, intimacies and passions of

certain persons of unnatural habits, tastes and practices." The second was that in December 1894 he published a "certain other immoral and obscene work in the form of a magazine entitled *The Chameleon*," containing similar references and "certain immoral maxims entitled 'Phrases and Philosophies for the Use of the Young.' "(*Star*, 3 April)

He [Sir Edward Clarke] did not intend to mention the names alluded to in the pleadings, but he would deal with certain suggestions made in those pleadings that Mr. Wilde was the writer, or at all events the publisher, of articles of a remarkable and unnatural tendency. One of the publications called in question was the "Picture of Dorian Gray," a book that, strangely enough, had been publicly sold for several years. The learned counsel outlined the story, and defied the other side to prove that the author had done more than use a novelist's privilege to portray the vices and passions of human nature. (*Echo*, 3 April)

In the accounts appearing in the *Evening Standard*, the *Daily Telegraph*, and the *Star*, Clarke's quotations from the plea of justification are almost reported verbatim with the crucial exception that the words used to describe the text's "sexual characteristics" explicitly there are rendered euphemistically here. Yet unlike the initial descriptions of the defense allegations against Wilde himself, which by and large represented the original legal language through the complex structure of mediation discussed above, these versions follow the syntax of the defense pleading exactly with only tactical omission (e.g., the word "sodomitical" in the *Standard*) or substitution (e.g., the word "vice" in the *Telegraph*). The emergence of this manifestly legal formulation into texts that had heretofore abjured such explicit expression calls attention both to the ostensible subject of the statement (i.e., Wilde's writings) and to the imputations made against them/him. This attention becomes especially critical when the repetition of the phrase "the relations, intimacies, and passions of certain persons guilty of unnatural practices" (or "vice") as a description of Wilde's texts becomes the precursor for the corollary suggestion that this interpretation casts Wilde as "a person inclined to certain practices." While in the course of his statement Sir Edward Clarke was obviously attempting to interrupt this defense equation between Wilde's writings and his "character," the reports of his argument seem to create the opposite effect in the press: by representing Clarke's denial of the defense's interpretations, the newspapers transform it into the very means of introducing these interpretations to a reading public that had no other access to them. As the paraphrase of the defense position provided by the *Echo* suggests, "a remarkable and unnatural tendency" comes as easily to describe Wilde's "character" as it does his texts, thereby constituting these writings as a primary locus for publicly defining his sexual identification.

Having just rendered Clarke's statement for the prosecution in terms of—or more accurately, as the negation of—the defense's attempt to establish a (sexualized) equivalence between writer and text, the papers then turn to their depictions of Wilde's appearance as the primary witness which followed immediately upon the conclusion of the opening statement. While in the courtroom this movement was part of the trial's flow and as such was punctuated by numerous spatial and temporal gestures that marked these out as distinct moments, in the journalistic representations their immediate juxtaposition necessarily works against Wilde since the accounts of his entrance into the witness box appear to confirm Queensberry's characterization of him. As with the opening statement, this textual formulation was to some extent determined by the prosecution itself, since the apparent purpose of Wilde's testimony was to preempt the defense's ability to define his actions (both physical and verbal) as sexually transgressive. Appearing in the box on his own behalf, Wilde was lead through a series of questions that allowed him to recount in his own uniquely flamboyant style, the "story" of his harassment by the Marquis of Queensberry. While much of the narrative had been outlined by Sir Edward Clarke in his opening address to the court, Wilde's reiteration was not simply designed to underscore the gravity of the allegations, but rather sought to co-opt the defense's characterization of Wilde by establishing a more compelling counterinterpretation *in his own voice*. In this struggle for meanings, the deployment of Wilde's ability as a storyteller proved to be the most powerful resource—even if it was not ultimately a persuasive one—for the prosecution, and the force of his narration came to organize the journalistic accounts of his testimony.

Beginning with a short catechism designed to establish him as a scholar, author, popular playwright, husband, and father, Wilde's direct examination consisted primarily of a series of interlocking anecdotes that circled back upon and then extrapolated from the question of blackmail introduced in the opening statement. But since the details of the blackmail scheme had already been largely laid out, it was Wilde's rendering of them and not the "facts" themselves that constituted their newsworthiness. As the *Morning* notes in its commentary on his testimony, Wilde's self-(re)presentation was really the focus of journalistic attention:

> He answered the friendly questions addressed to him in a modulated
> voice, though his affected manner rendered his replies rather difficult
> to catch. During that portion of his examination which treated of
> the interviews he had with three men regarding the letters sent by
> him to Lord Alfred Douglas, Mr. Wilde asked for and obtained
> permission to explain in his own way exactly what took place. With
> eyes fixed on the ceiling and in a deliberate style, he narrated with
> remarkable precision the exact words used on the occasion. (5 April)

In reflecting on Wilde's appearance as a witness, the *Morning* constructs an opposition between Wilde's verbal self-control (i.e., his
"modulated voice") and his (re)presentational style (i.e., his "affected
manner") noting that the latter undermined the public comprehension
of the former. The report then compounds the implications attributed
to this contradictory effect by indicating that Wilde's narration comes
to occupy a unique, (self-) identifying positioning in the courtroom,
thereby conspicuously foregrounding the relation between his words
and his person. That his distracted gaze is conjoined with his "deliber-
ate style" to signify the point of origin of his "remarkably precise
narration" underscores the extent to which Wilde's verbal effect comes
to represent—and indeed (re)produce—his "character." Thus, in depicting Wilde's testimony the newspaper implicitly suggests a way of
reading his words so that they come to signify not just semantically
but also behaviorally: that is, they begin to identify him as a complex
source of meaning that can then be understood (or interpreted) as a
particular kind of (sexual) person.

Since the fascination with Wilde's verbal talent was so central to the
public interest in the trial—and rightly so, as his performance in the box
was an incredible *tour de force*—it is not surprising that it should figure
prominently in almost all the accounts of the case. The *Daily Telegraph*
and the *Evening Standard*, for example, provided what appear to be
largely unedited versions of the examination process detailing both
Wilde's tale and the manner of its telling. These reports are textually
constructed as dramatic dialogues between the witness and his counsel
so that the dynamics of their interaction emphasize the power of Wilde's
wit in contrast to his interlocutor's staid legal language. Since the efficacy
of Wilde's unmediated verbal skill is legendary and since the depiction
of his lengthy testimony is foregrounded in H. Montgomery Hyde's
treatment of the case, it seems more profitable here, for the sake of brevity, to consider the effect of Wilde's language when it is not explicitly
showcased—or, indeed, when it is manifestly constrained—in order to
illustrate the extent to which his representation as a "speaking subject"

came to be understood as "characteristic."[19] As the following extract
from the *Times* (5 April) suggests, the capacity of Wilde's narration to
interrupt even the most powerfully monologic textual strategies became
a primary index for his "personality."

In April 1893, Mr. Beerbohm Tree handed the witness what purported to be a copy of a letter. A man named Allen subsequently
called upon the witness, who felt that Allen was a man who wanted
money from him, and he said, "I suppose you have come about my
beautiful letter to Lord Alfred Douglas. If you had not been so
foolish as to send a copy to Mr. Beerbohm Tree I should have been
very glad to pay you a large sum for the letter as I consider that it
is a work of art." Allen said a curious construction could be put on
the letter. The witness said, in reply, "Art is rarely intelligible to the
criminal classes." Allen said, "A man had offered me £60 for it."
Witness said, "If you take my advice you will go to him and sell my
letter to him for £60. I myself have never received so large a sum for
any prose work of that length, but I am glad to find that there is
someone in England who will pay such a large sum for a letter of
mine." Allen said that the man was out of town. The witness said
that the man would come back, and added, "I assure you on my
word of honour that I shall pay nothing for the letter." Allen,
changing his manner, said he had not a single penny and was very
poor, and that he had been on many occasions trying to find the
witness to talk about the letter. Witness said that he could not
guarantee his cab expenses, but handed him half a sovereign. Witness
said to Allen, "The letter will be shortly published as a sonnet in a
delightful magazine, and I will send you a copy." That letter was
the basis of a sonnet which was published in French in the *Spirit
Lamp* in 1893. Allen went away. About five or six minutes after a
man called Clyburn came in. Witness said to him, "I cannot be
bothered anymore about the letter. I don't care twopence about it."
Clyburn said, "Allen has asked me to give it back to you." Witness
said, "Why does he give it me back?" Clyburn said, "Well, he says
that you were kind to him, and that there is no use trying to rent
you, as you only laugh at us." Witness looked at the letter, and
seeing that it was extremely soiled said, "I think it unpardonable
that better care was not taken of an original letter of mine." He said
he was very sorry—it had been in so many hands. Witness took the
letter then and said, "Well, I will accept the letter back, and you can
thank Mr. Allen from me for all the care he has shown about the
letter." He gave Clyburn half-a-sovereign for his trouble. Witness
said, "I am afraid you are leading a wonderfully wicked life." He
replied, "There is good and bad in every one of us." Witness told
him he was a born philosopher.

Here the *Times'* homogenizing prose style attempts to contain Wilde's dialogic testimony within its standard rhetoric for trial reporting. Thus, Wilde's name is effaced behind the generic designation "Witness" and his plurivocal narrative style is rendered as a patchwork of direct and indirect discourse. Yet in spite of the power of these rhetorical strategies to (re)produce the effects of a quasi-official documentation (in which the authority of the court is inscribed and legitimated in the very language of the reporting), the humor and the eloquence of Wilde's speech cannot be entirely circumscribed. In this passage, the juxtaposition of selected quotations from Wilde's testimony to the "standard prose" paraphrases (translations?) of the nonquoted portions underscores both the particularity of Wilde's style and its "difference" from official language. Foregrounding the facility of his wit, the use of direct discourse illustrates how Wilde sought both to recast the question of the letter's economic value in aesthetic terms ("I consider that it is a work of art") thus challenging the sexual assumptions presupposed by the blackmail scene ("a very curious construction could be put on the letter") and to humorously undermine the legitimacy of these sexual implications by insinuating that the blackmailers are not proper interpreters ("Art is rarely intelligible to the criminal classes"). However, since the effect of Wilde's humor is predicated on a self-referential display of linguistic prowess that continually calls attention to its own uniqueness (here in opposition to Clyburn and Allen and, in an ensuing anecdote, to the Marquis of Queensberry himself), its journalistic representation ironically seems to confirm the defense suggestion that Wilde's language is an indicator of his personal (sexual) difference.

While this imbrication of Wilde's linguistic and sexual difference remains implicit in most of the accounts of his direct examination, it is made strikingly explicit as soon as the papers begin to narrate his cross-examination by defense barrister, Edward Carson. Indeed, since Carson went to great lengths to prove the defense contention that there was an identity created between Wilde's sexual and literary "tendencies," it is not surprising that the journalistic representations of his cross-examination thematized this "identity" as Wilde's own "tendency." As the lead paragraphs of the *Evening News'* second day of coverage suggest, Carson's questioning not only constituted the climax of the dramatic events—or at least of their "dramatic" representation—but also "revealed," as any good story should, the "true nature" of Wilde's "character."

> Today was the second day of the hearing of the prosecution of the Marquis of Queensberry for criminal libel by Oscar Fingal O'Flaher-

tie Wilde. The accounts of the first day's proceedings had generated tremendous interest. "I never write anything that is not extraordinary," Oscar had said in the witness-box and in addition to his extraordinary writings, the extraordinary character of some of his doings, as related by himself under cross-examination, had been "highly stimulative to thought," and had brought crowding into the Old Bailey corridors a bigger press of would-be hearers than ever.

The fame of yesterday's performance—it was little else—had gone abroad, the accounts of the strange attitude adopted by this "lover of things beautiful," who thinks "books cannot be moral or immoral," and who is "not concerned to do good or evil but only to create the beautiful," had excited no less interest than the reports of the wonderful intellectual force and flow of perfect language with which he defended his positions, and the curious tone of his epistolary prose sonnets, and the bizarre nature of his choice of chance acquaintances, had aroused a deeper interest still, which was mirrored in the packed court that patiently awaited the resumption of the trial, in which this strange personality is nominally accusing a relentless pursuer of libel, but is actually defending himself against one of the gravest charges that can be brought against an English gentleman. (4 April)

The progression of meanings outlined in these paragraphs illustrates precisely those connections between Wilde's "extraordinary writings" and "the extraordinary character of some of his doings" and his "strange personality" that the defense took pains to produce in the trial. Appearing under the heading "OSCAR TODAY" and interrupted by a crude line drawing depicting "Mr. Oscar Wilde" (see figure 8), this account quickly establishes "Oscar" as the point of reference from which the meanings ascribed to the "performance" must be drawn. By stringing together quotations from Wilde's epigrammatic replies to Carson's questions—quotations that are then reiterated at length in a feature following the "story" itself entitled "Oscar's Epigrams: Some Excerpts from Yesterday's Evidence"—in order to illustrate the "strange attitude adopted by this 'lover of the beautiful,'" the *Evening News*'s reporting foregrounds Wilde's words as the source of evidence about "the strange personality." That the newspaper text conjoins Wilde's "wonderful intellectual force and flow of perfect language" with the "curious tone of his epistolary prose sonnets" and "the bizarre nature of his chance acquaintances" in order to report his "performance" as a witness reveals the constellation of meanings from which Wilde's "extraordinary character" emerges. Yet, since Wilde's replies to Carson also called into question the very logic of interpretation upon which such characterological claims were predicated, the repre-

MR. OSCAR WILDE.

Figure 8. *The Evening News,* 4 April 1895.

sentations of his cross-examination once again inscribe Wilde's texts as a primary site over which the contest of meanings takes place.

At a schematic level, Carson's cross-examination can be chronologically divided into two parts: the first occupied the terrain of Wilde's writing and the second his life/style. While this division unfolded temporally in the courtroom, however, its mediated appearance in the press established a logic of insinuation in which the sexual presumptions attributed to Wilde's writings during the earlier part of the questioning were reiterated in the second part (conveniently occurring almost entirely on the second day of testimony) as evidence of the sexual quality of his relationships with several younger, working-class men. To this end, Carson began his inquiry by addressing what he perceived as the sexual implications of a series of "literary" works: Alfred Douglas's poems "Praise of Shame" and "Two Loves," a short story by John Francis Bloxham in *The Chameleon* called "the Priest and the Acolyte," Wilde's "Phrases and Philosophies for the Use of the Young" (appearing in the same issue of *The Chameleon*), *The Picture of Dorian Gray*, Huysmans's *A rebours*, as well as several letters from Wilde to Alfred Douglas. In each case Carson sought to introduce to the court a text whose "meaning" he asserted was "improper," "immoral," "blasphemous," or "unnatural" and then to deduce from these "meanings" a moral equivalence between the writing and Wilde—even when he was not the text's author. While the pattern of questioning is quite similar for all the texts named: Carson asking Wilde if a "certain" interpretation could not be drawn from the work in question and Wilde replying that such interpretations were predicated on a naive reading process, the interrogation concerning *The Picture of Dorian Gray* surpassed all others in developing this strategic exchange. Here the activities and attitudes ascribed to Wilde's characters become the pretext for direct imputations made about Wilde's own "character." Since the *Daily Telegraph* (4 April) provides one of the the most detailed versions of this metonymic slide, it is worth considering its somewhat lengthy account here.

> This is your introduction to "Dorian Gray": "There is no such thing as a moral or immoral book; books are well written or badly written." That expresses your view?— My view on art, yes.
>
> Then a well written book putting forth certain views might be a good book? —No work of art ever puts forth views of any kind. Views belong to people who are not artists.
>
> Is "Dorian Gray" open to certain interpretations? — Only to brutes and illiterates. The views of the Philistine on art are incalculably stupid.
>
> The majority of people would come within your definition of Philistine and illiterates? —I have found wonderful exceptions.
>
> Do you think the majority of people live up to the pose you are giving us? —I am afraid they are not cultivated enough.
>
> Not cultivated enough to draw the distinction you have done between a good book and a bad book? —Certainly not. It has nothing to do with art at all.
>
> You don't prevent the ordinary individual from buying your books? —I have never discouraged it. (laughter)

. . .

  Mr. Carson then read a passage describing the introduction of the
artist to Dorian Gray and asked: Do you consider the feeling there
described as a proper or improper feeling?

  Witness: I think it is the most perfect description possible of what
an artist would feel on meeting a beautiful personality that he felt
in some way or other was necessary to his art and his life.

  You think that is a moral kind of feeling for one man to have
toward another? —I say it is the feeling of an artist toward a beautiful
personality.

  You have never known the feelings you describe there? —No. I
have never allowed any personality to dominate my art.

Although the accounts appearing in other papers differ substantially
at times from this one,[20] the movement from text to (authorial) context
remains constant in each. As the *Telegraph* represents it, the cross-
examination seems to juxtapose Carson's assertions about *Dorian
Gray*'s "(im)morality" to Wilde's claims that the power of art obviates
such monologic "views." Yet, since Carson seems to have quickly
subsumed the question of morality under that of public opinion,
Wilde's "aesthetic" replies situate him in opposition to "the ordinary
person" so that he seems to constitute himself as "extraordinary." In
the courtroom where the audience was to a large extent comprised of
highly educated legal officials, such an implication might have been
received with relatively little disapprobation, if not actual approval, as
the reported laughter seems to suggest. But as soon as the remark
was reiterated in the daily press where the readership was necessarily
constituted by—and was perhaps even definitive of—the "ordinary
reader," Wilde's remarks could be seen as corroborating the defense
suggestions made against him (see the *Evening News* use of "ordinary"/
"extraordinary" above). By foregrounding the issue of Wilde's "character," then, this questioning privileges the interpretation of Wilde
through his texts, so that there is little room for distinguishing between
them. The newspaper report makes this association between writer
and writing even more explicit when it omits the passages from *The
Picture of Dorian Gray* read aloud in the trial, so that instead of
appearing to refer to the characters in his novel, the references to
"the artist" seem to evoke Wilde himself. Hence, Wilde's statement
concerning "what an artist would feel on meeting a beautiful personality" can appear quite logically to signify his own relation to Lord
Alfred Douglas, thereby undermining his assertion that he had "never
allowed any personality to dominate [his] art."

  This effective equation between Wilde's aesthetic and sexual ideologies appears even more unequivocally in the more "dramatic" press accounts of the "literary" testimony that appeared in the *Echo*, the *Star*, and the *Morning Leader*. For these highly condensed, overly and overtly narrated versions do not hesitate to emphasize the (sexual) implications that the testimony itself usually leaves unspoken, even when such emphasis leads to blatant misreporting.

As to your works, you pose as not being concerned about morality or immorality. The aim is to try to make the thing have some quality of beauty or of emotion? —I really [*sic*] think anything I write is true. (laughter) With regard to the story of "Dorian Gray," he said additions were made to it when published in volume form, and one in particular, in consequence of its being pointed out to the witness that the sin of Dorian Gray might be misconstrued. . . .

Mr. Carson—In your introduction to "Dorian Gray" you say, "There is no such thing as moral or immoral literature; a book is either good or bad? —Yes.

A novel suggesting a serious offense might be a good book according to you? —I don't know what you mean by such a book.

I suggest "Dorian Gray." —There are things that cannot be appreciated by brutes and the illiterate.

Mr. Carson read further passages from the novel, and the witness in every case repudiated the insinuation that felonious conduct was necessarily suggested. (*Echo*, 3 April)

Presently the cross-examination got into deeper and deeper waters still, and Oscar was found saying, "I don't believe that any book or work of art ever produces any effect on conduct at all"—and was forthwith launched upon a long discussion of the art and morals question with Mr. Carson. He presently said that his writings must not be tested by truth in the sense of correspondence with fact. Anything was good he said, which stimulated thought. To realize oneself through pleasure was finer than to realize oneself through pain. And so forth, and

DEEPER AND DEEPER STILL

till the Irish Q. C. was left hopelessly floundering. Oscar blandly ran his fingers through his hair, and beamed on his cross-examiner, while overwhelming him with metaphysical definitions and "half truths put in an amusing and paradoxical form."

"What the sins of 'Dorian Gray' are no one knows," Mr. Wilde had written in answer to a reviewer. "People might think it meant unnatural vice?" suggested Mr. Carson. "Every man would see his own son [*sic*] in Dorian Gray," said Mr. Wilde. (*Star*, 3 April)

"What the sins of 'Dorian Gray' are no one knows," Mr. Wilde had written in answer to a reviewer. "People might think it meant unnatural vice?" suggested Mr. Carson. "Every man would see his own sin in 'Dorian Gray," said Mr. Wilde.

"A book which puts forward vicious views might, if you are right, be called a good book?" suggested Mr. Carson.

"No work of art ever puts forward views," Oscar sententiously replied. "Dorian Gray could only be called vicious when misinterpreted by the vulgar and the illiterate. The

VIEWS OF THE PHILISTINE

upon art are incalculable" and Oscar had "no knowledge of the ordinary individual."

"You don't mind the ordinary individual buying your book? —I have never discouraged him.

Mr. Carson asked the prosecutor if he had ever experienced the sentiments he attributed to the painter Basil, and whether he thought them natural.

"I should think it perfectly natural," Oscar replied, "to intensely adore and love a younger man. It is an incident in the life of almost every artist."

Is it an incident in your life? Have you every adored a man some 20 years younger than yourself? —No—not madly. (*Morning Leader,* 4 April)

In the *Echo*'s account, Wilde's testimony is first misquoted ("really" is substituted for "rarely") so as to obscure both the force and the humor of his speech and then in a supposed paraphrase is transposed so that it appears to imply that Wilde accepted the suggestion "that the sin of Dorian Gray might be misconstrued" and altered his manuscript as a consequence (when indeed he had denied that any such motive underlay the revisions for the bound volume). Yet beyond simply misreporting "the facts," the *Echo*'s text selectively juxtaposes apparently direct, but actually deracinated, quotations from the exchange between Wilde and Carson to its narrative conclusion that "the witness in every case repudiated the insinuation that felonious conduct was necessarily suggested," and thereby paraleptically affirms this "necessity" in the person of Wilde himself. The *Star*'s version similarly misreports Wilde's testimony (tellingly substituting the word "son" for "sin" in the sentence "Every man would see his own son in Dorian Gray") and uses paraphrase to privilege the "immoral" interpretation of Wilde's text. Here however, the narrative interventions overshadow the effects of these (mis)reporting techniques: The emphatic repetition (in bold-faced, capital letters) of the phrase "deeper and deeper . . . still"—which suggests both getting closer and closer to the "truth" of the matter and getting more and more enmired in the morass of iniquity where the upright Carson "hopelessly flounder[s]"—is juxtaposed to the description of Wilde's physical and verbal presence. Hence, Wilde is represented as sharing his character's trajectory through the Victorian underworld, which "people might think . . . meant unnatural vice." The *Morning Leader,* in turn, first singles out Wilde's manner for explicit disapprobation ("Oscar sententiously replied") which it then compounds by conspicuously reiterating Wilde's apparent claims to self-distinction: "Oscar had 'no knowledge of the ordinary individual.'" "Oscar" thus comes to signify an "extraordinary individual" who believes that "it is perfectly natural to intensely adore and love a younger man." While perhaps in many ways this statement approaches the philosophy that Wilde asserted in his life, it is certainly not the one he enunciated in the courtroom; however, the *Morning Leader* abjures the actual testimony given so that it can move from the imputation made against Wilde's novel to the imputation made against Wilde himself ("Have you ever adored madly a man 20 years younger than yourself? —No—not madly."). That all three newspaper texts portray Wilde through Carson's reading of *The Picture of Dorian Gray* illustrates how the journalistic representations of the legal proceedings conjoin "the sexual" and "the textual" and underscores the way that Wilde's "character" served to mediate between them.

Since this representational conjunction effectively introduced the accounts of the ensuing cross-examination—which proceeded to question the (sexual) implications of Wilde's relationships with the men named in the plea of justification—it established an interpretive frame for how these relations between men could/should be read. Conveniently, the transition between the literary and life/style portions of the testimony occurred during Carson's interrogation about the "prose sonnet" from Wilde to Alfred Douglas where the shift to interpreting Wilde's behavior as a signifier of his "character" appeared to derive logically from the interpretation of his text. As Carson moved from the close scrutiny of the letter's rhetoric to the issue of the blackmail itself, he carefully imbricated his interpretation of the text's "meanings" with a salacious description of the milieu in which it had monetary value. Accordingly, he shifted the focus of his inquiry from the implications of Wilde's writing to the implications of Wilde's relationships. As the descriptions of these interactions were then subjected to the same hermeneutic process that had been established for the textual interpretations that preceded them, they came to define the basis for an indictment both of Wilde's prose and of his "pose." To a large extent, then, Carson's questions to Wilde were not intended to elicit the explicitly sexual aspects of his interactions with the various men named in the plea. Instead, they sought to reiterate the parallel between the textual and the sexual by foregrounding precisely those aspects of Wilde's life that seemed to corroborate the "immorality" of his texts.

In the next chapter, which addresses the reporting of Wilde's prosecutions for committing "acts of gross indecency with another male person," the process by which Wilde's acts became the signifiers of a certain kind of sexual actor will be considered at length. Suffice it to say here that the press reports of these acts that emerged from the libel proceedings articulated them as elements in a story whose narrative development was predicated on establishing the kind of person that Wilde was. As the defense undertook to incriminate Wilde's behavior in his relationships with several younger, (usually unemployed) working-class men, it did not overtly charge him with sexual transgressions but instead intimated that his ·"friendships" with them could not be "proper" because they were marked by gross disparities in class, age, position, and social and educational background.

> There was the fact that in not one of these cases were the parties upon an equality with Wilde in any way. They were not educated parties such as he would naturally associate with and they were not his equal in years, and there was a curious similarity between the ages of each of them. . . . They were out of employment, and of their antecedents Wilde professed to know nothing. All of them were from 18 to 20 years of age, or thereabouts, and in the manner of their introduction to Wilde and his subsequent treatment of them all were in the same category, leading to the same conclusion that there was something unnatural and what might not ordinarily be expected in the relations between them. (*Evening Standard*, 4 April)

The defense statement makes the implications of Carson's questioning explicit: Wilde had transgressed those boundaries of difference (class, age, education, etc.) that delimited the realm of "natural association" for the Victorian middle class and hence his relationships could "logically" be perceived to signify "something unnatural," or at least "what might not ordinarily be expected." These signifiers of difference(s) then were reiterated as Wilde was asked to describe the rooms in which he met with the younger men, the restaurants in which they ate, the gifts that passed between them, all in order to underscore the implication that these relationships could not have taken place within the sphere of "normal" behavior. Although it appears that Carson did ultimately ask Wilde in most cases whether or not he had engaged in what the papers concur in referring to as "improprieties" with the men in question, his intention was not to prove that Wilde had committed any specific acts (since Wilde would hardly have admitted this in any case) but instead to suggest that the very fact of these relationships was improper. Thus, in glossing this testimony, the *Evening News* described it atmospherically by alluding to the milieu that Carson evoked rather than any sexual behavior *per se*:

> [T]he Old Bailey recoiled with loathing from the long ordeal of terrible suggestion that occupied the whole of yesterday when the cross-examination left the literary plane and penetrated the dim-lit, perfumed rooms where the poet of the beautiful joined with valets and grooms in the bond of silver cigarette cases. (5 April)

Here the personified court becomes a metonym for the larger public whose values it (supposedly) enforces and hence serves to emphasize the public horror provoked by the "ordeal of terrible suggestion." However, when the content of this ordeal is actually specified, it seems to consist entirely in the "bond" between "the poet of the beautiful" and "valets and grooms." By denoting these (sexual) actors solely by their occupations—and implicitly by their class and social status—the *Evening News* underscores the suggestion that no matter what might actually have or have not happened between them, the very conjunction of these men from different social positions itself constituted an "unnatural" relation. It is this interaction across what were (ideologically) defined as "natural" differences, then, that constituted the basis for the press reporting on Carson's indictment of Wilde's actions.

In the opening statement for the defense that followed the conclusion of the cross-examination, Carson carefully laid out the grounds on which he deemed the Marquis of Queensberry justified in claiming that the text "For Oscar Wilde, Posing as a somdomite" was both true and for the public benefit. Detailing the terrain that he had staked out in his cross-examination, Carson summarized the "literary portion" of the case and then explicitly connected it to the imputations made against Wilde's friendships with the younger men by claiming that Wilde's (sexual?) influence on Alfred Douglas—the very influence that Queensberry's card was allegedly attempting to disrupt—could be read in the text of Douglas's poems. As the *Evening Standard* provides a version substantially identical to those appearing elsewhere, it can serve as a model for the journalistic representation of Carson's tactic:

> The poem was written by Lord Alfred Douglas and was seen by Mr. Wilde before its publication. Was it not a terrible thing that a young man on the threshold of life, who had been for several years

dominated by Oscar Wilde, and who had been "loved and adored"
by Oscar Wilde as his letters proved, should thus show the tendency
of his mind upon this frightful subject?

That Douglas's poem (presumably "Two Loves") becomes a site for
interpreting the effects of Wilde's "domination"—which the rhetorically deft narrator syntagmatically links to his "love" and "adora-
tion"—illustrates the extent to which Wilde's "character" is continually articulated not as merely an embodied sexual proclivity but as a
"tendency of mind." This mental inclination serves to identify Wilde
both as one who has a "frightful" habit of thought (or at least subject
matter) and who inscribes this habit in his words and deeds. Thus, two
sentences later the *Standard* will paraphrase Carson's discourse on
The Picture of Dorian Gray by parenthetically noting: "The learned
Counsel read a long extract from 'Dorian Gray' with a view of maintaining that his contention was, as to the tendency of the book, right."
It is this "tendency" then that the court affirmed when on Sir Edward
Clarke's withdrawal of Wilde's prosecution, it found that the Marquis
of Queensberry was justified in his statement about Wilde's "pose."

Since my intention here is not to analyze the legal proceedings themselves but rather the effects of their public mediations in the press, I will
not address the complex legal issues raised by the abrupt termination of
Wilde's prosecution (which occurred at this point in Carson's opening
for the defense). Instead, I will conclude this chapter by considering
two editorials that appeared on Saturday 6 April 1895, the day after
the conclusion of *Wilde v Queensberry* and the day of Wilde's indictment for committing "acts of gross indecency with another male person." The first of these pronouncements appeared on the front page of
the *Westminster Gazette* under the headline "ART" and contained the
following assessment of the case:

> Every reader of our columns, as he passed his eye over the reports
> of WILDE'S apology for his life and work at the Old Bailey must
> surely have realized, with accumulating significance at every line,
> the terrible risks involved in certain artistic and literary phases of
> the day. Art we are told has nothing to do with morality. But even
> if this doctrine were true, it has long ago been perverted, under the
> treatment of the decadents, into a positive preference on the part of
> "Art" for the immoral, the morbid, and the maniacal. It is on this
> narrower issue that the proceedings of the last few days have thrown
> so lurid and convincing a light. We have no desire to revive here
> the memory of any of the degraded literature which it was Mr.
> CARSON'S painful duty to exhibit in its true tendency at the Old

Bailey. . . . No man—and still more, no community—has ever suc-
ceeded in setting "Art" and thought in a vacuum and, hermetically
sealing it off from emotion and conduct. The theory that you may
think anything without being immoral is followed in due course, if
it is not even preceded, by the theory that you may do what you
think. Then at length comes the discovery that the whole thing rests
on a base of rottenness and corruption. There is nothing new in this;
it has been seen over and over in the history of the world, and the
end is always the same. It has not gone far in England, for the
Philistine element is strong to check the excesses of the artistic
temperament. But it has gone far enough, and the crushing exposure
which has come in this case will, we hope, give pause to some who
have followed, either in sheer thoughtlessness or in the perverted
notion that they have a mission to emancipate "Art" from the
discipline of civilized mankind.

Here the *Westminster Gazette* offers its commentary as a form of moral
didacticism which it then juxtaposes to the "immoral" claims proffered
in "Wilde's apology for his life and work." As such its concluding
query ("[W]ho can doubt that the public attention called to the present
case will have a most salutary effect, in many different directions, upon
those who are hovering in a state of moral obfuscation caused by the
decadent theory of "Art for Immorality's sake?") underscores the role
that the press coverage had in (re)producing the "proper" public meanings that could be culled from the proceedings. Yet what precisely were
those meanings that the *Westminster Gazette's* editorial sought to
privilege? The paper first attempts to foreground the "naturalness" of
the case's "significance" by asserting that its readers "must surely have
realized . . . the terrible risks involved in certain artistic and literary
phases of the day"—even while the necessity for an extended analysis
would appear to belie the very obviousness of these meanings. Articulating the "true tendency" that Carson was able to discern in Wilde's
texts as its "natural" meaning, this interpretation marks out the aesthetic as a realm of social instability. Estranged by the "decadents"
from the healthy influences of "morality," "Art" becomes simply a
catalogue of degenerate pathology: it is "perverted," "immoral,"
"morbid," "maniacal," and "degraded." Yet, as this list of adjectives
suggests, the art works that are illuminated in the "lurid light" cast by
the trial are not themselves at issue; rather, they are significant only in
so far as they represent the negation/antithesis of normative social
standards (i.e., the "normal," "moral," "healthy," "sane," and "valued"). In this (con)text, "Art" functions as a metonym for the proliferation of "painful" counterhegemonic meanings and practices that

Wilde's voice (here equated with his "decadent" writings) introduced during the trial. For clearly, even in choosing "ART" as its title, the text signals its attempt to displace the revelations about Wilde's transgressive—or perhaps subversive—sexual and artistic practice onto the desexualized abstraction of aesthetic production. Thus, "Art for Immorality's sake" becomes a metaphor that knowingly alludes to the sexual implications made against Wilde while simultaneously suppressing the direct expression of this knowledge.

In enunciating its own counteraesthetic, then, the *Westminster Gazette* is not just propounding a theory of artistic production, or even simply trying to situate this production within a social context; rather, it is defining the position of hegemonic (re)production and reinscribing Wilde within it. Through the strategic use of negation, the text rhetorically invokes its authority to speak with the voice of universal truth ("no man," "no community," "nothing new") so that it implies the timelessness of its utterance. Since from this transcendent vantage point, "Art" and "thought" stand in an inextricable relation to "emotion and conduct," intellectual transgressions such as Wilde's must necessarily, or at least by way of a broken syllogism, provoke social anarchy and lead to cultural degeneration. Asserting that this regressive sequence reiterates a pattern that "has been seen over and over in the history of the world, and the end is always the same," the passage links Wilde's artistic and sexual practices to the fall of empires, even as it disdains to mention these practices explicitly. Thus, as the (pseudo)logical movement of this passage reveals, what is ultimately at stake in this moral evaluation of "Art" is the future of—in the author's unconsciously imperialist terminology—"the discipline of civilized mankind." Simultaneously evoking both a belief in the "natural" superiority of the British empire (over and against the "uncivilized" both at home and abroad) and a sense of the precariousness of this national and global ascendency (dependent as it was on a strict adherence to discipline), this last phrase must have conveyed to its presumably middle-class audience the importance of affirming their own moral and cultural rectitude. That Wilde's case should become the impetus for such a radical reassertion of "civilization's" moral ground suggests that the unarticulated assumptions that underlay the newspaper coverage of the trial negatively infused into the figure of Wilde those presumptions that define the "British" masculine norm.

The *Daily Telegraph's* assessment of the verdict against Wilde made this connection even more explicit. Beginning with a brief summary of the trial's denouement, the *Telegraph* foregrounds Wilde's exemplary role both in the proceedings and in the nation.

As for the prosecutor, whose notoriety has now become infamy, he made no appearance yesterday upon the scene, and he has since been arrested at the insistence of the Treasury on a charge of a very grave character. This being so, as regards any further influence which he can exercise upon social, literary, or artistic matters, and the contempt and disgust felt for such a character being fully met by the hideous downfall of the man and of his theories, we may dismiss the prisoner without further remark. We have had more than enough, of Mr. Oscar Wilde, who has been the means of inflicting upon public patience during this recent episode as much moral damage of the most offensive and repulsive kind as any single individual could well cause. If the general concern were only with the man himself— his spurious brilliancy, inflated egotism, diseased vanity, cultivated affectation, and shameless disavowal of morality—the best thing would be to dismiss him and his deeds without another word to the penalty of universal condemnation. But there is more than the individual himself to be considered in the matter. The just verdict of yesterday must be held to include with him the tendency of his peculiar career, the meaning and influence of his teaching, and all those shallow and specious arts by which he and his like have attempted to establish a cult in our midst, and even to set up new schools in literature, the drama, and social thought.

The "very grave character" of the charge on which Wilde was arrested serves to define Wilde as "such a character" as embodies the "social, literary, or artistic"—not to mention sexual—implications of the unnamed offense. By rendering Wilde's name in small caps, the text constructs him as the point of origin of the "moral damage of the most offensive and repulsive kind" thereby obscuring the fact that it was not Wilde *but the newspapers themselves* that "inflicted" these indignities upon the "public patience." Yet the editorial does not attempt to confine the "immoral" meanings that "Wilde" generates to "the man himself," even though it takes pains to articulate them very specifically, but instead seeks to transform his "character" into an example of "the tendency of his particular career." This movement from "character" to "tendency" then constructs "Wilde" as an "immoral character" who comes to signify the unnamed "charge of a very grave character" in order to warn the public against the dangers of "h[im] and his like."

But what are these dangers that the *Telegraph* so emphatically seeks to warn its readers of? In elucidating the implications of Wilde's transgressions, the paper leaves no doubt as to what it believes to be at stake.

It will be a public benefit, compensating for a great deal that has been painful in the reports of this trial, if the exposure of a chief representative of the immoral school leads to a clearer perception of its tendency and a heartier contempt for its methods. There is nothing difficult to understand in the principles of such people or in the results to which they lead. The aestheticism which worships a green carnation or a perfume has lost so much the sense of what is precious in parental and filial relations that we saw in this case a son addressing his father in terms which in ancient days would have involved his death. The superfine "Art" which admits no moral duty and laughs at the established phrases of right and wrong is the visible enemy of those ties and bonds of society—the natural affections, the domestic joys, the sanctity and sweetness of the home. We may judge this curse of an outrageous cult best when we find it the sworn and desperate opposite of the sacred verse which runs, "Whateverso things are true, whateverso things are honest, whateverso things are just, whateverso things are pure, whateverso things are lovely, whateverso things are of good report, if there be any virtue, and if there be any praise, think on these things." A nation prospers and profits precisely by those national qualities which these innovators deride and abjure. It goes swiftly to wreck and decay by precisely that brilliant corruption of which we have just had the exposure and the demonstration.

Characterizing the "tendency" of which Wilde is "a chief representative" as antithetical first to the authority of father over son and then by extension to the larger social organization articulated as the "nation," this quotation identifies the social order with the "natural affections" embodied within Victorian domesticity and simultaneously inscribes Wilde as their "visible enemy." In other words, it foregrounds the "sacredness" of the bourgeois home as the condition of "national prosperity" by representing "Oscar Wilde" as the "sworn and desperate opposite" of all that seems to guard against "wreck and decay." Here the "immorality" of Wilde's aesthetic ideology serves as an index for his transgressions, which, by moving across those boundaries that seem to guarantee national security, place him outside the world symbolized by the "sanctity and sweetness of the home." This positioning then serves to construct Wilde as the embodiment of a threatening "difference" so that he becomes the figure for a counternormative masculinity that both violates and transforms Victorian opposition between domestic and public spheres.

It was this threat that the crown's prosecution of Wilde was intended to contain.

6

DIS-POSING THE BODY
"Gross Indecency" and the
Remapping of Male Sexualities

> I awoke the imagination of my century so that it created myth and
> legend around me.
>
> Oscar Wilde, De Profundis

The withdrawal of Wilde's prosecution and the determination that
the Marquis of Queensberry was "justified" in his claim that Wilde
had "posed as a sodomite" terminated the libel proceedings in *Wilde
v. Queensberry*. Yet this was far from the conclusion of Wilde's legal
ordeal. For the moment Queensberry was released from the dock and
was dismissed as the nominal defendant in the case, the legal purview
could turn to consider what the journalistic gaze had taken in all along:
that it was really Oscar Wilde himself who was on trial. Thus, instead
of offering Wilde any legal redress against a man who had relentlessly—
and defiantly—harassed him, the proceedings in *Wilde v. Queensberry*
formed the basis for the ensuing prosecution of Wilde himself on
charges that he committed "acts of gross indecency with another male
person." Based on the evidence gathered in Queensberry's defense and
outlined in his plea of justification, Wilde was arrested in the evening
of 5 April 1895 and charged on a warrant at Bow Street Police Court the
next day. As the *Echo's* lead paragraph on Saturday 6 April described it,
the irony of Wilde's situation was far from subtle:

> How completely have the tables been turned in the Queensberry
> case! The man who for two days parried the verbal attacks of
> counsel, who lolled indolently and smilingly in the witness-box at
> the Old Bailey, who gave vent to his polished paradoxes with careless
> nonchalance, and who expressed his utter contempt for all things
> mundane, is now in the hands of the police charged with one of the

> most heinous crimes that can be alleged against a man—a crime too
> horrible and too revolting to be spoken of even by men.

As the last chapter attempted to suggest, in the three days prior to his
arrest Wilde's person(a) had been publicly redefined so that both in
the court and in the press he came to exemplify the "kind" of man
who had a "tendency" toward the commission of "certain" (sexual)
acts with other men. Indeed, the representational practices through
which Wilde's "exemplary" status was widely disseminated produced
"Oscar Wilde" as an iconic (sexual) "character" whose particular
attributes could then be read off as evidence of a more general type.
However, since in the libel case this characterization emerged without
the specification of any corresponding sexual activity, it was instead
articulated as a conjunction of behavioral, verbal, sartorial, and cultural styles. In the *Echo's* florid prose, Wilde's "indolent lolling," his
"polished paradoxes," his "careless nonchalance," his "utter contempt
for all things mundane" underscore the playwright's personification as
the figure for a counternormative male "type" that can now be mapped
onto a specific sexual accusation: "a crime too horrible and too revolt-
ing to be spoken of even by men." Although the *Echo*—both in the
above quotation and more explicitly later in the same article[1]—incor-
rectly plays on the suggestion that Wilde was charged with "sodomy,"
the syntactical conjunction of Wilde's "character" with a particular
sexual charge illustrates the ways in which the paper mobilized the
narrative effects of its previous coverage in order to make the criminal/
sexual offense meaningful. While this construction of meaning might
have been more conventional had Wilde actually been charged with
"sodomy" (for which a specific legal if not colloquial interpretation
could easily have been produced), the actuality of his indictment, trial,
and ultimate conviction under section 11 of the Criminal Law Amendment Act initiated a process of semiotic/semantic production in which
a newer legal definition of Wilde's behavior as "acts of gross indecency"
could be quite literally "fleshed out."

It could hardly have been more fitting that this process of sexual and
legal (re)definition should have been instigated concurrently in the
courts and in the press. For, Wilde's immediate indictment on charges
of "gross indecency" occurred only after Queensberry's solicitors for-
warded the evidence gathered against Wilde to the office of the public
prosecutor, Hamilton Cuffe, along with a letter *that was simultaneously released to the London newspapers*:

> Dear sir, —In order that there may be no miscarriage of justice, I
> think it my duty at once to send you a copy of all our witnesses'

statements, together with a copy of the shorthand notes of the the
trial. —Yours faithfully, Charles Russell. (*Echo*, 5 April)

Setting in motion the legal mechanisms that would result in Wilde's
arrest later the same evening, this communication also established
the interpretive grounds upon which Wilde's prosecution would both
proceed and be made meaningful. On the one hand, the evidence culled
in Queensberry's defense provided the strategic basis for the crown's
case against Wilde so that the conflation of characterological and
literary "tendencies" established in the libel proceeding came to frame
the legal interpretation of Wilde's (sexual) acts as they were construed
in the trials for gross indecency. On the other hand, the publicity given
to the incitement to prosecute was implicitly juxtaposed to the alleged
"miscarriage of justice" in the "Cleveland Street scandal" (see chapter
4) so that the very fact of Wilde's prosecution itself could be perceived,
both politically and popularly, as the symbolic reversal of the earlier
events. Given this legal and cultural context, Wilde's indictment, trials,
and conviction were necessarily constituted as public spectacles in
which the particularity of the charges and the unfolding of the legal
process also seemed to legitimate the impartiality of legal "justice"
along with its concomitant jurisdiction over a new province of sexual
"crimes." As the *Evening Standard* (6 April) paraphrased prosecutor
C. F. Gill's opening speech at Wilde's committal hearing, even though
"it was a most unpleasant case to go into . . . it was enormously
important that it should be known to those young men the Prisoner
had come into contact with that there was only one end to such a life
as that of the Prisoner Wilde, and that was at the hands of justice."
From the outset, then, Wilde's treatment "at the hands of justice" was
clearly intended to be exemplary, so that the meanings ascribed to
"such a life" both in the courtroom and in the press came to have
significance far beyond the strictly legal issues upon which Wilde's
guilt or innocence would be determined.

Not surprisingly, the sequence of legal events that concluded on 26
May 1895 with Wilde's sentencing to two year's imprisonment with
hard labor unraveled amidst an almost unprecedented amount of publicity during the spring of that year. Schematically, the judicial process
can be chronicled as follows: After his initial arrest (5 April) and
subsequent formal indictment (25 April) for committing acts of gross
indecency and conspiring to commit such acts along with Alfred Taylor—an unemployed gentleman of Wilde's acquaintance who had recently run through a small inheritance, arrested on 6 April, and addi-
tionally charged with procuring young men for Wilde—the two

defendants were remanded to police custody without bail until the indecisive conclusion of the first prosecution on 1 May. During the four days of testimony given in *Regenia v. Wilde and Taylor*, Wilde once again assumed the witness stand, this time followed by his codefendant, and their appearances—especially Wilde's eloquent defense of "The love that dares not speak its name"—seem to have been instrumental in causing the jury to disagree as to their guilt or innocence on the charges. The Crown then arranged to retry the case at the next session of the Old Bailey, at which time the prosecution was assumed by the solicitor general, Sir Frank Lockwood, a move that both signaled the political/symbolic importance of the prosecution and shifted the weight of presumption against the defendants. (Under British legal practice the solicitor general, unlike any other prosecuting barrister, always has the right to speak last before the jury.) Since the conspiracy charges were determined to be unfounded during the course of the first trial, the second prosecution separated Wilde and Taylor's adjudications so that Taylor was brought up again on 21 May and found guilty on 22 May, whereupon the prosecution against Wilde recommenced and he was found guilty on 25 May of seven counts under section 11 of the Criminal Law Amendment Act. Both men were then sentenced together to two years' imprisonment with hard labor, the maximum penalty allowed by law.

Throughout this sequence of court appearances, the claims made against both defendants were based almost exclusively on those outlined in the Marquis of Queensberry's plea of justification discussed in the last chapter. Indeed, so repetitive were these arguments that by the time of Wilde's second prosecution, the newspaper accounts frequently commented on—in the *Evening News'* (23 May) phrase—the "now familiar story" by way of glossing over their coverage of the testimony. Since the evidence presented in all the proceedings derived from an essentially unvarying sequence that the newspapers then reiterated with minute narrative and/or descriptive embellishment, it will be helpful here to briefly describe the major accusations and witnesses.

The charges against Wilde fundamentally rested on the interpretation of his relationship with several younger men, Charles Parker, Alfred Woods, Edward Shelly, Fredrick Atkins, as well as with one or more unidentified men whom he was accused of entertaining at the Savoy Hotel. Concomitantly, Alfred Taylor was indicted along with Wilde for his relationships with Charles Parker and his older brother, William, as well as for procuring these men for Wilde and for conspiring with him to commit various acts of gross indecency. Although nominally both defendants were equally implicated, it was apparent from the outset that the charges against Wilde constituted the main focus of legal *and* journalistic attention, while Taylor was relegated to being a marginal figure at best. The main testimony against Wilde came from Charles Parker and Alfred Woods, both of whom were in their early twenties, unemployed, and had already been involved in a variety of blackmail schemes when they first met Wilde. Parker was apparently introduced to Wilde by Taylor who brought the younger man along with his older brother William to dine with Wilde at Kettner's restaurant in March of 1893. In the newspaper accounts, this repast was represented as a luxurious affair in honor of Taylor's birthday at which the brothers Parker—an unemployed valet and groom—were treated to a feast in "a private room [where] the table was laid for four, and was lighted by candles with red shades . . . [and where] there was champagne followed by cognac" (*Star*, 26 April). Afterward, Wilde was alleged to have taken the younger Parker back to his rooms at the Savoy Hotel, plied him with more drink, and thereupon committed the "indecencies" for which he was indicted, giving Parker several pounds on his departure. The same sort of interaction was also reported to have occurred on several other occasions both at The Savoy and in rooms that Wilde rented in St. James Place. Woods seems to have made Wilde's acquaintance through a telegrammed introduction from Lord Alfred Douglas (although he also claimed to have been recommended by Taylor); Woods testified that he approached Wilde in the Cafe Royal, was invited to dine in a private room at the Florence, and was then taken back to Wilde's family home in Tite Street, where the absence of Wilde's family and the influence of alcohol facilitated the (supposed) commission of the "criminal" acts. Not coincidentally, Woods had also figured prominently in the Queensberry libel proceedings: he was the man to whom Lord Alfred Douglas gave the suit containing several letters from Wilde including the famous "prose poem" and he was also the one to whom Wilde gave money to go to America. In the course of the first indecency trial, it was further revealed that Woods along with a man named Allen (who was reported in the libel trial to have attempted to blackmail Wilde with the "prose poem") paid Charles Parker to sexually entrap an unnamed older man from whom they extorted several hundred pounds.

In addition to these allegations for which Wilde was eventually convicted, two other witnesses testified that they had engaged in indecencies with Wilde, although their statements were ultimately dismissed as unfounded. The first of these witnesses was a man named Fred Atkins who contended that Wilde took him to Paris, put him up in an adjoining hotel room, paid for him to have his hair cut and curled, but swore that he "never committed any act of impropriety with anyone" (*Reynolds'*, April 28). He alleged however that he saw Wilde in bed with another young man named Maurice (a.k.a "Jennie") Schwabe and that Wilde had tried unsuccessfully to introduce himself to Atkins's bed as well. Atkins's grudging admissions under cross-examination, that he had also been involved in blackmail and extortion schemes for which he was arrested (though never tried) in 1891 and that his partner in that case, a man named Burton, also "worked" with Charles Parker under similar circumstances, did much to discredit his testimony. The second witness Edward Shelly was apparently the only one of the men testifying against Wilde who was not in some way implicated in either male prostitution or blackmail. Shelly was a clerk in a publishing firm that handled Wilde's books; he met Wilde in 1892 and was taken by him to dine at the Albemarle Hotel, "had champagne with his dinner and afterwards whiskey and soda and smoked cigarettes in Wilde's sitting room" until Wilde committed "this outrage" upon him (*Reynolds'*, 26 April). Afterward he saw Wilde again under similar circumstances until, under "the painful sense of having committed sin," he unsuccessfully attempted to break off the acquaintance. However, during the course of his testimony, it transpired that that Shelly was rather emotionally unstable and had written Wilde a series of conflicting—and conflicted—letters entreating Wilde for assistance that seemed to contradict his sworn statements in the case. As his testimony could not be corroborated, it was ultimately dismissed.

The remaining charges on which Wilde was tried and convicted came to be referred to in the press as the "Savoy Hotel evidence." This designation described the testimony of a series of employees from the hotel where Wilde frequently stayed, who provided circumstantial evidence of the claim that Wilde had on several occasions been found in bed with or appeared to have been in bed with one or more unidentified men. As part of this testimony, the hotel bookkeeper corroborated the dates of Wilde's stays at the hotel, a chambermaid reported on the condition of Wilde's sheets, the housekeeper testified that she had seen Wilde with a young man in his room, a waiter deposed that he had served dinner to Wilde and a younger man, and Wilde's masseur claimed that he had entered Wilde's unlocked room to find him in bed with someone whom he at first believed to be a young woman and then realized was a young man.

In addition to this direct testimony as to Wilde's relationships with a series of men and his subsequent appearances in the dock on his own behalf, the transcripts of Wilde's performance in the Queensberry libel proceeding were read aloud at both gross-indecency trials. Yet, while these readings apparently occupied a great deal of time during the trials and indeed were constantly referred to in the prosecution's cross-examination of Wilde, the newspapers universally abjured from reiterating this earlier material, focusing instead either on the quality of the reading or on Wilde's response to it. To take just one example: "For the first time Wilde began to show uneasiness as counsel rapidly and with a minimum of expression, ran through the wonderful series of Oscarisms which made up a day and a half of cross-examination unparalleled in the history of the Old Bailey. There was now an intolerable irony in such flippancies and paradoxes as made amusing reading when Wilde was in the witness box" (*Star*, 29 April). Here the juxtaposition of Wilde as prosecutor to Wilde as prosecuted foregrounds the ironic mapping of Wilde's "characteristic" use of language in the libel trial onto the (sexual) interpretation of his physical behavior in the trials for indecency—a mapping that is then underscored as the *Star* elaborates its description by commenting on Wilde's body: "As refuge from the ghosts of his own intellectual fireworks, Wilde took to playing with a quill pen. He is grown perceptively thinner since the first trial." As I will argue below this pattern of somatic displacement became the conduit through which the unverbalized/unverbalizable aspects of the sexual charges against Wilde were made available to the reading public, inasmuch as the specific acts detailed in the trial fell outside the limitations of "reportability." Suffice it to say here that embedding the references to the proceeding of *Wilde v Queensberry* in the newspaper accounts of *Regenia v. Wilde* served to reinforce the characterological implications of the charges against him, while simultaneously shifting the (re)definition of "acts of gross indecency" away from narrowly delineated sexual practices to a larger sexual/behavioral context.

The evidence against Taylor was considerably less developed than that against Wilde, as was the significance derived from it. The only direct accusations made against him came from Charles and William Parker who claimed that they had slept with Taylor on several occasions and that he had introduced them to Wilde; from Alfred Woods who claimed that Taylor had introduced him to Wilde; from a police inspector who stated that he had found women's clothes, a wig, and a brooch in Taylor's rooms; and from the woman who lived downstairs from Taylor who claimed that young men were continually visiting him. In large part, then, the charges against Taylor were circumstantial and were aimed not at proving the extent of his particular "indecencies" but rather at portraying Taylor's lodgings as what the *News of the World* called "the snuggery at Little College-street" (26 May), i.e., as a male brothel where Taylor introduced men "like Wilde" to younger men for sexual purposes. To this end, much of the testimony against Taylor concerned the "bohemian" decor of his rooms, the kind of incense he burned, the frequency of his guests, and where men slept when they stayed with him (i.e., in his bed), thereby providing an environmental metonym for the indecencies he was supposed to have perpetrated: "Taylor's rooms with their heavily draped windows, their candles burning on through the day, and the languorous atmosphere [were] heavy with perfumes" (*Star*, 26 April).[2] By characterizing Taylor's abode as a demimonde milieu, both the press and the prosecution effectively represented it as a liminal space whose decorative perversions of bourgeois domesticity came to signify larger violations of the sexual/moral codes that such domesticity (re)produced and reflected. In so doing, these representations construed Taylor's and Wilde's movements in and through this space as confirmation of—if not the source for—the "indecencies" of which they were accused.

It is important to note here that such contextual confirmations were structured in part by the nature of the evidence presented against the two defendants and by the rules of jurisprudence that governed the validity of such testimony. For under British legal precedent, testimony as to "acts charged not against the will of the persons called upon to prove them" demanded corroboration lest "innocent people be exposed by designing or spiteful adversaries" (*Times*, 2 May). Since the Criminal Law Amendment Act decreed that all parties to the commission of an act of gross indecency were equally culpable, and hence the witnesses who testified that they had committed such acts with Wilde and Taylor were potentially as responsible as were the named defendants, their claims against Wilde and Taylor needed corollary substantiation before they could provide the basis for a conviction. Yet because the charges in the case related to acts that occurred in private, the judge, Mr. Justice Charles, determined that it was not reasonable to expect eyewitness corroboration, and thus evidence as to the "acquaintanceship of the defendants with the witnesses and as to many particulars of the narrative which they gave" was sufficient substantiation. This finding transformed the mere fact that Wilde and Taylor knew younger men who were not of their class, educational, or social status into proof of the "indecency" of these relationships and thereby located the determination of the sexual crime as much in the context as in the act. This contextualization received a succinct formulation in the *Echo's* account (21 May) of Taylor's second trial, when it reported the solicitor general's response to Taylor's barrister J. P. Grain's objection that the corroboration had not been sufficient to warrant conviction:

[I]f corroborative evidence of actual offenses were obtainable there would be no need to call as witnesses accessories to the crimes. It was obvious that such corroboration as Mr. Grain asked for could not be obtained, but there was other corroborative evidence that answered the requirements of justice. The general mode of Taylor's life, his associations, the manner in which he addressed his youthful friends, and the manner in which they addressed him—these things threw a curious light upon the nature of the relations which existed between Taylor and the young men who had been mentioned.

By arguing that "the general mode of Taylor's life" provided the needed verification of the criminal/sexual charge against him, the solicitor general effectively blurred the distinction between the specificity of a new, relatively unformed statutory definition ("acts of gross indecency") and a range of manifestly "nonsexual" behaviors and attributes. In so doing, he expanded the purview of legal determination beyond the consideration of "acts" per se to a constellation of relationships, interactions, preferences, and affects that would then refer back as circumstantial confirmation of the "actual offenses." This strategy of investing the patterns of everyday life with a significance that evokes/invokes a hidden sexual origin—not coincidentally echoing the strategies used to define "masturbatory insanity" discussed above in chapter 2—shifts the locus of the new legal definition from a consideration of the particularity of a sexual practice to the generality of a gender identity. Since Taylor's retrial immediately preceded, and indeed was immediately eclipsed by Wilde's, this shift would come to take on even more importance there: The plethora of detail ascribed to Wilde's "character" in the libel proceeding along with his popular status as a self-marketed public figure provided a unique opportunity for mapping a highly visible set of critically nonnormative public behaviors onto an obscure but apparently transgressive set of sexual practices.

Given this legal and journalistic frame, it is hardly surprising that the newspaper reporting of Wilde's prosecution conjoined the spectacular and the characterological in order to figure "Oscar Wilde" as embodying a new type of sexual offender. As soon as Wilde himself became the subject of legal scrutiny, it was very clear that it was his body—and metonymically the constitution of the male body—that was at stake in the production of public meanings engendered by the case. Since, unlike the earlier libel proceeding, the trials in which Wilde stood accused of "acts of gross indecency" were not organized around the interpretation of written texts, but rather were focused on determining the legal status of particular somatic relations, the disposition of

Wilde's body became the key to understanding the meaning of these "crimes." In part, this somatic concern derived from the ambiguities inhering in the legal shift from sodomy to gross indecency discussed in chapter 4: when the specificity of the criminal act could no longer be defined by the particularity of a sexual practice (i.e., anal penetration), then the quality of the sexual "indecency" could only be derived from the "nature of the relations"—to use the Solicitor General's phrase—within which the acts occurred. Hence "acts of gross indecency" were determined to be "grossly indecent" precisely because they involved the conjunction of two or more male bodies and not because of the "nature" of the acts per se. Accordingly, when a witness reported that he sat on Wilde's lap or that he "allowed" Wilde to kiss him, this testimony could then be adduced as corroboration of the crime even though the actions themselves would have been lawful—if not laudable—had they transpired in a relationship between a man and a woman. This transformation in the definition of sexual crime, therefore, necessitated an explicit attention to the contexts and relationships within which the bodies in question were situated and the locations where the indictable activities took place, since it was the situational and not the intrinsic quality of the somatic arrangements that rendered them subject to legal control.

In reporting the process of Wilde's arrest, indictment, incarceration, trial, sentencing and imprisonment, the newspaper accounts foreground this somatic orientation by organizing their narratives around the movements of Wilde's body across London's geopolitical terrain. For example, in their coverage of the events of 5 and 6 April, they usually elide Wilde's arrest, formal charging, and incarceration, so that the images of Wilde in the dock and in his jail cell became the *points de capiton* for the play of legal, sexual, and social meanings (figure 9). Moreover, in reporting the testimony that was subsequently given against Wilde, the papers follow the prosecution's lead in highlighting his passage through a series of social spaces (e.g., hotel rooms, private dining rooms, the theater, his home in Tite Street, Taylor's "bohemian" lodgings, etc.) rather than using chronology to organize the story of Wilde's "indecencies." This strategy moves simultaneously in two directions: first, they consign the representations of these criminalizable somatic arrangements to locations outside the middle-class family[3] and second, they use this extra familial milieu to designate the specificity of the "crime story." Since, as was discussed in the previous chapter, naming the sexual charges made against Wilde would exceed the limits of journalistic representation, it was the coincidence of Wilde's body with those of the young men named in the charges against him *in these*

Figure 9.

particular geopolitical contexts that came to signify the "unnatural"
or "improper" quality of their relationships.

Although it seems impossible that, in examining the case's primary
witnesses, the prosecution did not elicit stories about the sexual acts
in which they claimed to have engaged with Wilde, with only one
exception—which was itself far from explicit[4]—*no newspaper reported
the details of any sexual charge against Wilde*. Indeed, the criminal
activities themselves were never directly named in *any* newspaper account of the case but instead were designated by a virtually interchange-
able series of euphemisms (similar to those used in the coverage of
the libel trial) that directly conveyed nothing substantive about the
practices in question except perhaps that they were nonnormative:
e.g., "certain misdemeanors," "indecencies," "misconduct with lads,"
"immoral relationships," "improper relations," "certain practices,"
"certain matters," "the offense," "acts of impropriety," "disgraceful
charges," "gross misconduct," "gross immorality," "grave offenses,"
"terrible offenses," "wicked acts" and "unmentionable acts." Thus,
rather than depicting the criminal behaviors that Wilde was alleged to
have engaged in with the men who testified against him, behaviors
whose absence from the journalistic accounts might be supposed to
have rendered these reports nearly unintelligible, the newspapers produced a metonymic web in which the situation of male bodies dis-
placed/replaced the unarticulated and indeed unarticulable "sexual"
meanings. Simultaneously, the implicit juxtaposition of these somatic
situations to what was deemed the "proper" or "decent" placement of
the bourgeois male body (e.g., in the boardroom, the drawing room,
the club, or even the brothel) mapped onto these "sexual" signifieds
differences of class and generation that became constitutive elements
in the popular representations of Wilde's gendered, social identity.

Not coincidentally, then, the journalistic "story" of the case often
begins even before any legal actions have transpired with descriptions
of—as the *Weekly Dispatch's* subhead labels them—"OSCAR WILDE'S
MOVEMENTS." From the moment that Wilde's absence was noted on
the final morning of the libel trial, reporters from London's press army
were scouting for the whereabouts of the body in question. Tracking
him from a consultation with Sir Edward Clarke at the Old Bailey to
the Viaduct Hotel in Holborn where he was joined by Lord Alfred
Douglas, to his bank, and finally to the Cardogan Hotel where he
remained until his arrest several hours later, reporters quickly fixed
Wilde's person as the site of signification upon which all subsequent
interpretations would be inscribed. As they obsessed about the possibilities for his future movements; as they sought to interrogate any and

all who may have seen him as to his "condition"; as they made themselves ready to track him wherever he might try to flee; the press corps anticipated the legal attachment of Wilde's body by confining/defining him within their interpretive gaze. The focus on Wilde's presence/ absence thus came to isolate the origin for the legal proceeding in the man himself, thereby conjoining the offense for which he would be indicted to movements of his body.

The subsequent depictions of the arrest and incarceration of—in the *Morning Leader's* telling phrase—"the strange being whose mental and personal vagaries have compelled the attention of even those who laughed at or contemned [*sic*] Oscar Wilde since 'Patience' laughed him for a time out of society" then became a set piece in the newspaper versions of the events, so that Wilde's physical disposition is narratively encoded as the source/site of meaning. As the *Evening News's* sensational headline of Saturday 6 April framed it:

IN THE CELLS
Oscar Wilde Spends a Night at Bow Street
HE CANNOT EAT
But Drinks Police Coffee With Relish

the image of "the poet of the beautiful in the cell" became the locus from which all subsequent action departed so that even the most mundane details of Wilde's incarceration served symbolically to underscore the positioning of his body vis-à-vis the state: "Then the heavy door swung to, and the man was alone. The eye of a minion of the law was ever upon him through the small barred latchet-hole in the door. The chicken was brought and the water. No intoxicants are admitted in a prison cell." The ironic or even melodramatic depiction of the these transformations in Wilde's personal privilege foregrounds the limitations inscribed upon his body by the law, so that narration of these strictures itself seems to align the journalistic gaze with "the eye of a minion of the law." By positioning the reader of the article to "know" Wilde through the represented disposition of his body, the article shifts the epistemological frame of its coverage from the iconic representation of "Oscar Wilde" (re)produced in the libel proceedings to an exemplary (con)figuration constituted by the "subjecting" effects of the journalistic-cum-legal "eye."

This alignment of the newspaper narrative with the legal gaze is best illustrated in *The Echo's* 6 April account of Wilde's first night in jail:

> [The messenger] returned attended by one of the hotel servants
> bearing a waiter piled with soup, fish, chicken and a small bottle of
> champagne. For this repast, *recherché* although it might be, Oscar
> displayed only the slightest partiality, and it was returned but little
> diminished in quantity. Then he requested to be provided with a
> book, in order to wile away the time in reading. The light in the cell
> however prevented this. He slept very lightly, and now and then
> paced his cell. As soon as the morning broke he stepped up to the
> door of the cell, and, catching sight of the constable who had been
> detailed for the duty of watching him during the night, had a brief
> conversation with him. At eight o'clock a messenger arrived from
> the Tavistock Hotel again with his breakfast. This consisted of coffee
> and bread and butter. The coffee he drank, but the solid food he
> returned untouched. A curious feature however was that before this
> food could be taken away from the cell, another messenger arrived
> with coffee, bread, and butter, and two eggs. This, of course, was
> returned.

Offering what was ostensibly a chronology of "THE NIGHT IN THE
CELLS," this passage indeed underscores the extent to which "Oscar's"
incarceration constituted him as an object of legal and journalistic
observation. From the failure of his appetite to the fitfulness of his
sleep, the detailed reporting on the hours Wilde spent in jail prior to
his arraignment focus the newspaper's consideration on the knowledge
produced by scrutinizing the somatic effects of his imprisonment. And
since the narrative description of his actions necessarily foregrounds
the legal circumscription of his body, the narration (re)produces this
embodiment as both the site and the result of the meanings engendered
by the legal process.

As the *Echo* then turns to report Wilde's appearance before the Bow
Street Police Magistrate under the subhead "VISIBLY AFFECTED," it
invokes his physical transformation to signify the "truth" of his position: "the terrible anxiety he had undergone during the previous day
and night had left evident traces upon his face. Very different he
appeared from the playwright who had bowed his acknowledgements
to a London audience only a few weeks previously." This description
of the popular playwright's altered visage introduces the *Echo's* version
of the Crown case against Wilde almost as if it were offering to read
the "evident traces upon his face" as somatic inscriptions of his "story."
Thus, the *Echo* effectively juxtaposes its interpretation of Wilde's transformed body in the courtroom to the subsequent evocations of his
somatic "appearances" in other, less "proper," locations that immediately follow upon it:

Tracing the course of the dinners given to youths of various names, Mr. Gill went on, and visibly affected, Wilde at length sank upon the seat in the dock, drawing a deep sigh, and leaning his head upon his hand. Pitilessly Mr. Gill proceeded to trace the acts alleged for the prosecution, stating all he said would be corroborated in every detail, both by the boys and the prisoner himself, who was an available witness upon this charge, and by the youths. Evidence, he also remarked, would be called to prove the character of the various places which had been mentioned, while the procuration of youths for the prisoner and men like him would also be proved.

In this synopsis of the effects produced by C. F. Gill's opening statement for the prosecution, the *Echo* foregrounds the constellation of themes that will organize its ensuing coverage. With Wilde's drooping body providing the site to which all subsequent meanings are referred, the newspaper subsumes the "alleged acts" (which are neither described or defined) under the supposed fact of Wilde's relationship with "the boys." Moreover, it metonymically suggests that "the character of the various *places* . . . mentioned" in some way corroborates the charge of "procuration" not only for Wilde but also for "*men like him*" (my emphasis). In so doing, the reporting necessarily underscores Wilde's somatic (dis)placements as evidence of his alleged crimes, thereby over-determining his body *and its dispositions* as the origins from which the social meanings of such incriminating acts can be adduced.

In the ensuing "DETAILED REPORT," then, the *Echo* elaborates "the charges against [Wilde] related to immoral conduct" precisely by linking the presence of "the lads" to a series of social spaces whose "character" is clearly neither that of business nor of bourgeois domesticity. For example, in the following account of the crucial testimony presented by the unemployed valet, Charles Parker, the *Echo* moves back and forth between direct and indirect quotation so that the environmental details of the former come to overcompensate for the transparent sexual omissions in the latter.

The witness proceeded to say that he was introduced to Wilde two days later. He was given the address in Little College Street by Taylor at a restaurant, and he and his brother called there. He forgot who admitted him, but when inside he saw the rooms which Taylor lived in. They were three in number—a bedroom, drawing room and kind of kitchen. One, the drawing room, was very well furnished. He did not see a servant there, and then went on to describe the furniture.

Mr Gill —Do you remember whether the rooms at the time you went were lit up ? —No.

Was anyone there but Taylor? —No.

What did he say to you? —He said that he had arranged for me to be introduced to Mr. Wilde.

Did he say where? —I forget where; it was a restaurant.

When were you introduced? —That evening, after dinner, at half past seven.

Then you and your brother left? —Yes, I think we all three came out together, we left very shortly after this.

That evening did you go to the restaurant, you and your brother? —Yes.

Where did you go when you got there? —Upstairs, in a private room.

Where did you see the prisoner [Taylor]? —I met him at a bar and then went on with him and my brother.

Was there a table set for four? —Yes.

How was it lit? —By candles, with red shades.

Did you wait for him in that room? —Yes.

Did the prisoner Wilde then come in? —Yes.

Had you seen him before? —Never.

When he came in what took place? —Taylor introduced us.

Visits to the Hotel

What did you have with your dinner? —Champagne.

Did you see who paid for the dinner? —I saw Wilde write out a cheque.

In answer to further questions the witness then detailed the visit to the Savoy Hotel. There the prisoner and himself went into a sitting room alone. Wilde then ordered whiskey and soda. He was given £2 by the prisoner who also told him to call again in a week's time. He did so, and had supper and champagne with the prisoner alone. On this occasion he stopped for an hour, or an hour and a half, receiving when he left £2.

Here the absence of any mention of sexual activity makes the details of Parker's visit to Taylor's rooms, to the restaurant, and to the Savoy increasingly significant. The use of direct quotation to evoke the context of Wilde's relationship with Parker seems to underscore the impropriety of Wilde's entertaining an unemployed valet and groom in such an "extravagant" fashion. Appearing to reiterate the voice of the younger, working-class male, this quotation thereby attempts to render sexually meaningful the implicit connection—embedded only by way of a caesura in the much-abridged paraphrase of Parker's testimony— between their presence in "a sitting room alone" and a gift of £2. Hence, the appearance of an unemployed, working-class man in a context that is deemed inappropriate to both his age and his social position comes to represent an "indecent" relationship even in the absence of any specific representation of "indecent acts."

This strategy of displacing the sexual onto Wilde's somatic (dis)position receives a clearer formulation in the *Evening News*'s 6 April paraphrase of the same testimony, where the charges against Wilde are reduced to what is practically a list of place names.

> In the beginning of 1893, Wilde was staying at the Savoy Hotel from March 2 til March 29. At the same time there was living at Little College-street, Westminster, a man named Alfred Taylor, a man closely connected with Wilde. The prisoner was in the habit of visiting Taylor at Little College-street, as to the conditions of things at which house evidence would be given. Parker and his brother were approached by Taylor in St. James' Restaurant and asked to visit him at Little College-street. He spoke to them of immoral practices and mentioned to them Wilde's name.
>
> Shortly afterwards, they were taken by Taylor to Kettner's where they were entertained at a sumptuous dinner given by Wilde at the close of which Wilde said to Taylor, "Charlie is the boy for me." He then took Charles Parker to the Savoy Hotel, plied him with drink, and committed the offenses charged, giving the young man money.

That the *Evening News*'s story chronicles the narrative of Wilde's "immoral practices" in terms of the places in which these were allegedly organized and then committed underscores the extent to which the journalistic representation of these "offenses" was determined contextually. While in the courtroom questions concerning the specificity of "the offenses" were almost certainly put directly to the witness, the absence of such questioning in the newspaper accounts shifts the burden of explicating the charges away from the particularity of the acts to the "impropriety" of the relationship. Such displacement then allows for the overdetermination of the unspecified "indecency" so that in addition to the increasingly obvious—yet manifestly unarticulated—erotic implications ascribed to the term, meanings of class, age, status, and moral conduct could be mapped onto the emerging definitions of the "sexual" offense.

This nexus of signification provides the frame within which all subsequent depictions of Wilde's behavior will be portrayed. For as the prosecution sought to establish sufficient grounds on which the jury might convict Wilde for committing acts of gross indecency, the newspapers interpreted this courtroom (re)presentation for the larger reading public by excising those elements of the case that transgressed the limits of reportability, simultaneously rearticulating these notable absences within a web of signifiers that sutured the gaps characterologically. To this end, the journalistic versions of the trials continually foreground the juxtaposition of the defendants to the witnesses testifying against them in order to construct a topology of difference(s) across whose boundaries of age, class, social, and educational status, Wilde and Taylor's transgressions are then mapped. However, since the (ideological) efficacy of such mappings necessarily depends upon simultaneously inculcating and reiterating the implicit assumption that such differences are not constructed but "natural," these representations mobilize the larger play of difference(s) that organizes the production of "normal" (bourgeois) masculinity described in the first half of the book. As both sides of the ópposition between Wilde and "the boys" come to signify distinct deviations from—if not antitheses of— such normative, middle-class masculinity (figure 10), the definition of their "indecent" relationships begins to crystallize into a set of behaviors, attributes, and affects whose existence will negatively confirm the superiority of all that is "decent."

Since the newspapers continually capitalize upon the courtroom appearance of the male body—and especially Wilde's body—as a descriptive trope that personalizes the criminal proceedings, they contextually portray these patterns of "indecent" relationship as inhering in the modes of embodiment attributed to the individuals in question (figure 11). Wilde and Taylor as the named offenders are cast as morally, if not physically, "degenerate," so that their crimes are evinced by the symbolic significance ascribed to their bodily presence.[5] The following example from the *Star's* introduction to the first day's arguments in *Regina v. Wilde and Taylor* (and repeated verbatim in *Reynolds'*, 28 April) illustrates the extent to which such somatic description casts the defendants as the embodiment of the "sexual" transgressions that the ensuing text narrates (but never actually names):

> The prisoners were almost at once brought into the dock. Wilde looking almost haggard and fallen away from his old fleshiness, wore the dark overcoat and suede gloves that have been his attire throughout these painful cases and still carried his scrupulously-brushed silk hat. Taylor for the first time wore an overcoat, of light brown cloth with a collar of slightly-darker velvet and was suede-gloved like his companion. He was neatly groomed as ever but his fresh-colored effeminate face wore a much more serious expression than when he was first brought up at Bow Street. Wilde leaned heavily on the front of the dock, Taylor stood erect and looked

Figure 10. *News of the World,* 14 April 1895.

curiously about the court, which he last saw from a very different point of view.

Here the precise attention given to the defendants' clothing seems a bit curious as the prelude to a legal report, suggesting descriptions that might have been given more familiarly in the accounts of a society event or an art exhibition. However, in this (con)text such detail serves to underscore both the incongruity and the irony of the defendants'— and especially Wilde's—position in the courtroom by emphasizing

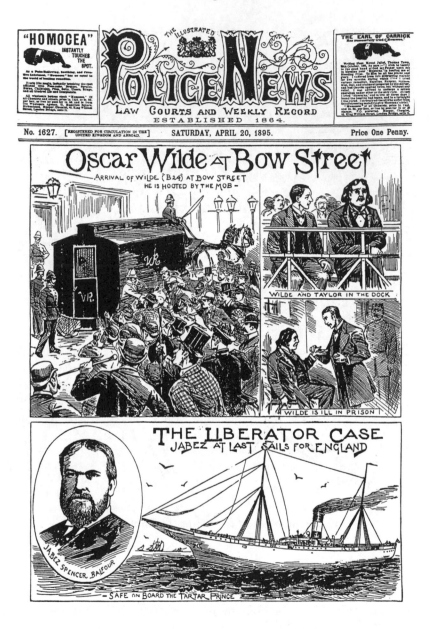

Figure 11.

their radical transformation in social status. Moreover, the initial evocation of Wilde, "haggard and fallen away from his old fleshiness"— a characterization that unsubtly contrasts a somatic mnemonic for Wilde's "extravagant" lifestyle to the somatic consequences induced by the legal process that interrupted it—is then juxtaposed to this sartorial elegance so that the discontinuity between the clothing and the body seems to signify a hidden (somatic) corruption that lurks beneath an apparently refined appearance. On the other hand, the depiction of Taylor's "fresh-colored effeminate face" in conjunction with the very meticulous portrayal of his "neatly groomed" person links the physical traces of "effeminacy" to a scrupulous attention to appearance, thereby mapping the qualitative attributions of nonnormative masculinity onto a visible somatic trait. Thus, the concluding opposition between Wilde's drooping frame and Taylor's "erect" posture suggests that as different as they might appear, it is the defendants' bodies in the dock that will provide the site upon which the trial's diverse sexual significance will be written.

Given the symbolic importance of this somatic siting, it is easy to understand how the unceasing journalistic attention to Wilde's progressive physical disintegration becomes both a metaphor for and the proof of the charges made against him. From the opening subhead "HOW WILDE LOOKED," appearing in several papers on the first day of the proceedings, through the repeated descriptions of Wilde's physical reactions to the testimony against him, to the concluding images of the convicted Wilde, "his huge body shr[u]nk into littleness . . . as the gaoler touched him on the shoulder" (*Evening News*, 27 May), Wilde's physical collapse bore the added significance of testifying to the "truth" of the "unspeakable" evidence against him.

> Wilde looked worse this morning than ever previously during this terrible period of his history. His hair was unkempt and his face pale. (*Evening News*, 26 April)

> The prisoners had followed [the] cross-examination with close attention. Taylor showed some excitement, but Wilde, lolling wearily in the corner of the dock with his head on his hands was inscrutable. (*Reynolds'*, 28 April)

> Wilde was thinner, and his hair was shorter. He sighed audibly during the reading of the long indictment. . . . (*The Weekly Dispatch*, April 28)

Wilde had grown positively grey in the face and can no longer keep out of his eyes the haggard consciousness of his terrible position. (*Star*, 1 May)

Anxiety and suspense told their tale, and in the first moment as [Wilde] stood moistening his parched lips, he looked more haggard and troubled than before. (*Evening News*, 2 May)

When the accused were placed in the dock, it was noticed that a marked change had taken place in the appearance of Wilde since he was first charged at Bow Street. He looked exceedingly careworn and in this respect presented a very different appearance to his companion, who was seen frequently to smile during the proceedings. (*Illustrated Police News*, 4 May)

There is little improvement in Wilde's appearance. Mental trouble has cut very deeply into his face. (*Star*, 20 May)

Wilde reached the court early. He looked haggard and ill and his hair which has a slight natural wave and is usually parted neatly from the middle was somewhat in disorder. (*Star*, 22 May)

Wilde listened to the whole of the Savoy evidence with an air of stolid indifference, occasionally looking round at the clock as if it bored him. But every now and then his right hand stole in front of his face, and concealed in the palm was a small bottle of smelling salts. (*Evening News*, 23 May)

WILDE
WEAK, ILL, AND UTTERLY DEJECTED IN THE DOCK

When Wilde was called upon to surrender he stumbled on mounting the steps leading up to the dock and seemed

WEAK AND UNCERTAIN

on his feet. There is no truth to the report which was yesterday circulated that the prisoner was seized with illness in the dock, but he is very obviously enfeebled and upset by his recent experiences. His fixed attitude, when he wedges himself in the angle of the dock with his head resting heavily on his right hand, bespeaks unutterable weariness. (*Star*, 23 May)

WILDE IS WEARY

Wilde looked more weary still this morning. He listened listlessly to the Solicitor-General's sneers at his "love of praise and delight in discussing that most interesting topic—himself." Occasionally he sighed, occasionally he took up his quill pen and drew heads on the sheet of paper before him. On the ledge of the dock stood his bottle of smelling salts, the application of which was a frequent relaxation. He looked to be suffering from a headache, and again his eyes were the eyes of a sleepless man. (*Evening News*, 25 May)

Then people looked at the face of the prisoner, and it was like the face of a corpse. (*Star*, 27 May)

While it was almost certainly the case that the ordeal of the trials did cause Wilde's physical and emotional breakdown so that by the time of his sentencing his appearance in the courtroom would have in itself provided cause for note, the newspapers' continual foregrounding of this process also becomes a counterpoint to the loud silences in their expurgated reports of the testimony about Wilde's physical/"sexual" relationships. Since they could not explicitly narrate the stories of the "acts of gross indecency" for which Wilde was actually being tried, the newspapers instead displaced the significance of these unarticulated acts onto the body of the supposed actor. Indeed, by the time of his conviction, the repeated representation of Wilde's physical being was so imbued with the significance of these "criminal behaviors" that it itself became almost a character in the journalistic stories of the trial—a character whose "nature" seemed to account for the unreportable behaviors in which it engaged and whose guilt could be read off from its suffering (see figures 12 and 13).

In contrast to this concerted attention to Wilde's body, the newspaper accounts are entirely restrained in their physical descriptions of the men testifying against him with one crucial exception: the importance placed upon their youth. While to a large extent the journalistic interest in the case revolved around the evidence given by the men who swore to their "indecencies" with the defendants, their presence was rendered significant only in so far as it was linked with the charges to which they were attesting. In this context, the generational disparity between them and Wilde—of which their young bodies became both the focus and the proof—served as a symbolic index of the "unnaturalness" of their relationships. Thus, the recurrent designation of these witnesses as "youths," "young men," "lads," and "boys" collected them into a set whose defining characteristic was their age so that in the newspaper reports their individuation as social actors was effectively diminished in favor of their role as metonyms for cross-generational "impropriety." To take just one example, in their narration of the first day's proceedings in *Regenia v. Wilde and Taylor* both the *Star* and the *Evening News* foregrounded age as Charles Parker's preeminent physi-

IN PRISON.

CAN YOU IMAGINE WHAT THE MENTAL AND PHYSICAL SUFFERINGS OF A
MAN OF THE OSCAR WILDE TEMPERAMENT MUST BE!

Figure 12. *Illustrated Police Budget,* **20 April 1895.**

SCENE AT THE OLD BAILEY.
THE MOST SENSATIONAL TRIAL OF THE CENTURY.

Figure 13. *Illustrated Police Budget,* **4 May 1895.**

cal feature: "Charles Parker is now 21 years of age, a slim cleanshaven lad with a fair girlish face" (*Star*, 26 April) and "Charles Parker is just 21 years old. He is gaunt and boyish still" (*Evening News*, 26 April). In both instances, the announcement of Parker's age is conjoined with a physical description that seems to suggest that he is somatically even younger than his chronological age. In the *Star* this implication is further emphasized by the evocation of his "fair girlish face" to create Parker as the image of the diminutiveness—if not even innocence—of "youth."[6] Since these portrayals locate the qualitative attributions being ascribed to the disparity in age between Wilde and Parker at the level of the temporal body, they render the constellation of difference(s) being (re)produced in the representations as "natural" (i.e., "biological") and thereby stabilize their normative effects.

Yet this representational practice was itself not unproblematic since throughout the course of the trials it was continually suggested that many of these "youths" had knowingly participated in what the *Star* so eloquently called "the depraved life of certain lads" (30 April). Indeed, the newspapers' obsessive concern with the effects of Wilde's "corrupting influence" on the younger men with whom he consorted— admittedly a concern essential to the prosecution's case against him— can be interpreted as both an attempt to fix Wilde as the responsible "sexual" agent, thus mitigating the complicity of those testifying against him, and to circumvent the possibility that these men might choose to earn their income from engaging in sexual relations with other men. Indeed, given the limited means for obtaining gainful employment by lower-class, undereducated, unskilled males during the last decades of the century (e.g., Charles and William Parker were out of work as a valet and a groom respectively, Alfred Woods had been a bookmaker's assistant, and Edward Shelly a publisher's clerk), it does not seem unreasonable to suggest that the lucrative possibilities promised by male prostitution, especially when accompanied by the potential for blackmail, and perhaps also by personal inclination, might make it a not entirely objectionable choice of occupation.[7] While it is hard to document the extent to which the structural unemployment resulting from the so-called "Great Depression" overdetermined the cultural significance attributed to the witnesses' lack of "respectable" employment, it seems hardly coincidental that just two columns over from the *Star's* gloss on "the depraved life of certain lads" the following squib appeared:

THE UNEMPLOYED
A HUNT BY THE COMMITTEE FOR A SUITABLE REMEDY

> The first report of the Committee on Want of Employment was issued today. The committee mention a number of suggestions that have been made for meeting the difficulty, and while anxious to make recommendations, state that no plan has been suggested which fulfills the required conditions. They therefore give the evidence received, while they proceed with further investigations.

That this (albeit terse) reminder of the "want of employment" should be situated in such close typographical proximity to—and yet bear no apparent logical connection with—a story foregrounding the (sexual) behaviors of particular unemployed "youths" underscores the degree to which the newspaper's narrative of the legal proceedings adumbrated the larger social factors at play in the case only by rendering them as individual anomalies. Indeed, by focusing so extensively on the ages of the men who were (allegedly) Wilde's sexual partners, both the legal and the journalistic interpretations undertook to represent Wilde as the sole responsible party. They therefore attempted to corroborate Wilde's "indecency" precisely to the extent that they sought to exclude both the possibility that these men had willingly chosen to enter into sexual relations with Wilde and the likelihood that contemporary social and historical conditions shaped their sexual practices.[8]

The most extensive elaboration of this attempt to fix Wilde as the source of sexual contamination is found in the detailed coverage of his cross-examination during both indecency trials. Having been placed in the dock by his barrister, Sir Edward Clarke, in order to refute under oath the claims made against him, Wilde was then subjected to a sequence of searching questions that sought to force him to characterize his relationships with the younger men named in the case in the terms of conventional bourgeois morality. In other words, the prosecution challenged Wilde to legitimate his interactions with a series of men whose class, age, educational, and social status situated these relations outside the sphere that the dominant cultural codes designated as "proper" so that his refusal to reiterate these normative ideologies under oath seemed to confirm the truth of the "sexual" charges against him. Inasmuch as the newspapers were restrained from describing any of the sexual activities that may have been narrated in the courtroom, the reporting of these exchanges between Wilde and his interlocutors took on increased significance in the journalistic versions of the trials. For it was in the accounts of the cross-examinations that the newspapers could extrapolate on the sexual inferences derived from the prosecution's case by linking them to the characterizations of Wilde produced during the libel trial.

The pattern for this connection of the characterological and the

sexual crystallized during prosecutor C. F. Gill's cross-examination in
Regenia v. Wilde and Taylor. Here the questioning begins by initially
reiterating Edward Carson's cross-examination in *Wilde v. Queensberry* and only then moving on to the specific sexual charges made
against Wilde under the Criminal Law Amendment Act. Starting with
the "literary" evidence that had featured so prominently in the earlier
case, the prosecutor apparently sought to evoke from Wilde the aesthetic ideology that he had so eloquently propounded in the court
several weeks earlier and then to juxtapose this ideology to the materiality of his relations with Parker, Atkins, Mavor, etc. In the newspapers,
however, this strategy was largely reworked, as the "literary" materials
repeated from the libel proceedings were only noted in the most abbre-
viated forms. For example, in the *Star*, which provided the most detailed account of this portion of the testimony, the "literary" cross-
examination merited only a few sentences. However, as the questioning
entered onto new territory and Wilde moved beyond the verbal spar-
ring of the first trial, the newspapers shifted abruptly from their circumspect paraphrase to an elaborate if indirect quotation in order to report
in amazing detail (for it is amazing that it appeared at all) Wilde's
apology for the love between an older and a younger man. As the *Star*
provides the fullest account of this quite eloquent statement, it is worth
quoting here:

> [Mr. Gill:] The other sonnet [by Lord Alfred Douglas] was entitled
> "The Two Loves." It concluded, " 'I am true love, I fill the heart of
> girl and boy with mutual flame.' Then sighing, said the other, 'Have
> your will. I am the love that dare not speak its name.' "
> Witness: That is clear.
> Mr Gill: Clear that it refers to natural love and unnatural love?
> "Oh, no," said the witness, "most certainly not," and entered
> upon an explanation which unfortunately was not at times perfectly
> audible. The love that dare not speak its name, he said, was the great
> affection between an elder and a younger man, as between David
> and Jonathan, such as Plato made the basis of his philosophy, such
> as you find in the sonnets of Michael Angelo and of Shakespeare,
> that deep spiritual affection that is as pure as it is perfect, and that
> pervades great works of art, like those of Michael Angelo and
> Shakespeare "and those two letters of mine." It was a love so
> misunderstood that it might be described as "the love that dared not
> speak its name." There was
>   NOTHING UNNATURAL
> about it. It was beautiful, it was fine, it was noble, it was intellectual,
> this love between an elder man with his experience of life and a
> younger with all the joy and hope of life before him. (30 April)

The effects of this passage within the full report of the day's proceedings are highly contradictory. On the one hand, this very moving statement (whose delivery, it is noted "drew a burst of spontaneous applause from the small public gallery") was easily the most widely disseminated public justification of emotional—if not explicitly physical—intimacy between two men. Couched in metaphors of pedagogy and aesthetics, Wilde appealed to the same cultural genealogy used by his contemporaries to legitimate the "greatness" of Victorian Britain's imperial traditions in order to assert the centrality of his own marginalized emotional/physical relationships. In so doing he very effectively interrupted the opposition between "natural" and "unnatural" within which the prosecution sought to situate the "love that dared not speak its name," and offered instead by way of a double negation ("nothing unnatural")—which the *Star* then underscored by employing it as a subhead—the possibility for opening up the field of significance in a way that was certainly enabling for those seeking such a possibility.

Yet even though the power of this rhetorical strategy clearly pervades the *Star's* account, it is also circumscribed by its (con)text so that the immediate effect of Wilde's apology must also be set against the delimiting testimony that follows. Since the quotation marks set around "and these two letters of mine" call attention to Wilde's self-justification in evoking his genealogy of "great" male lovers and suggest the dubiousness of his inclusion in it, the ensuing depiction of Gill's cross-questioning as to the import of these letters seems to undermine the idealism of Wilde's speech.

> Mr. Gill tried to apply this definition to the two letters to Lord Alfred Douglas—the first containing the references to the slim gilt soul and the rose-leaf lips, and the second saying "You are the divine thing I want," and describing Lord Alfred Douglas' letter as being "delightful red and yellow wine to me."

By foregrounding these extracts from Wilde's correspondence with Douglas the paper invokes the significance placed upon these same phrases in the earlier case. Assuming that its readers would already be familiar with the texts and their interpretation, the *Star's* account effectively links the textual implications highlighted in the finding that Wilde "posed as a sodomite" with the meanings produced in the "indecency" proceeding and thereby conjoins the notion that Wilde was the type of man who had an inclination to commit "certain sexual offenses" with the elaboration of the kind of relationships within which those "offenses" took place. As the account then abruptly shifts to the specific claims made about these relationships both directly by the witnesses themselves and indirectly by inference from the locations in which they transpired, this conjunction comes to specify the unarticulated sexual meanings that pervaded the reports of the libel trial.

While the accounts of Wilde's cross-examination during the first indecency trial crystallized many of the ambiguous or unvoiced elements from the earlier libel proceedings, it was only with the coverage of the solicitor general, Sir Frank Lockwood's cross-examination of the defendant during his retrial that this process of increasing specification received its most precise definition. In part, the increased specificity was a direct result of the first jury's inability to reach a decision based on the evidence presented. For, it was quite clear from the moment the chief Crown barrister assumed responsibility for the case that he was zealously committed to achieving a conviction by delineating as clearly as possible the inferences he wished the jury to draw.[9] In the journalistic versions of the second indecency trial, then, the solicitor general's presence in the courtroom served to focus the meanings produced by the evidence in a way that had not been heretofore possible, so that the testimony given against Wilde by the men named in the charges was almost entirely eclipsed in the newspaper accounts by Lockwood's questions to the defendant. However, it is also important to note that this choice of emphasis did not merely reflect the charisma or the aura of the prosecutor's courtroom presence—although both seem to have been extraordinary—but was also partially determined by the newspapers' need to continually stress the "currency" of its reporting. Since witnesses' testimony remained essentially unchanged from the initial versions given at the committal hearing almost two months before, the reiteration of these "now familiar stories" (*Evening News,* 23 May) no longer sufficed to justify its commodification as "news." Not surprisingly, then, the "newsworthiness" of the long, drawn-out legal process was now centered upon the connections that Sir Frank Lockwood was attempting to forge between the earlier characterizations of Wilde as a certain type of person and the contested assertion that Wilde had engaged in relationships whose "impropriety" confirmed the commission of unseen "acts of gross indecency."

Like prosecutor C. F. Gill before him, Lockwood began his questions to Wilde by going over the "literary" evidence from the Queensberry case before turning to the specific charges made against Wilde himself. As the subheads from *The Evening News*'s account of the 24 May proceedings suggest, the trajectory of this inquiry was designed to circumscribe the evidence presented against Wilde within a particular "criminal" interpretation of its significance: "WILDE IN THE WITNESS BOX,"

"CROSS-EXAMINED," "A QUESTION OF DECENCY," "TAYLOR'S TEA PAR-
TIES," "HE IS FOND OF PRAISE," "PLENTY OF WINE," "WOOD [*sic*] AND THE
£15." Not surprisingly, the first sentence following the initial marker of
Wilde's testimony begins with a description of his physical appearance
on the stand: "Wilde, looking very haggard was given a chair in the
witness-box and a glass of water placed at this elbow." Once again making Wilde's body the point of departure, the *Evening News*'s narrative
then abruptly shifts from its descriptive mode to recapitulate the trial's
chronology by tracing out the interrogation as it was (apparently) con-
ducted at the Old Bailey. Moving quickly through the brief direct examination in which Wilde was simply called upon the deny under oath the
charges against him, the bulk of the story is devoted to the solicitor general's catechism of Wilde's transgressions, beginning with his insinuations
about the nature of Wilde's relationship with Alfred Douglas. As the
evidence for the "impropriety" of this connection derived solely from
the letters that passed between them, the report of the cross-examination
was quickly immersed in the textual exegesis that had consumed so much
of the libel proceedings. Yet in this case, since the goal of the interpretation was no longer simply to determine the quality of Wilde's "pose," its
journalistic representation necessarily underscored the somatic implications contained in the charges against Wilde. Since the *Evening News*
(24 May) provides one of the best examples of this pattern it is worth
quoting here at some length:

> Are these two letters a sample of the letters you have written to
> Douglas? —No; I don't think you can take them as a sample.
> "My own boy," proceeded Sir Frank Lockwood, reading the
> letter, Is that the way you usually addressed him? —Oh yes, often.
> He was much younger than I was.
> You adopted this phraseology on account of his being so much
> younger? —Yes.
> "Your sonnet is quite lovely, and it is a marvel that those red rose-
> leaf lips of yours should be made no less for the music of song than
> the madness of kissing." May I ask you Mr. Wilde: Do you consider
> that a decent way of addressing a youth? —It is a little like a sonnet
> of Shakespeare. I admit it was a fantastical and extravagant way of
> writing to a young man. The question whether the thing is proper
> or right is—
>
> A QUESTION OF DECENCY
> The word I used, Mr. Wilde, was decent? —It was a beautiful
> way for an artist to write to a young man who had a love of art.
> Do you consider that a decent mode of addressing a young man?
> (emphatically) —It was a literary way of addressing a prose poem
> to—

I ask you if you know the meaning of the word decent? —Yes (quietly).

And do you consider that decent? —It was an attempt to write a prose poem in beautiful phraseology.

Did you consider it a decent phraseology? —Oh yes, yes.

"Your slim-gilt soul walks between passion and poetry. Hyacinthus, whom Apollo loved so madly, was you in Greek days." You were speaking of love between men? —What I meant by that phrase was that he was a poet and Hyacinthus was a poet, and— (then the voice became inaudible).

"Always with undying love," read on Sir Frank. —It was not a sensual love, said Wilde.

Is that again poetic imagery or an expression of your feelings? —That is an expression of my feelings (with a smile and a bow).

Here the transition from Wilde's mode of addressing Alfred Douglas (which not coincidentally foregrounds both Douglas' "youth" and the disparity in age between him and Wilde) to his "poetic letters" is circumscribed by—if not typographically centered upon—"A QUESTION OF DECENCY." Indeed, given the significance that the word "decent" bears in this case both as the antonym for and as the root of the charge under which Wilde was being prosecuted, the "QUESTION OF DECENCY" becomes the crux around which the earlier interpretations placed upon Wilde's epistles can be reinterpreted here as evidence of somatic as well as proprietary transgressions. That Wilde is shown to respond to Lockwood's reading of the letter's envoi by paraleptically introducing the phrase "sensual love" seems to underscore this heretofore unmentioned physical concern which is then once again narratively linked—by way of parenthetical description—to Wilde's own body.

In moving from the overdetermined significance of Wilde's textual practice to a more—but far from entirely—explicit gloss on his sexual practice, the *Evening News* divides the subsequent account of Wilde's cross-examination so that it emphasizes precisely those meanings that the prosecution sought to stabilize. Thus, the banner "TAYLOR'S TEA PARTIES," appearing the day after Taylor was found guilty of the same charges on which Wilde was in the process of being tried, frames the ensuing testimony by effectively "framing" Wilde. In depicting the solicitor general's exceedingly direct questions about Wilde's knowledge of the witnesses' (lack of) occupations and social status, about the nature of his enjoyments in interacting with them, about his "extravagant" treatment of them (buying them dinners, giving them gifts, serving them drinks, etc.), the paper situates its narrative so that the preferred meanings derived from it are at least in part structured by a conclusion that has already been confirmed (i.e., Taylor's conviction). In this light, the last three sections of the narrative, "HE IS FOND OF PRAISE," "PLENTY OF WINE," and "WOOD AND THE £15," come to overdetermine the characterological interpretations of Wilde's behavior as signifiers of the same sexual practices that led to Taylor's conviction—even before Wilde himself will be found guilty. Hence, by eliding the distinctions between them, this substitution of Wilde's social behaviors for the sexual practices that cannot/do not appear in the text comes to confirm Wilde's "identity." In so doing the account structures the representation of the unarticulated/unarticulable (but ever present) "acts of gross indecency" as elements in a range of characteristic practices that are determined to be intrinsic elements of—to use the phrase that Lockwood applied to Taylor—Wilde's "general mode of life."

Inasmuch as it confirmed the "indecency" of his life by validating and legitimating the "truth" of the charge that he had committed "acts of gross indecency," Wilde's conviction and sentencing then provided a singular opportunity for consolidating the social, sexual, and somatic meanings engendered by the extended sequence of trials that precipitated it. Culminating the months long legal proceedings, the finding that Wilde had committed the newly defined criminal offense retroactively imbued the earlier interpretations of his speeches, writings, movements, manners, relationships, etc., with a significance that could then be stabilized by reference to the fact of his sentencing and imprisonment. Indeed, when in his summation for the jury Mr. Justice Charles chronicled the various stages by which Wilde had arrived as the defendant charged with acts of gross indecency, he began by confirming the essential contiguity between the Queensberry libel proceedings and the subsequent criminal cases in which Wilde stood accused of consorting with men who were "not his equals . . . [but] illiterate boys" (*Globe*, 25 May). This merging of the issues raised in distinctly different legal contexts, formally conjoined a constellation of attributes that had been determined to justify the statement that Wilde had "posed as a sodomite" with the proofs necessary to establish Wilde's culpability for committing certain legally punishable sexual acts. Thus, when after deliberation the jury returned with its verdict that Wilde was indeed guilty on seven counts of "committing acts of gross indecency with another male person," it simultaneously imbricated the qualities attributed to Wilde's "pose" with the now legally legitimated "fact" of his sexual practice.

In the newspaper accounts, this nexus of significance was once again represented by the descriptive foregrounding of Wilde's physical presence. While in some cases, they editorially condemned Wilde by expressing moral outrage at what the *Westminster Gazette* called his "unwholesome tendencies" (27 May), by and large the journalistis reports eschewed drawing elaborated conclusions from the verdict. Yet given the narrative implications evoked by their earlier depictions of his somatic disposition, it seems clear that these unarticulated meanings were deemed to be implicitly marked in the lineaments of Wilde's body. Thus, the story of Wilde's conviction and subsequent sentencing and imprisonment almost inevitably yielded crucial descriptions of Wilde's physical response to the verdict.

> Wilde was brought up from the cells and placed in the dock. The last shadow of pretense of insouciance was gone from his haggard face. He was not pale—his face might more accurately be described as swollen and discolored—and he looked at the jury with dead eyes. "Gentlemen," said the Clerk of Arraigns, "have you agreed upon your verdict?" (*Star*, 27 May)

> [T]he prisoner was brought back to the dock. He walked up the stairs with a heavy step, seemingly having a difficulty in lifting his feet from one stair to another. He closely scrutinized the faces of his judges and then stepped to the front of the dock, leant over the rail, and began playing, with fingers that would not keep still, with his suede gloves. His face was flushed, and his eyes were heavy and swollen. He bent his head forward to listen for the word which was to decide his fate. . . . The clerk of arraigns put the formal question, "Gentlemen, are you agreed upon your verdict?" "Yes," replied the foreman, whereupon the prisoner turned his face full upon the jury. A twitching of the muscles of the face showed that he was now suffering great mental agony. What the verdict was to be it would be a relief to him to know it. After a moment's pause the clerk of arraigns asked whether they found the prisoner guilty or not on the first count. "Guilty," came the response. (*Illustrated Police News*, 1 June)

> Wilde, on hearing his sentence, raised his arm and gazed forward with a despairing look, as though about to speak. His mouth moved, but all that could be heard was a hollow cry, "Can't I say something?" The warders gently motioned him back, and he stepped towards the stairs. Just before reaching them however, he turned his horror stricken face once more towards the court, and seemed to desire to say something. This was prevented by his being handed down to the cells below. (*Lloyd's Weekly Newspaper*, 26 May)

WHAT WILDE WILL DO NOW

After sentence on Saturday, Wilde was conveyed in a depressed and nervous condition to the cell at Newgate, and immediately after when the warrants authorizing his detention for two years had been prepared, was taken in a prison van to Holloway. Here he found the reception warder waiting for him to deprive him of all loose cash and valuables; he was stripped to his shirt and placed before an officer, who proceeded to "take his description"; to write down in the prison ledgers a minute account of his appearance, his distinctive marks, the color of his eyes, hair, complexion, any peculiarities, a broken finger, tattoo marks, moles and so forth. Not being an old hand, having no previous convictions against him, he was not measured under the Bertillion system.

After the "description" was recorded, a matter of 10 or 15 minutes, he passed into the bath-room, where a hot bath awaited him, and while he was refreshing himself his shirt, the last vestige of his days of freedom, was removed. Emerging from the water, he found a full suit of prison clothes ready for him, from under linen to the loose shoes to the hideous Scottish cap. The clothes are of the well-known dirty drab color, plentifully adorned with broad arrows. (*Evening News*, 27 May)

As these passages suggest, the conclusion of Wilde's months-long legal ordeal culminated with the public gaze focused on the disposition of his body. Since, in a strictly legal sense, this somatic disposition defined both what was at issue in the courtroom (i.e., the "crime" was defined by the interpretation placed upon certain physical acts) and what was at stake in the criminal proceeding (i.e., the possibility of conviction and imprisonment problematized the orientation/movement of Wilde's body through the social space), it is not entirely surprising that the image of Wilde awaiting the verdict or Wilde being taken to prison should have been so compelling. However, in these reports the significance of such images was also overdetermined in so far as it made Wilde's body into a hieroglyph of the "crime" that he had committed. Indeed, by organizing the disparate meanings that the trial and its journalistic representations had engendered into a single, well-known, easily identifiable figure, the newspaper accounts effectively constituted Wilde's body as the meaning of the crime. In so doing, they foregrounded the emergence of a mode of understanding sexual acts that had only become possible in the ten years since the Criminal Law Amendment Act had been passed. For, the definition of Wilde's sexual "crime" was predicated first upon the "justification" that he had "posed as a sodomite"—i.e., that he represented himself as having the

TWO YEAR'S HARD LABOUR!
"You, Taylor, have kept a kind of male brothel, and you, Wilde,
have been the centre of a circle of extensive corruption, among
young men, of ???? hideous kind.—Justice Wills.

Figure 14. *Illustrated Police Budget,* 1 June 1895.

attributes of one who might be inclined to commit a highly specific form of sexual act (which he was never found to have engaged in)—and then upon the mapping of this attribution onto an emergent category of legal offense whose specificity was determined by the context within which Wilde's body was situated—i.e., in hotel rooms and restaurants with unemployed, younger, working-class men. Thus, the determination of his criminality and its publication for a national reading audience effectively constituted Wilde himself as a metonym for the "crime," especially as the newspapers could not offer any more concrete representation of the physical acts that were ostensibly at issue than a physical description of the actor who was legally determined to have performed them (figure 14).

EPILOGUE
What's in a Name?

On 25 May 1895, Wilde's imprisonment began and the newspaper stories about him—like his body itself—largely disappeared from public view. With the exception of a brief set of court appearances during his adjudication for bankruptcy later the same year, when crowds gathered near the court buildings in the hope of catching a glimpse of the infamous prisoner and the newspapers briefly noted this renewed interest, Wilde's moment as the focus of public attention had passed. After his emergence from prison on 19 May 1897, Wilde was never able to resume his earlier writing career, publishing only "The Ballad of Reading Gaol" before his death on 30 November 1900. In the years between his release from prison and his untimely demise, he lived primarily in France, sometimes under a pseudonym, Sebastian Melmouth—so overdetermined had his own name become that it was difficult even for its bearer to acknowledge in the land of his exile. However, even though the anonymous ignominity in which Wilde passed the years preceding his death is still, almost a century later, both indescribably moving and indescribably painful, this is not this consequence of Wilde's trials that I wish to call to your attention in closing this book. For, even as I recognize that it is perhaps the most egregious limitation of my project, it is not the personal but the discursive consequences of Wilde's legal proceeding that I wish to foreground for you now.

In the decade and a half since Michel Foucault wrote that: "[t]he nineteenth-century homosexual became a personage, a past, a case history, and a childhood in addition to being a type of life, a life form, and a morphology, with an indiscreet anatomy and possibly a distinct morphology,"[1] much intellectual if not emotional energy has been expended by gay historians in dating the "birth" of "the homosexual." Some have argued that "homosexual" denotes a set of sexual activities between men that have existed in a recognizably modern form for as long as several hundred to perhaps well over a thousand years. Others contend that the "homosexual" acquired a unique specificity in the nineteenth century that marks the concept as a socially and historically determinant frame for comprehending and experiencing a set of sexual practices between men in such a way that they are distinguishable from earlier ways of knowing/experiencing the "same" practices. While clearly my approach is much more closely aligned with the latter view than with the former, it seems important to underscore that the polemical divide is itself constructed upon political questions represented through concrete historical and semantic issues. For what appears to be at stake in the historiographic debates about dating "homosexuality" is how we ought to evaluate the ways this concept still organizes our own engagements with and transformations of the current historical moment.

Since it is my belief that the values we assign to any categories—sexual or otherwise—must be derived from the differentials established within the fields across which they are defined, it seems difficult for me to comprehend how "the homosexual" can exist, let alone be analyzed, apart from historical constellations within which this subject (position) emerged. Now this is not to say that I deny that there may have been men, or even communities of men, in earlier historical moments who were marked by virtue of their erotic preferences for other men. Nor even to say that these men may not have been publicly designated in terms of their sexual difference. Rather, it is to argue that what distinguishes the emergence of "the homosexual" during the second half of the nineteenth century is the fact that at this time it became inseparable from and literally incomprehensible without its "normal" twin, "the heterosexual." Indeed, it has been the underlying concern of this book to demonstrate that the emergence in England of "the male homosexual" as a distinctly counternormative category, signifying not only the presence of sexual and/or emotional bonds between men *but also* the absence of (re)productive male (hetero)sexuality, could only occur once the normative terms themselves had been rendered throroughly problematic.

Now if I were a better historian, I probably would have tried to examine this conceptual transformation through a more detailed consideration of the material challenges posed to "proper" bourgeois masculinities from such social changes as the expansion of the franchise, the growth of trade unionism, the economic stagnation of the 1870s and 1880s, the challenges to Empire both in Ireland and Africa, the emergence of the "New Woman," among many, many, others. As it is however, I have focused instead on a single, if highly visible, instance of discursive proliferation in which the structures of meaning underlying how middle-class standards for male propriety could be signified were rearticulated in order to signify an oppositional type of sexual subject whose imputed behaviors exceeded the standards for acceptable public representation. In doing so, I have chosen to consider the material effects that derive from such public (re)productions of meaning, in part because I believe that over the last two centuries, this has been *and indeed, very much continues to be* one of the primary fields across which the struggles to legitmate sexual differences and different sexualities have occurred. For, as the recent political interventions by groups like ACT UP, Queer Nation, WAC, and WHAM have demonstrated, contests for the production of sexual meanings—especially as mediated through the popular, mass-market press—still provide important opportunities to challenge, if not renegotiate, the public limits on how human (erotic) pleasures can be both embodied and represented.

For me, then, the political aim of my project lies in its attempt to historically situate the conditions under which the "homo/hetero" pairing emerged, both within and against the imaginary but material (re)productions of bourgeois masculinities in nineteenth-century Britain. In this way I have tried to suggest that all subsequent representations of masculinity structured by this putative opposition are necessarily inscribed within a mode of embodiment that simultaneously seeks to "fix" the incommensurate dispositions we have come to know as "class," "sex," "age," "gender," "race," and "nationality." My purpose in this analytic undertaking has been twofold: On the one hand, I believe that by historically positioning "male homosexuality" within the field of male subjectivity per se, we may come to better understand the exclusionary—if not aggressively repressive and violent—effects that the castigation of sexual and emotional intimacies between men has engendered. Indeed, such a relational understanding may enable us to explore more concretely why many men tacitly accept, as well as actively engage in, manifestly hateful and bloody attacks on "other" men to whom such intimacies can be attributed (whether reliably or not). For, if one of the ways that the stability and dominance of normative masculinity has been shored up over the last century is by (re)producing it in opposition to its antithetical "other(s)," then the (violent) repudiation of those who are categorically defined as antagonistic to it can be imagined by those interpellated as "manly men" to fix the vicissitudes of their own subjectivity. This interpretation might also open up a way of historically considering other recent social problems largely attributed to otherwise "normal" men such as domestic violence, rape, hate crimes, and child abuse.)

On the other hand, I hope by illustrating that the "pathological" emergence of "the homosexual" always bore within it the trace of its "normal" fraternal twin to suggest a further strategy for those interested in challenging the constraints that currently circumscibe the expressions—at once somatic and imaginary—of human (erotic) pleasures and relationships. Within the contemporary political context, the recent move to profess "queer" identifications as an alternative to self-affirming lesbian and gay "identities" represents an attempt to redefine the (imaginary) terrain of sexuality (here visibly stripped of the gender specificity that marked the earlier categories) over and against the hegemonic practices of "straight" society. This epistemological as well as political desire is well summed up by the button a seventeen-year-old friend of mine recently brought back from a Queer Nation demonstration, proudly proclaiming: "How dare you presume I'm straight?" While I believe this question quite rightly and directly addresses the unmarked dominance of "the heterosexual" as a foundational category for how sexual subjectivities continue to be known, I'm not certain that the same can be claimed for the recuperation of "queer" as the position from which such a question can be posed. For in attempting to reclaim a signifier that has served throughout much of this century as a homophobic epithet, this recent political denomination inscribes within itself the traces of an oppositional relation that has long structured the field of sexual meanings. Now I don't want to seem to suggest that this is an adequate reason to reject "queer" as a rubric within which diverse individuals and groups can organize their personal and political practices. Nor do I even advocate such a rejection. Rather what I'd like to suggest is that we might provisionally want to begin to imagine how we can historically problematize the ways the "oppositional" terms of dominance come to be embedded within the categories of resistance. My own current attempt to theorize such an analysis invokes the notion of "ec-centricity" as a way of moving beyond the binary structure of either/or. My hope is that a notion like "sexual ec-centricity" might enable us to abjure the fixing of any particular erotic practice or object as "essential," while offering the possibility for articulating an imaginary relation between all those "different" individuals who somehow find themselves off-center.

In raising questions about how nomination and denomination give telling shape to the field we have come to know as male "sexuality," therefore, this book has sought to explore the conditions within which the knowledges produced about male sexualities have concomitantly (re)produced the centrality of those modes of embodiment that are defined as "masculine." Indeed, what I hope to have suggested here is that the mapping of masculinities across those categories that designate male sexual subjects with respect to their sexual object choices— whether male and/or female—makes sense only to the extent that they continue to imbricate (male) gender and sexuality within the articulations of power that organize our contemporary social forma- tions. Thus to ask "What's in a name?" by way of concluding is not to ask how language engenders "reality," but rather to inquire into how the ways we name and narrate our (e)motions inscribe the limits within which we are constrained to experience what we come to "know" as real. For it is my belief that by exploring the historical transformations of such epistemological limitations we may be better able to transform the possibilities for imagining alternative, more ex- pansive, more pleasurable, more equitable modes of embodiment in the future. And it is with this at once political and personal desire that I have tried to *Talk on the Wilde Side.*

NOTES

A Funny Thing Happened on the Way to the Trials

1. In fact they paled so much that they were quickly removed from production: During the course of the trials both *Lady Windermere's Fan* and *The Importance of Being Earnest*—which had been playing to enthusiastic audiences—closed. On the significance of this rapid reversal in popularity, see my essay "Laughing in Earnest: The Trying Context of Wilde's 'Trivial' Comedy," *LIT: Literature, Interpretation, Theory* 3 (1991): 57–64.

2. H. Montgomery Hyde, *The Trials of Oscar Wilde* (New York: Dover, 1962). All further references will be incorporated in the text.

In fact Hyde's book on the trials is the only text published within the last fifty years to treat the trials as its primary concern. The absence of information on Wilde's trials seems a serious omission not only for the emerging historical genres of gay or sexual history but also for the more canonical study of legal history as well. In fact, it was as legal history that Hyde's book initially appeared, constituting one work in a "Famous Trials" series, as did the only other book on the trials, *Oscar Wilde: Three Times Tried* (London: Ferrestone Press, 1912), by Stuart Mason (Christopher Millard), which appeared anonymously in a series of "Great Trials of the Nineteenth Century." The only other work to focus exclusively on the trials (but only the second and third) is another monograph entitled "The Trials of Oscar Wilde—From the Shorthand Reports" by Charles Carrington and printed privately in Paris in 1906 (actually the text is not taken from shorthand reports, but—as with all of the works on the subject—derives from compilations and/or abstractions from the newspaper clippings on the trials).

While references to the trials abound in late-nineteenth- and early-twentieth-century biographies, memoirs, and even fiction, these treatments are primarily anecdotal reminiscences or post facto defenses of Wilde. Good examples of this genre include Frank Harris, *The Life and Confessions of Oscar Wilde* (1916; London: Fortune Press, 1925); Alfred Douglas, *Oscar Wilde and Myself* (London: J. Long, 1914) as well as his later works *Without Apology* (1938), *Oscar Wilde: A Summing Up* (1940), and his *Autobiography* (1929), titled in the American edition *My Friendship with Oscar Wilde* (New York: Coventry House, 1932); André Gide, *Oscar Wilde*, trans. Bernard Frenchtman (New York: Philosophical Library, 1949); and Vivian Holland, *Son of Oscar Wilde* (London: R. Hart-Davis, 1954). Robert Sherard provided a virtual production line for such works, becoming what Hyde calls "Wilde's most chivalrous defender in print." His works on Wilde include *Oscar Wilde: The Story of an Unhappy Friendship* (1902), *Life of Oscar Wilde* (1906), *The Real Oscar Wilde* (1915), *Oscar Wilde Twice Defended* (1934), and *Bernard Shaw, Frank Harris, and Oscar Wilde* (1934). Marc-André Raffalovich published the first full account of Wilde's trials in his *Uranisme et Unisexualité* (1896).

Other early works which treat the trials include Arthur Ransome, *Oscar Wilde* (1912), Vincent O'Sullivan, *Aspects of Wilde* (1936), Boris Brasol, *Oscar Wilde: The Man, the Artist, the Martyr* (1938), and Percy Colson and Francis, the Tenth Marquis of Queensberry, *Oscar Wilde and the Black Douglas* (1949). Hyde draws extensively upon these works, as well as from his own large collection of Wildeania to produce the biographical introduction to *The Trials of Oscar Wilde*.

Even the contemporary works on Wilde continue in this anecdotal tradition. Most recently, Richard Ellmann, *Oscar Wilde* (New York: Knopf, 1988) but also Rupert Croft-Cooke's *The Unrecorded Life of Oscar Wilde* (New York: D. McKay and Co., 1972); Martin Fido's *Oscar Wilde* (New York: Viking Press, 1973); and J. E. Chamberlin, *Ripe was the Drowsy Hour: The Age of Oscar Wilde* (New York: Seabury Press, 1977). In addition, there are several fictionalizations of Wilde's life which utilize Wilde's energetic self-dramatization for their own artistic ends. These include Lester Cohen, *Oscar Wilde: A Play* (New York: Boni and Liverwright, 1928); Leslie and Sewell Stokes, *Oscar Wilde: A Play* (New York: Random House, 1938); John Furnell, *The Stringed Lute: An Evocation in Dialogue of Oscar Wilde* (London: Rider and Co., 1955); Eric Bently, *Lord Alfred's Lover: A Play* (Toronto: Personal Library, 1981); Desmond Hall, *I Give You Oscar Wilde: A Biographical Novel* (New York: New American Library, 1965); Clement Wood, *The Sensualist, a Novel of the Life and Times of Oscar Wilde* (New York.: J. Swift, 1942); Peter Ackroyd, *The Last Testament of Oscar Wilde* (New York: Harper and Row, 1983); and Robert Reilly's *The God of Mirrors* (Boston: Atlantic Monthly Press, 1986). Even Ken Russell's recent movie, *Salomé's Last Dance* uses (an apocryphal version of) Wilde's arrest as its dénouement.

3. Richard Ellmann's much-acclaimed recent biography of Wilde repeats Hyde's "tragic" structure exactly, as the book's section headings confirm: "Beginnings," "Advances," "Exaltations," "Disgrace," "Exile." For an analysis of the problems with this structure, see Ed Cohen, "Nothing Wilde," *The Nation* 246. 6 (1988). For a detailed "ideological" reading of Hyde's text, see Ed Cohen, "Hyding Wilde," *Talk on the Wilde Side: Towards a Genealogy of the Discourse on Male (Homo)Sexuality* (Ph.D. diss., Stanford University, 1989), 1–40.

4. It's probably useful to note here that Wilde himself was not English but Irish. While I believe that it is not insignificant that Wilde's trials occurred within a period of increasing agitation over Irish independence, there was no reference to the fact of Wilde's "Irishness" either in the courtroom or in the press. It is certainly beyond my own ken to comment intelligently on this absence. Yet what it enabled was the coding of Wilde's behavior as paradigmatic of a "type" of sexual actor who was then juxtaposed to normative versions of *English* masculinity.

5. My first copy of Hyde's book was a used hardback published in 1956. The blurb on the front of the dust jacket read:

The first complete account of all three sensational trials Oscar Wilde underwent. It includes the complete transcriptions of all three trials—with Wilde's witticisms competing with legal terminology. A postscript adds the opinions of Krafft-Ebing and Bloch and other psychoanalysts and penologists whose findings have greatly altered the treatment and the punishment of this particular social offense.

6. Personal correspondence, 10 June 1985.

Part I. Against the Norm

1. Even this text only appeared in English after having first been published in German under joint authorship with John Addington Symonds, who along with Edward Carpenter was largely responsible for collecting the male case histories that constitute much of the book. Symonds, a well-known British literary historian and apologist for sexual relations between men—whose privately printed *A Problem of Greek Ethics* (1883) and *A Problem in Modern Ethics* (1891) presented literary and historical precedents for such relations—was instrumental in crystallizing Ellis's approach to "sexual inversion." Owing to pressures from the Symonds family after his death in 1893, Ellis was required to revise the text and remove Symonds name from it before its British pressing (1897). Shortly thereafter (in May 1898), *Sexual Inversion* became the catalyst for a criminal prosecution against London bookseller George Bedborough against whom the chief charge was that he had "sold and uttered a certain lewd wicked bawdy scandalous and obscene libel in the form of a book entitled *Studies in the Psychology of Sex: Sexual Inversion.*" After Bedborough pled guilty on 11 October, Ellis removed the book from British publication and it has not been reprinted in Britain. For accounts of the controversy generated by *Sexual Inversion* see Phyllis Grosskurth's biographies of both Havelock Ellis (London: Allen Lane, 1980) and John Addington Symonds (London: Longmans, 1964). Also see Jeffrey Weeks's essay, "Havelock Ellis and the Politics of Sex Reform," in Shelia Rowbotham and Jeffrey Weeks, *Socialism and the New Life* (London: Pluto Press, 1977), 139–85; and Arthur Calder Marshall's account in *Lewd, Blasphemous and Obscene* (London, 1972).

2. See, for example J. C. Shaw and G. N. Ferris, "Perverted Sexual Instinct," *The Journal of Nervous and Mental Disease* 10.2 (April 1883): 185–204. Also, Julius Krueg, "Perverted Sexual Instincts," *Brain* 4.3 (October 1881): 368–76.

3. R. von Krafft-Ebing, *Psychopathia Sexualis with especial reference to Contrary Sexual Instinct: A Medico-Legal Study*, trans. Charles Chaddock, 7th edition (London: F. J. Rebman, 1892). The O.E.D. entry for "homosexual"—conspicuously absent from the standard 1933 edition—first appears in the 1976 "Supplement," and confirms this emergence in the translation of Krafft-Ebing. An earlier use of the term "homosexual" can be found in Symonds's *A Problem in Greek Ethics* but as there were only ten privately printed copies of this text until it appeared publically, first as an appendix to the short-lived British pressing of Ellis's *Sexual Inversion* (1897) and then in a pirated 1901 edition, its influence prior to the Chaddock translation cannot have been widespread. However, it does indicate the importance that medicoforensic discourse had, at least for an educated elite, in providing the terms through which men came to describe, if not understand, their sexual and emotional intimacies with other men. For a bibliographic history of this text see Robert Peters' forward to the recent reprint of Symonds's essays in *Male Love: A Problem in Greek Ethics and Other Writings* (New York: Pagan Press, 1983).

4. This term was first used in an anonymous pamphlet written as an open letter to the Prussian Minister of Justice to protest the criminalization of sexual acts between men. It was subsequently taken up by Krafft-Ebing and Hirschfeld among others where it coexisted with the competing formulations "sexual inversion" or "contrary sexual instinct" until early in this century, when the latter were eclipsed by "homosexual" (as opposed to "heterosexual"). On Kertbeny see, Manfred Herzer, "Kertbeny and the Nameless Love," *Journal of Homosexuality* 12.1 (1985): 1–26; Jean-Claude Féray and Manfred Herzer, "Homosexual Studies and Politics in the 19th Century: Karl Maria

Kertbeny," *Journal of Homosexuality* 19.1 (1990): 23–47; and Hurbert Kennedy, *Ulrichs* (Boston: Alyson, 1988), 149–56. On "sexual inversion," see George Chauncey, "From Sexual Inversion to Homosexuality," *Salmagundi* 58–59 (1982–83): 114–46. See also David Halperin's analysis in *One Hundred Years of Homosexuality* (New York: Routledge, 1990), 151.

5. In his discussion of this relation, Halperin notes that while Kertbeny used the word "heterosexual" in his private correspondence to the German sex radical Karl Heinrich Ulrichs in his printed texts he opposes "homosexual" to *normalsexual* (for Kertbeney's text see, Kennedy, 152–53). This explict juxtaposition foregrounds what I take to be implicit in all subsequent uses of the term "homosexual": i.e., that it signifies a type of sexual act(or) by referring to an opposing, normative gender category. Herzer suggests that "heterosexual" may have first appeared in print in the second edition (1880) of Gustav Jager's *The Discovery of the Soul* (6).

6. Krafft-Ebing, *Psychopathia Sexualis* 324.

7. Ibid. 185.

8. The phrase "contrary sexual instinct" derives from Carl Fredrich Westphal's seminal essay "Die conträre Sexualempfindung, Symptom eines neuropathischen (psychopathischen) Zustandes" (1870). Halperin translates Westphal's definition as follows: "The phrase is intended to express the fact that 'contrary sexual instinct' does not always coincidentally concern the sexual drive as such but simply the feeling of being alienated, with one's inner being, from one's own sex—a less developed stage, as it were, of the pathological phenomenon" (163). For Halperin—as for Foucault—the importance of this formulation lies in the shift from earlier ways of understanding sexual practices between men in terms of proscribed acts (e.g., "sodomy," see chapter 4 below) to a characterization predicated not upon acts but upon "inner dynamics, [a] distinctive *orientation* of the inner life of the individual" (Halperin 163). While I would obviously concur with this assessment, what I would like to underscore here is that the impulse that defines this "orientation" is designated only in so far as it moves athwart "appropriate," i.e., normative, gender expectations: "the feeling of being alienated, with one's entire inner being, from one's *own* sex." Here the "contrary sexual feeling" emerges as a disjunction within the individual between "one's own sex" and "one's entire inner being" such that the propriety of the former fails to become the property of the latter. It is this disruption in the field of "proper" masculinity in which sexual and gender "identities" are aligned, I will argue, that the emerging designations for sexual relations between men seek to "fix."

9. Krafft-Ebing, *Psychopathia Sexualis* 185.

10. Tim Calligan, Bob Connell, and John Lee, "Towards a New Sociology of Masculinity," *Theory and Society*, 14.5 (1985): 587 (emphasis in original).

11. This is not to say that "gay" and "lesbian" have no relation to the terms they are intended to supersede. Indeed, as the recent controversies in the gay press about "outing" suggest, the current affirmations of "gay" and "lesbian" no longer seek to produce the political effects that they sought to engender twenty years ago (when they referred not just to "identities" predicated upon sexual object choices but also to how one made one's sexual object choices the basis for a critique of dominant sexual cultures) and instead have come today to signify generically—in much the same way that "homosexual" does—a type of person who is inclined to engage in sexual acts with people of the same sex.

12. Paula Treichler, "AIDS, Homophobia and Biomedical Discourse: An Epidemic of Signification," *October* 43 (Winter 1987): 44–45. As Treichler astutely points out the construction of this list of "risk groups" serves to mask the comprehension of HIV

transmission among women generally and "heterosexuals" specifically, so that the disappearance of the former from the early AIDS discourse served to naturalize the latter as "innocent victims." Yet, as Treichler quips, heterosexual "begins with the letter H after all" (45).

13. For a discussion of this process, see Paula Treichler's excellent article, "AIDS, Gender and Biomedical Discourse: Current Contests for Meaning," in Elizabeth Fee and Daniel Fox, *AIDS: The Burdens of History* (Berkeley: University of California Press, 1988), 190–266.

14. *New York Times*, 18 June, 1991, C1.

15. This formulation unnecessarily—and mistakenly—collapses the transmission of a retrovirus with the symptoms of an immune disorder only retroactively correlated with it. Thus it foregrounds a kind of sexuality as the origin of the "disease" rather than indicating that the transmission of HIV constitutes the precondition for developing the symptoms that are clinically ascribed to AIDS.

16. This interest is also inflected across another pathological demarcation through the casual, though highly moralizing, reference to "intravenous drug abusers" as a further qualification upon "heterosexual AIDS." The point here is that it is intravenous drug *use*, not "abuse," that transmits HIV, since even one use of a needle carrying the retrovirus can lead to infection. Hence the seemingly gratuitous prefix "ab" precisely specifies the normative force of the characterization, especially as it comes to define a category of person, "intravenous drug abusers."

17. Simon Watney, "The Spectacle of AIDS," *October* 43 (Winter 1987): 75.

18. Jacques Derrida, *Positions*, trans. Alan Bass (Chicago: University of Chicago Press, 1981), 41.

1 Embodying the Englishman

1. Max Nordau, *Degeneration* (London: Heinemann, 1895). This English translation appeared in February 1895, the same month that the Marquis of Queensberry left his now-famous calling card at Wilde's club.

2. B. A. Morel, *Traité des dégénérescences physiques, intellectuelles, et morales de l'espèce humaine* (Paris: Ballière, 1857). Caesar Lombroso, *Criminal Man* (New York: G. P. Putnam, 1911) and *The Female Offender* (London: Unwin, 1895). For a historical survey of materials on "degeneration," see Daniel Pick, *Faces of Degeneration: A European Disorder 1848–1918* (Cambridge: Cambridge University Press, 1989). For an excellent summary of Morel's work and its influence on "degeneration theory," see Eric Carlson, "Medicine and Degeneration: Theory and Praxis," *Degeneration: The Dark Side of Progress*, ed. J. Edward Chamberlin and Sander Gilman (New York: Columbia University Press, 1985), 121–44. The most comprehensive treatment of Morel's work can be found in Ruth Friedlander, *Benedict–Augustin Morel and the Theory of Degenerescence: The Introduction of Anthropology to Medicine* (Ph.D. diss., University of California at San Francisco, 1973). Also, Colin Martindale's article "Degeneration, Disinhibition, and Genius," *Journal of the History of the Behavioral Sciences* 7.2 (April 1971) provides a good elucidation of the intertextual relationships between Morel, Lombroso, and Nordau, especially in reference to their common interest in establishing connections between "genius" and "degeneration."

3. See Greta Jones, *Social Darwinism and English Thought: The Interaction between Biological and Social Theory* (Brighton: Harvester Press, 1980); W. Houghton, *The Victorian Frame of Mind, 1830–1870* (New Haven: Yale University Press, 1957), 209–

13; also R. J. Halliday, "Social Darwinism: A Definition," *Victorian Studies* 14 (1971). On Lamarck's influences see, P. Corsi, *The Age of Lamarck* (Berkeley: University of California Press, 1988); Ludmillia Jordanova, *Lamarck* (London: Oxford University Press, 1984); and R. W. Burkhard, *The Spirit of System: Lamarck and Evolutionary Biology* (Cambridge, Mass.: Harvard University Press, 1977).

4. Nordau, *Degeneration* 317–21.

5. Explicit references are found in the *Westminster Gazette*, the *Daily Chronicle*, *Reynolds's Weekly Newspaper*, and *News of The World* among others. See chapter 6.

6. On "othering" as a strategic practice see Mary Louise Pratt, "Scratches on the Face of the Country; or, What Mr. Barrow Saw in the Land of the Bushmen," *Critical Inquiry* 12.1 (Autumn 1985): 119–41. In this regard it is interesting to consider another front-page article entitled "Sex Mania" which appeared in *Reynolds's Newspaper* during the course of Wilde's trials on Sunday, 21 April 1895. This one also refrains from mentioning Wilde directly but considers the phenomena of which he is clearly an example by castigating the "decadents." However, unlike the *Weekly Sun* piece on *Degeneration* which focuses primarily on famous artists and writers, this front page editorial considers another aspect of what it perceives as "degeneration": the "New Women." Here the challenge to male autonomy—which is here explicitly elided with the nation (indeed "nation" is literally the editorial's "final word")—comes from across the "natural" male/female binary; yet the problem is "fixed" here as in the *Weekly Sun* article by characterizing both the New Women and other "uncontrollable sexual tendencies" as "unnatural offences." Given the paper's more "radical" political history, however, the return to "nature" in *Reynolds's* is also conjoined with an attack on aristocratic and class privilege: "These alarming symptoms of our national life are likely to spread with the increasing luxury of our age and the ever-growing population who live on the labours of others." See chapter 6 below.

7. While the discussions of race as a salient social and somatic distinction are also central to these hegemonic formations—especially after the mid-Victorian period when the effects of British imperialism came home as what Hazel Carby calls "internal colonization" in, for example, the discussions of urban poverty—it is beyond the scope of this discussion to adumbrate such a connection here.

8. This difficulty is true both during the period and subsequently in recent historiography. Indeed, the distinction made between the middle class and the middle classes indicates not just a semantic attempt to gesture toward multiple cultural identities but also to a real difficulty in producing coherence within the social designation that we (and they) understand as "middle class." For a recent discussion of this problem see R. S. Neale, "Class and Class-Consciousness in Early 19th-century England: Three Classes or Five?" *Victorian Studies* 12 (1968): 4–32.

9. Raymond Williams, *Keywords: A Vocabulary of Culture and Society* (New York: Oxford University Press, 1976), 53. See also Eric Hobsbawm's comment in *The Age of Capital 1848–1875* (London: Abacus, 1975):

> social mobility and educational progress, both essential to bourgeois society, blurred the distinction between the middle strata and their social inferiors. Where, in the great and increasing mass of 'respectable' workers and lower-middle classes who adopted so much of the values and, insofar as their means allowed, the behavior of the bourgeoisie was the line to be drawn? (122–23)

10. Marcia Ian, "Two's Company, Three's a Construction: Psychoanalysis and the Failure of Identity," paper delivered at the Rutger's Center for Historical Analysis, New Brunswick, New Jersey, 6 February, 1990.

11. Quoted in Richard Altick, *The English Common Reader: A Social History of the Mass Reading Public, 1800–1900* (Chicago: University of Chicago Press, 1957), 82. A more recent commentator, Richard Sennett, notes in *The Fall of Public Man: On the Social Psychology of Capitalism* (New York: Vintage, 1978):

we can identify the bourgeois classes of London . . . beginning with the proprietors of businesses with at least one other employee, with officeworkers, clerks, bookeepers and the like, and with the professional and managerial strata above them. They were a surprisingly large group of people; with their families they comprised between 35 and 43% of London's population in 1870 . . . . (138)

12. P. Thane, "Social History 1860–1914," *The Economic History of Britain since 1700,* ed. Roderick Floud and Donald McCloskey (Cambridge: Cambridge UP, 1981), 223.

13. See W. A. Armstrong, "The Use of Information about Occupation," *Nineteenth Century Society,* ed., E. A. Wrigley (Cambridge: Cambridge University Press, 1972), 191–310; and "The Interpretation of the Census Enumerators' Books for Victorian Towns," *The Study of Urban History,* ed. Harold J. Dyos (New York: St. Martin's, 1968). The Victorian statistician R. Dudley Baxter attempted to provide a breakdown of class distinctions based on income in his book *National Income* (1867). He designated six class categories drawing the gross distinction between "upper and middle classes" and "manual labour class" at £74 per year. Using this breakdown he found that the former constituted around 20% of the population and the latter 80%. See Thane, "Social History." For a discussion of the conflicts and compromises within the middle class(es) which were endemic in the period, see Robert Gray, "Bourgeois Hegemony in Victorian Britain," *Class, Hegemony and Party* (London: Lawrence and Wishart, 1977), 77–93.

14. Hobsbawm, *The Age of Capital 1848–1875* 259.

15. Houghton, *The Victorian Frame of Mind* 62. For details on boom/crisis fluctuations see Donald Read, *England 1868–1914: The Age of Urban Democracy* (London: Longman, 1979), 6–23 and 382–99. On the emergence of an understanding of the business cycle in the 1860s, see S. G. Checkland, *The Rise of Industrial Society in England, 1815–1885* (New York: St. Martin's Press, 1964), 425. On "crises," see Charles Kindleberger, *Manias, Panics, and Crashes: A History of Financial Crises* (New York: Basic, 1978).

16. Barbara Weiss, *The Hell of the English: Bankruptcy and the Victorian Novel* (London: Associated University Presses, 1986), 47. Weiss provides numerous statistical tables documenting bankruptcy in the period, as well as a discussion of the difficulties in interpreting them (176–89).

17. Leonore Davidoff and Catherine Hall, *Family Fortunes: Men and Women of the English Middle Class 1780–1850* (Chicago: University of Chicago, 1987), 71–192.

18. Hobsbawm, *The Age of Capital 1848–1875* 286 (original emphasis).

19. I obviously do not mean to suggest here that there were no middle-class women; rather, that by and large middle-class women, for whom there were increasingly complex "technologies of gender" (to steal Teresa de Lauretis's phrase) as the recent feminist historiography on public/private spheres attests, were defined in their class position as it correlated with their "proper" gender, i.e., usually in relation to a "middle-class man." See Davidoff and Hall; also Nancy Armstrong, *Desire and Domestic Fiction* (Oxford: Oxford University Press, 1986).

20. Foucault uses this term in an interview with Lucette Finas (trans. Leo Marshall, in Colin Gordon, ed., *Power/Knowledge* (New York: Pantheon, 1980)) where he says:

As to the problem of fiction, it seems to me a very important one; I am well aware I have never written anything but fictions. I do not mean to say, however, that truth therefore is absent. It seems to me that the possibility exists for fiction to function in truth, for a fictional discourse to induce the effects of truth, and for bringing it about that a true discourse engenders or "manufactures" something that does not as yet exist, that is, it "fictions" it. One "fictions" history on the basis of a political reality that makes it true, one "fictions" a politics not yet in existence on the basis of a historical truth. (193)

21. Michel Foucault, *The History of Sexuality*, trans. Robert Hurley (New York: Vintage, 1980), 1:124.

22. Ibid. 47.

23. Ibid. 154.

24. Ibid. 125–26.

25. Ibid. 123.

26. For a parallel discussion of the production of "the nation" as a historical artifact which reciprocally "produces" individuals as national subjects, see Benedict Anderson, *Imagined Communities: Reflections on the Origin and Spread of Nationalism* (London: Verso, 1983).

27. Foucault, *History of Sexuality* 125.

28. Russell C. Maulitz, *Morbid Appearances: The Anatomy of Pathology in the Early 19th Century* (Cambridge: Cambridge University Press, 1987), locates the emergence of modern mappings of the human body at precisely this moment. See also, Ludmilla Jordanova, *Sexual Visions: Images of Gender in Science and Medicine between the 18th and 20th Centuries* (Madison: University of Wisconsin Press, 1989); Londa Schiebinger, *The Mind Has No Sex? Women in the Origins of Modern Science* (Cambridge, Mass.: Harvard University Press, 1989); and Thomas Laqueur, *Making Sex: Body and Gender from the Greeks to Freud* (Cambridge, Mass.: Harvard University Press, 1990).

29. Foucault, *History of Sexuality* 123.

30. Charles Taylor, *Sources of the Self: The Making of the Modern Identity* (Cambridge, Mass.: Harvard University Press, 1989), 193.

31. George H. Sabine, *A History of Political Theory*, 3rd edition (New York: Holt, Rinehart and Winston, 1961), 463.

32. Christine Di Stephano, *Configurations of Masculinity: A Feminist Perspective on Modern Political Theory* (Ithaca: Cornell University Press, 1991), 80–81, makes a similar point in a rather different context. Her reading of Hobbes by way of feminist object-relations theory attempts to interpret his writing as quintessentially "masculine" by evaluating it in terms of the refusal of the "(m)other." While I don't share this project, I was happy to find that her analysis corroborates my own.

33. For a historical survey of the introduction of "identity" as a description of human individuation, see Philip Gleason, "Identifying Identity: A Semantic History," *Journal of American History* 69.4 (March 1983): 910–31.

34. John Locke, *Essay Concerning Human Understanding*, (London: George Bell & Sons, 1892) 2, chpt. 27, sec. 8.

36. Ibid. 6. The O.E.D. uses the first sentence of this quotation as its example of how "identity" qualifies the character of human individuation. John Yolton in his book *Thinking Matter: Materialism in 18th-Century Britain* (Minneapolis: University of Minnesota Press, 1983) glosses this quote as follows:

Locke was rejecting the same *soul* as sufficient to make the same *man*. He was searching for some ways of excluding the possibility that "those men, living in distant Ages, and of different Tempers, may have been the same Man." Locke turns to matter for the answer. There must be, he argued, something 'in the Nature of matter, why the same individual Spirit may not be united to different Bodies." (35, original emphasis)

While Yolton is concerned here with the way Locke's philosophy anticipates various later forms of materialism, his analysis underscores the extent to which the idealized "material" body serves to ground Locke's rejection of "soul" as the guarantee of human individuality.

36. C. B. Macpherson, *The Political Theory of Possessive Individualism* (Oxford: Oxford University Press, 1962), 3.

37. John Locke, *Two Treatises of Government*, II, 27.

38. It is important in this regard to specify—even if Macpherson does not—that we are speaking of an adult male identity, since in this theory neither women nor children were granted possession of either their bodies or their labor. For a compelling feminist critique of the gendered terms within which "liberal" political theory has constructed "individual rights," see Carole Pateman, *The Sexual Contract* (Cambridge: Polity Press, 1988).

39. The first edition of Malthus's book, *An Essay on the Principle of Population, as It Affects the Future Improvement of Society. With Remarks on the speculations of Mr. Godwin, M. Condorcet, and other writers* appeared in 1798. The significantly revised second edition—upon which all future editions were based—appeared in 1803 with the altered title *An Essay on the Principle of Population, or, A View of Its Past and Present Effects on Human Happiness; with an Inquiry into Our Prospects Respecting the Future Removal or Mitigation of the Evils Which it Occasions*. For a discussion of the publication history as well as a comparison of the editions, see Gertrude Himmelfarb's introduction to the volume of Malthus's writings collected as *On Population* (New York: Modern Library, 1960), as well as her related discussion in *The Idea of Poverty: England in the Early Industrial Age* (New York: Knopf, 1983). See also Kenneth Smith, *The Malthusian Controversy* (London: Routledge and Kegan Paul, 1951) and Anthony Flew's introduction to the Penguin edition of Malthus's *Essay* (London: Penguin, 1970).

40. Smith, *The Malthusian Controversy*, illustrates how Malthus drew upon similar discussions of "population" by David Hume, Adam Smith, William Paley, and Benjamin Franklin, among others, in framing his theory. It is Malthus's contribution in assimilating these writings, however, to have placed the body (as the site of biological development) at the center of this concept.

Ludmilla Jordanova, *Sexual Visions*, provides a general description of the context:

It had become clear by the end of the 18th century that living things and their environment were continually interacting and changing each other in the process. This was true of sexuality, for, although sex roles were seen as being in some sense "in nature," because of their relationship to physical characteristics, they were also seen as mutable, just as physiology and anatomy in general were taken to be. The customs and habits of day-to-day life such as diet, exercise and occupation, as well as more general social forces such as mode of government, were taken to have profound effects on all aspects of people's lives; their sexuality was no exception. The foundation for this was a naturalistic conceptual framework for understanding the physiological, mental and social aspects of human beings in a coordinated way. This framework underlay the relationship between nature, culture and gender in the period. (25–26)

While Jordanova singles out gender and sexuality here as salient categories, my discussion attempts to situate these qualities as part of a particularized production of social distinctions that was "coordinated" significantly by and for middle-class men.

41. This is not to say that the only terms of social analysis were Malthusian, but rather that most analyses—even, or perhaps especially, those that opposed him, e.g. Marx— had to take account of his position. Himmelfarb characterizes the situation as follows:

> This was the extraordinary achievement of Malthus: to have formulated the terms of discourse on the subject of poverty for half a century—and not only in respect to social policy (debates over the poor laws, most notably), but in the very conception of the problem. It was Malthus who defined that problem, gave it a centrality it had not had before, made it dramatically, urgently, insistently, problematic. Whatever difficulties there were in his theory, however faulty the logic or evidence, it gripped the imagination of contemporaries, of all ranks, classes, callings, and persuasions, as few other books had ever done. (*Idea* 126–27)

While I think it an overstatement to attribute such absolute causality to Malthus's text, it seems to me that it functioned so ubiquitously precisely because it placed the body at the center of the social imagination.

42. For an elaboration of the relation between Malthus and Darwin (who explicitly credited his reading of Malthus for catalyzing his thought), see Robert Young, *Darwin's Metaphors: Nature's Place in Victorian Culture* (Cambridge: Cambridge University Press, 1985), 23–55.

43. Malthus, *Essay* 8.

44. Ibid. 129.

45. Catherine Gallagher, "The Body versus the Social Body in the Works of Thomas Malthus and Henry Mayhew," *Representations* 14 (Spring 1986): 85.

46. Michel Foucault, "About the Concept of the 'Dangerous Individual' in 19th-Century Legal Psychiatry," *International Journal of Law and Psychiatry* 1 (1978): 6–7.

47. Malthus, *Essay* 124.

48. Ibid. 142.

49. Himmelfarb, *On Population* xxxii.

50. Malthus, *Essay* (7th ed.) 495.

51. Ibid. 497.

52. Ibid. 497.

53. Davidoff and Hall, *Family Fortunes* 199.

54. Ibid. 229.

55. Isaac Taylor, *Self Cultivation Recommended; or, Hints to a Youth Leaving School* (London: Rest Fenner, 1817), 87.

56. Ibid. 115.

2 Taking Sex in Hand

1. The more complete title of James Barker's text is "A Secret Book for Men Containing Personal and Confidential Light, Instruction, Information, Counsel and Advice for the Physical, Mental, Moral, and Spiritual Wants of Boys, Youths, and Men; Being an Expose of the Vice of Boyhood, the Blight of Youth, the Curse of Men, the Wreck of Manhood, and the Bane of Posterity" (1891).

2. Mark Poster, *Critical Theory of the Family* (New York: Seabury Press, 1978), 143.

3. Jeffrey Weeks, "Sins and Diseases," *History Workshop Journal* 1 (Spring 1976): 212.

4. Leonore Davidoff, "The Family in Britain," *The Cambridge Social History of Britain, 1750–1950*, ed. F. M. L. Thompson (Cambridge: Cambridge University Press, 1990), 71–130. See also Davidoff, "Class and Gender in Victorian England," *Sex and Class in Women's History*, ed. J. Newton, M. Ryan, and J. Walkowitz (London: Routledge and Kegan Paul, 1983) and "Rationalization of Housework," *Exploitation in Work and Marriage*, ed. Diana Barker and Sheila Allen (London: Longmans, 1976).

5. John Gillis, *Youth and History: Tradition and Change in European Age Relations, 1770–Present* (New York: Academic Press, 1974); P. Aries, *Centuries of Childhood*, trans. R. Baldick (London: Jonathan Cape, 1962); J. Donzolot, *The Policing of Families*, trans. R. Hurley (New York: Pantheon, 1979); Deborah Gorham, *The Victorian Girl and the Feminine Ideal* (Bloomington: Indiana University Press, 1982); F. Musgrove, *Youth and Social Order* (London: Routledge and Kegan Paul, 1965); John and Virgina Demos, "Adolescence in Historical Perspective," *Journal of Marriage and the Family* 31 (Nov. 1969): 632–39; John Springhall, *Youth, Empire and Society: British Youth Movements, 1883–1940* (London: Croom Helm, 1977); and J. H. Plumb, "The New World of Children in Eighteenth Century England," *Past and Present* 67 (May 1975).

6. Joseph Banks, *Victorian Values: Secularizing and the Size of Families* (London: Routledge and Kegan Paul, 1981) cites *A New System of Practical Domestic Economy* (1824). Also Leonore Davidoff's *The Best Circles: Women and Society in Victorian England* (Totowa, New Jersey: Rowman and Littlefield, 1973) surveys a large variety of this literature, see especially chapter 3, "The Anatomy of Society and Etiquette."

7. For an example of how contemporaries interpreted the significance of such cultural practices see Sarah Stickley Ellis, *The Wives of England* (1843). See also Banks, *Victorian Values*, Chpts 5 and 7; Davidoff, "Class and Gender" 24; and Donald Read, *England 1868–1914: The Age of Urban Democracy* (London: Longman, 1979), 23–29.

8. In his article, "Explosive Intimacy: Psychodynamics of the Victorian Family" (*History of Childhood Quarterly* 1 3 (1974): 437–61), Stephen Kern comments:

The child of the Victorian period was subject to an extraordinary set of pressures, particularly through the social ambitions of the family. Children were to inherit, and to enhance, the fortunes of the large middle-class estates built up for over a century of aggrandizement that often included financially advantageous marriages. (457)

9. John Roach, *Public Examinations in England 1850–1900* (Cambridge: Cambridge University Press, 1971), 10.

10. F. Musgrove, "Middle-Class Education and Employment in the Nineteenth Century," *The Economic History Review* 12.1 (1959): 100–101. Also J. H. Plumb, "The New World of Children in Eighteenth Century England," *Past and Present* 67 (May 1975): 80, and D. P. Leinster-Mackay, "Private or Public Schools: The Educational Debate in Laissez-Faire England," *Journal of Educational Administration and History* 15.2 (July 1983): 1.

11. Thomas Hughes, *Tom Brown's School Days* (New York: New American Library, 1986). In a direct address to "all you boys who are getting into the upper forms," Hughes succinctly indicates what he takes to be the project of public schooling:

Now is the time in all your lives probably when you may have more influence for good or evil on the society you live in than you can ever have again. Quit yourselves like men, then; speak up, and strike out if necessary for whatsoever is true, and manly, and lovely, and of good report; never try to be popular, but only do your duty and help others do theirs, and you may leave the tone of feeling in the school higher than you found it, and so be doing good, which no living soul can measure, to generations of your countrymen yet unborn. (144)

This admonishment to boys to "quit yourselves like men" is based on their developing a practice of self-reliance that establishes a standard for collective activity. We should not underestimate the sincerity of Hughes's underlying belief here that the future of the nation will be predicated on the success with which young men embody such a practice.

12. Quoting figures from *The Schools Inquiry (Taunton) Commission in 1868*, Musgrove (102) estimates that over 10,000 proprietary schools were established in the second quarter of the nineteenth century. In the article he misquotes this figure as "100,000" but subsequently revises it in a later article responding to a rebuttal by H. J. Perkins. For the entire polemic see *Economic History Review* 14.1 (1961): 122–30 and 14.2 (1961): 320–29.

13. For a comprehensive overview of the educational terrain, see J. R. de S. Honey, *Tom Brown's Universe* (London: Millington, 1977). On the relation of "public" and "proprietary" schools, see D. Leinster-Mackay, "Victorian Quasi-Public Schools," *British Journal of Educational Studies* 29.1 (February 1981): 54–68. Beginning with *Tom Brown's School Days*, the references to Arnold's transformation of Rugby are innumerable, for one succinct recent example see T. W. Bamford, "Thomas Arnold and the Victorian Idea of a Public School," *The Victorian Public School: Studies in the Development of an Educational Institution*, ed. Brian Simon and Ian Bradley (Dublin: Gill and Macmillian, 1975), 58–71.

14. David Newsome, *Godliness and Good Learning: Four Studies on a Victorian Ideal* (London: John Murray, 1961), 195. Much of this account derives from chapter 4 of Newsome's Book. See also, Norman Vance, *The Sinews of the Spirit: The Ideal of Christian Manliness in Victorian Literature and Religious Thought* (Cambridge: Cambridge University Press, 1985) and "The Ideal of Manliness," in Simon and Bradley, *The Victorian Public School* 115–29.

15. As Leonore Davidoff and Catherine Hall suggest in *Family Fortunes: Men and Women of the English Middle Class 1780–1850* (Chicago: University of Chicago, 1987), such competing interpretations of masculinity were central to the consolidation of upper class values, such that the development of a discernibly "Christian" standard of masculinity was instrumental in challenging older codes of male behaviors:

Christian manhood had to be created anew from the tissue of ideas associated with masculinity in the 18th century. Many of the values associated with evangelical Christianity—the stress on moral earnestness, the belief in the power of love, and a sensibility to the weak and helpless—ran counter to the worldly pursuits of the gentry. Masculine nature, in gentry terms, was based on sport and codes of honor derived from military prowess, finding expression in hunting, riding, drinking, and "wenching." Since many early Evangelicals came from gentry backgrounds they had to consciously establish novel patterns of manhood. (110)

16. Kingsley provides an excellent summary of the range of his beliefs on bodily health in *Health and Education* (London: Macmillan, 1887). Especially interesting in this regard is the first essay, "The Science of Health." The popularization of Kingsley's ideal took different forms; among them were the works of his friend Thomas Hughes. Indeed,

the epigraph for the previous chapter of this book, which succinctly frames their shared understanding of the purpose of the male body, is taken from a chapter of *Tom Brown at Oxford* (the sequel to *Tom Brown's School Days*) entitled simply "Muscular Christianity."

For the distinction between Arnold and Kingsley, see Newsome, *Godliness* 195–216. Also Vance, *Sinews* 78–133. In another context, Bruce Haley, *The Healthy Body and Victorian Culture* (Cambridge, MA: Harvard UP, 1978) makes a similar distinction between Kingsley and Carlyle.

17. Newsome, *Godliness and Good Learning* 197.

18. In "Nationalism and Respectability: Normal and Abnormal Sexuality in the Nineteenth Century" (*Journal of Contemporary History* 17.2 (April 1982): 221–47), George L. Mosse sketches the broad outlines of the relation between normative definitions of male sexuality and the ideologies of nationalism in Germany and to a lesser extent, Britain. His essay suggests the intimate connection between these ideological practices of the middle class, to which I can only allude here in passing.

19. The two best comprehensive histories of the use of exams in Britain are John Roach's *Public Examinations in England, 1850–1900* (Cambridge: Cambridge University Press, 1971) and R. J. Montgomery's *Examinations: An Account of Their Evolution as Administrative Devices in England* (Pittsburgh: University of Pittsburgh Press, 1965). Also Gillis, *Victorian Values*, especially chapters 5, 6, and 9, presents an analysis of the examination structure as it influenced middle-class adolescence.

20. In *Discipline and Punish: The Birth of the Prison*, trans. Alan Sheridan (New York: Vintage, 1979), Michel Foucault considers the school examination as an integral part of a developing grid of normalizing practices that in the eighteenth and nineteenth centuries produced a "detailed political investment of the body" (139). He suggests that the exam provided a unique disciplinary strategy because it simultaneously operated at three levels of specificity: "an examination . . . will have the triple function of showing whether the subject has reached the level required, of guaranteeing that each subject undergoes the same apprenticeship and of differentiating the abilities of each individual" (158). These three "functions," surveillance, normalization, and ranking, constituted, according to Foucault, an "analytical pedagogy" that transformed educational experience into the "permanent competition of individuals being classified in relation to one another":

> The examination combines the techniques of an observing hierarchy and those of a normalizing judgment. It is a normalizing gaze, a surveillance that makes it possible to qualify, to classify and to punish. It establishes over individuals a visibility through which one differentiates them and judges them. . . . At the heart of the procedures of discipline, it manifests the subjection of those who are perceived as objects and the objectification of those who are subjected. The superimposition of the power relations and knowledge relations assumes in the examination all its visible brilliance. (184–85)

By bringing pedagogical practices into conjunction with the disciplinary effects of power, the examination allowed schools to subject adolescent males to analytical evaluation (on specified "subjects"), thereby establishing a tactical arrangement through which they came to understand their individual experience as examination "subjects" ("subject to"/ "subject of"). This nexus of "subjection" constituted the singular male student in relation to a standard that defined his success or failure as a member of his "class" (both educational and socioeconomic) in terms of employment or further education, and hence created an introjected mechanism of normalization.

21. The best source on the subject is J. A. Mangan, *Athleticism in the Victorian and Edwardian Public School: The Emergence and Consolidation of an Educational Ideology* (London: Cambridge University Press, 1981), from which much of this account is taken. See also, J. A. Mangan, "Athleticism: A Case Study of the Evolution of an Educational Ideology," in Simon and Bradley, *Victorian Public School*, and André Rauch, "La Politique scolaire en matière de gymnastique au XIXe siècle," *Historical Reflections* 9.3 (Fall 1982): 373–82.

22. It should also be noted that this concern was part of a wider middle-class concern with health and fitness. During the second half of the nineteenth century, games and "sport" (no longer defined solely in terms of the leisure activities of the aristocracy and gentry, e.g., hunting, riding, fishing, etc.) became a widely visible aspect of Victorian popular culture, as Bruce Haley demonstrates in *The Healthy Body and Victorian Culture*, especially chapter 6. James Warton documents a similar movement in the U.S. in his *Crusades for Fitness* (Princeton: Princeton University Press, 1982).

23. Quoted in Mangan, *Athleticis*, 29.

24. T. L. Papillion, quoted in Mangan, *Athleticism* 9.

25. Mosse, "Nationalism and Respectability," elaborates the outline of this connection. Also, Mangan, "Athleticism: A Case Study," 156–57 and Rausch, "La Politique scolaire," address this issue.

26. Honey's examples in *Tom Brown's Universe* (167–96) are compendious and I draw on them in the following analysis. See also, John Chandos, *Boys Together: English Public Schools* (London: Hutchinson, 1984), 284–319. For an excellent example of the horror of the "solitary vice" and the "dual vice," see Edward Lyttleton, *The Causes and Prevention of Immorality in Schools* (Westminster: Social Purity Alliance, 1887). Lyttleton was headmaster of Eton.

27. E. Thring, *Uppingham Sermons* (1886), vol. 2, 15, quoted in J. R. de S. Honey, *Tom Brown's Universe* 171.

28. In fact, the discourse was so circumspect that one of its major polemics revolved around whether or not it was more damaging to even raise the issue with young boys and risk tainting their innocence or to have them encounter it unawares (and hence unprotected) at school. See "A Lecture to Young Men on the Preservation of Health and Personal Purity of Life, Seventh Edition" by "A Graduate" (London: Henry Bradshaw, 1892). Also the Church of England Purity Society pamphlet, "To the Teacher in Elementary Schools," 19.10 (n.d.), argues that "circumstances may arise which would render it necessary that children who have fallen into sin from ignorance, should know something of the calamitous circumstances of impurity to the offender, to families, and to society" (3). This question marks the literature on masturbation from its earliest examples. The unnamed author of what is deemed to be the first of these works, *Onania, or the Heinous Sin of Self-Pollution* . . . (7th ed, rept. *The Secret Vice Exposed! Some Arguments against Masturbation* [New York: Arno Press, 1974]) sets the issue quite clearly if somewhat fanatically:

> It is a Rule I know among the most prudent People, never to mention anything concerning this Vice, to the Youth of either Sex, for fear that either desire after Things forbidden, or else Curiosity itself, might prompt the Pupils to what they might never have thought on, had it not been for the too instructive Caution of the Teachers. But there are other Methods: The Instruction of Youth I hint at, should commence from their Infancy. If Children were strictly forbid, never to touch

their Eyes or Nose, but with their Handkerchief, and that only upon very urgent Necessities; if likewise they saw every Body comply with this Custom, and it was counted abominable to touch them with their naked Hands, I can't see why this might not be so shocking to 'em when grown up, as now the most guilty Denudations are to well bred people. (4)

29. Indeed, the preface to *Onania* makes explicit the significance of this genre for educators and their pupils:

> Would all Masters of Schools have but a strict Eye over their Scholars; (amongst whom nothing is more common, than the Communication of this vile Sin, the Elder Boys Teaching it the Younger, as soon as ever they arrive to the Years of Puberty) tell them of the Heinousness of the Sin, and give suitable Correction to the Offenders: therein, and shame them before their School-Fellows for it I am persuaded it would deter them from the Practice, and by that means save them from Ruin; Thousands of the Youth of this Kingdom Learning it there, who probably might never have known of it elsewhere. (v–vi)

30. During the nineteenth century, doctors began to undertake the role of guardians of the public welfare, addressing the squalid conditions of urban life that gave rise to a series of epidemics throughout the century. This new role expanded the locus of medical intervention from the individual body to the social body. Increasingly throughout the century doctors intervened in debates about setting social policy, on questions such as housing, urban improvement, sanitation, working conditions, and sexual behavior. The issues raised by the passage of, protest against, and eventual repeal of the Contagious Disease Acts (1860s–1880s), which were designed to contain the spread of venereal diseases among members of the British armed forces, placed doctors in the position of testifying as experts on matters of sexual conduct (see chapter 3). Thus, by the third quarter of the nineteenth century, the medical profession had consolidated its authority to speak as "experts" about a wide range of issues related to the experience of the human body both in public and in private; on "public health," see F. B. Smith, *The People's Health* (London: Croom Helm, 1979) and Anthony Wohl, *Endangered Lives: Public Health in Victorian Britain* (Cambridge, Mass.: Harvard University Press, 1983).

31. R. P. Neuman, "Masturbation, Madness and the Modern Concepts of Childhood and Adolescence," *The Journal of Social History* 7.3 (Winter 1975) suggests that this conjunction itself must be seen as a crucial element in the production of middle-class identity and values:

> [T]he anxiety about masturbation after 1700 was primarily characteristic of middle-class doctors and educators, who provided their clients (parents, pupils, patients) with an anti-masturbatory theory which reinforced and gave medical support to a cluster of social and sexual attitudes inextricably bound to the bourgeois Trinity of work, family and paternal authority. (6)

32. Robert H. MacDonald, "The Frightful Consequences of Onanism: Notes on the History of a Delusion," *Journal of the History of Ideas* 28. 3 (July–September 1967): 426. For accounts of Tissot's theories, see E. H. Hare, "Masturbatory Insanity: The History of an Idea," *The Journal of Mental Science* 108.452 (January 1962): 2–3; H. Tristam Englehardt, Jr., "The Disease of Masturbation: Values and The Concept of Disease," *Bulletin of the History of Medicine* 48 (Summer 1974): 235–36; René Spitz,

"Authority and Masturbation. Some Remarks on a Bibliographical Investigation," *Yearbook of Psychoanalysis* 9 (1953): 116.

33. My quotations from Tissot are taken from a copy of a nineteenth-century American translation, *Treatise on the Diseases Produced by Onanism* (New York: Collins and Hannay, 1832) reproduced in *The Secret Vice Exposed! Some Arguments against Masturbation*. For an example of the colloquial use of Tissot's seminal equation see the example of Bishop Taylor-Smith's advice to his godson on sending him off to prep school: "He was always talking to me about it, how semen was 40 times as valuable as blood, how if one lost it one got dark rings under the eyes and deteriorated mentally, how it stunted growth even more than smoking." Quoted in Honey, *Tom Brown's Universe* 170.

34. Tissot, *Treatise* 34 (original emphasis).

35. Ibid. 40.

36. Effects to some extent counteracted in "natural" (heterosexual) intercourse by the "magnetic" effects of the beloved upon the lover.

37. Tissot, *Treatise* 9–52.

38. Ibid. 47.

39. R. P. Neuman, "Masturbation" 4–5.

40. Unlike those writers who followed him, Tissot does not stress the distinction between procreative and nonprocreative seminal emissions. Though in his preface he acknowledges a difference in the consequences of "too abundant a discharge of semen . . . lost in the natural way" and "those produced by onanism," he does not underscore this distinction since he concerns himself almost exclusively with the latter, obviating the possibilities for such a comparison.

41. J. L. Milton, *On Spermatorrhoea; Its Pathology, Results and Complications* (London: Henry Renshaw, 1881), 30–31.

42. R. P. Neuman, "Masturbation," suggests that this expansion of the medicalized terrain was instrumental in constructing an equation between the "moral" and the "healthy":

In effect, doctors and alienists, as psychologists called themselves in the nineteenth century, were becoming the arbiters of sexual morality in an era where the religious basis for morality was being challenged. Behavior condemned as sinful and immoral was now diagnosed by alienists as unhealthy and even insane. (9)

Peter Conrad and Joseph Schneider, *Deviance and Medicalization: From Badness to Sickness* (Toronto: C. V. Mosby, 1980) concur with Neuman's assessment, claiming that:

Early in [the eighteenth] century and throughout the next, a handful of physicians and their popularizers promoted conceptions of health and illness that viewed the body as a closed system of vital nervous energy. Health was defined vaguely in terms of nervous system stability, balance, and equilibrium, which, in turn, were thought to be products of the individual's integration with (read "conformity to") the larger moral and social environment. To the extent that one's activities in the larger realm were "healthy," that is morally proper, internal physiological and nervous system function would follow accordingly. Conversely, activities that made repeated, unusual, "unhealthy" (immoral) demands on one's body would lead inevitably to its depletion, debility, wasting, and disease. Thus, immorality, as evidenced by social behavior, was believed causal of sickness and disease.

43. See Frank Mort, *Dangerous Sexualities: Medico-Moral Politics in England since 1830* (New York: Routledge Kegan Paul, 1987).

44. Judith Walkowitz in her *Prostitution and Victorian Society: Women, Class, and the State* (New York: Cambridge University Press, 1980) explores Acton's role in the passage of the Contagious Diseases (C. D.) Acts. In the next chapter, I will explore the relation of the campaign to repeal the C. D. Acts to the public debates about the limits of male sexual behavior in detail.

M. Jeanne Peterson, "Dr. Acton's Enemy: Medicine, Sex and Society in Victorian England," *Victorian Studies* 29.4 (Summer 1986), 569–90, argues that Acton's views, though highly popular during the period, have taken on a disproportionate importance in recent historical accounts of Victorian medicine's role in the construction of sexuality. She claims that another eminent Victorian physician, James Paget, had a greater impact on Victorian medical practice and, indeed, contradicted Acton's positions on "normal sexual function." For example, apropos of masturbation, Peterson notes that "[Paget] insisted that masturbation did not cause insanity. And he argued that the 'so-called functional sexual diseases' do not lead to 'epilepsy . . . paralysis, wasting palsies . . . impotence, insanity, or idiotcy [sic],' or other fearful disorders" (580). While clearly Acton should not be taken as representing the entirety of the British medical establishment, and the recognition of the competing claims within the formation of medical ideology does much to further the understanding of medical history, it is still necessary to realize that Acton's influence outside the medical institution itself, as witnessed by the proliferation of his opinions in popular and political (con)texts—see the discussion of the C.D. Acts in the next chapter—makes a consideration of his positions valuable for examining the dissemination of medical discourse as a key element in the production of Victorian sex/gender ideologies.

45. William Acton, *The Functions and Disorders of the Reproductive Organs, in Youth, Adult Age, and Advanced Life, Considered in Their Physiological, Social, and Psychological Relations* (London: John Churchill, 1857), 1.

46. Stephen Marcus discusses the history of Acton's work in *The Other Victorians: A Study of Sexuality and Pornography in Mid-Nineteenth-Century England* (New York: Basic Books, 1964), 1–33.

47. Quoted in Marcus, *The Other Victorians* 12.

48. Thomas Laqueur, "Orgasm, Generation, and the Politics of Reproductive Biology" (*Representations* 14 (Spring 1986): 1–41), and *Making Sex: Body and Gender from the Greeks to Freud* (Cambridge, Mass.: Harvard University Press, 1990), suggests that during the late-eighteenth and early-nineteenth centuries, theories that constructed biological distinctions between the sexes displaced earlier Galenic conceptions of sexual difference that described homologies between male and female reproductive function (i.e., the female reproductive tract being envisioned as an inverted and somewhat contorted penis). This displacement, Laqueur argues, parallels a shift in the Enlightenment political conceptualization of sex roles, thereby affirming the historical ascendency of men over women on a more "scientific" basis:

> Writers of all sorts were determined to base what they had insisted were functional differences between male and female sexuality, and thus between man and woman, on discoverable biological distinctions. In 1803, for example, Jacques Moreau de la Sarthe, one of the founders of "moral anthropology," argued passionately against the nonsense written by Aristotle, Galen and their modern followers on the subject of women in relation to men. Not only are the sexes different, they are different in every conceivable respect of body and soul, in every physical and moral aspect. To

the physician or the naturalist the relation of woman to man is "a series of opposi-
tions and contrasts." Thus the old model, in which men and women were arrayed
according to their degree of metaphysical perfection, their vital heat, along an axis
whose telos was male, gave way by the late-eighteenth century to a new model of
difference, of biological divergence. An anatomy and physiology of incommensurability replaced a metaphysics of hierarchy in the representation of women in relation
to men. ("Orgasm" 2–3)

While Laqueur's concern is primarily with medical and political representations of
"women in relation to men," his findings suggest the necessity of a similar "anatomy
and physiology of incommensurability" of men. The redefinition of male sex roles as a
result of the economic and social changes during the period (considerations that Laqueur
entirely ignores in his analysis) would seem, then, to underlie the medical speculation
on masturbation, as the following consideration of Acton will attempt to demonstrate.

49. Acton, *Functions* 6 (my emphasis).

50. Ibid. 7.

51. Ibid. 9.

52. Ibid. 16.

53. Certainly, this is an optimistic assessment of connubial bliss. In actuality the
equation of marriage and intercourse was one that was increasingly contested throughout
the second half of the century with middle-class women increasingly abstaining from
intercourse, as a means of limiting conception, from fear of contracting venereal disease
from their husbands (for example, Dora's mother in Freud's famous case), and as a
protest against the limitations of women's domestic roles, among other reasons. See
Nancy Cott, "Passionlessness: An Interpretation of Victorian Sexual Ideology, 1790–
1850," *Journal of Women in Culture and Society* 2.4 (1978): 219–36.

54. An excellent account of cross-class relationships can be found in Davidoff, "Class
and Gender" and Davidoff, "Mastered for Life: Servant and Wife in Victorian and
Edwardian England," *Journal of Social History* 7 (1974).

55. On these contradictions within the definitions of middle-class "respectability," the
most notable sources are Peter Cominos, "Late Victorian Respectability and The Social
System," *International Review of Social History* 8 (1963): 18–48 and 216–50 and Keith
Thomas, "The Double Standard," *Journal of the History of Ideas* 20.2 (April 1959):
195–216.

56. Acton, *Functions* 18–9.

57. Ibid. 56.

58. Ibid.

59. Ibid. 61.

60. G. J. Barker-Benfield, "The Spermatic Economy: A Nineteenth Century View of
Sexuality," *The American Family in Social Historical Perspective* (2nd edition), ed.
Michael Gordon (New York: St. Martin's Press, 1978), 379.

61. Ibid. 377. In a similar argument, Gail Pat Parsons, "Equal Treatment for All:
American Medical Remedies for Male Sexual Problems," *Journal of the History of
Medicine and Allied Sciences* 32.1 (January 1977) states that:

Doctors believed that the healthy body, whether male or female, maintained an
equitable distribution of [a] static quantity of nerve force. Illness resulted when one
particular area of the body received too much or too little needed force. Too
much sexual excitement, they agreed . . . could upset a delicate health sustaining
equilibrium. Excessive sexual activity attracted this force to the genitals and with-

drew it from other areas of the body leaving the depleted portions susceptible to disease of an asthenic nature. With their physiology well grounded in eighteenth-century thought, and aware that masturbation was widely practiced, physicians confronted with any male ailment from melancholia to eyestrain suspected overactive genital stimulation. (59)

62. Barker-Benfield, "Spermatic Economy" 378.

63. In a related observation René Spitz, "Authority and Masturbation," characterizes the shift as one "cure" to "suppression," noting the rise in somatic technologies designed to combat masturbation ranging from general organization of life, to devices designed to prevent access to the genitals, to (especially after 1850) the use of sexual surgery on both boys and girls: "While up to 1849 masturbation was treated mostly with hydrotherapy, diet, etc., between 1850 and 1879 surgical treatment was recommended more frequently than any of the other measures (120)."

64. Skae's paper is reprinted in *The Journal of Mental Science* 9.47 (October 1863). These passages are located on pages 310 and 314 respectively (emphasis in original).

65. Daniel Skae, "Morisonian Lecture on Insanity for 1873," *Journal of Mental Science* 19.88 [new series no. 52] (January 1874): 498–99.

66. Excellent examples of the medical fear of "unauthorized" ministering to the ills of the masturbator can be found in John Laws Milton's railings against "quackery" and "charlatans" in the first chapter of his *On Spermatorrhoea*, 1–13. See also John Hamilton, M.D., *A Treatise on Nervous Exhaustion and Loss of Vital Energy: Their Causes, Symptoms and Consequences* (London: Medical Hall, n.d.).

67. On Maudsley's life and career, see Sir Aubrey Lewis, "Henry Maudsley: His Work and Influence," *The State of Psychiatry* (New York: Science House, 1967), 29–48. Also Elaine Showalter's "On the Borderland: Henry Maudsley and Psychiatric Darwinism," in *The Female Malady: Women, Madness, and English Culture, 1830–1980* (Harmondsworth: Penguin, 1987), 101–120.

68. Henry Maudsley, "Illustrations of a Variety of Insanity," *The Journal of Mental Science* 14.66 [new series no. 30] (July 1868): 149–62. These quotations are taken from pages 150–51. All further references to this text are noted in the body of the chapter.

69. Showalter, *The Female Malady* 109.

70. For one of the fullest elaborations of these concepts, see T. S. Clouston, *The Neuroses of Development* (Edinburgh: Oliver and Boyd, 1891).

69. For a discussion of the political/gender implications of body imagery, see Leonore Davidoff, "Class and Gender in Victorian England" 17–20.

71. The significance of such antiauthoritarian behavior by adolescent males, especially as it was expressed within the middle-class family, can be better understood in light of the larger divisions between "public" and "private" that seemed to guarantee the stability of the socioeconomic order. As Stephen Mintz claims in his book, *A Prison of Expectations: The Family in Victorian Culture* (New York: New York University Press, 1983):

In a home that was conceived as a place of peace and order amid the abrasive waves of social and intellectual change, a dispute between a child and a parent could be regarded as a rebellion against the institution that stood at the very basis of civilization, as a revolt against all larger conceptions of authority and order, as a challenge to the very foundation of morality and stability. (68)

73. Not surprisingly, then, Maudsley's concluding image incorporates the racial and animal imagery typical of much of this discussion: "once the habit is formed, and the

mind has positively suffered from it, the victim is less able to control what is more difficult of control and there is as much hope of the Ethopian changing his skin or the leopard its spots, as of his abandoning the vice" (161).

74. The first edition of the *Index-Catalogue of the Library of the Surgeon General's Office* (1887) which lists articles published in the U.S., England, France, Germany, Italy, Spain, Mexico, Russia, and Poland spanning the eighteenth and nineteenth centuries, lists over 103 articles and 47 books on the subject of masturbation.

75. D. Yellowlees, "Masturbation," in D. Hack Tuke, *Dictionary of Psychological Medicine* (London: J. & A. Churchill, 1892), 784–86.

76. E. C. Spitzka, "Cases of Masturbation (Masturbatic Insanity)," *Journal of Mental Science* 33 (April, July, and October 1887): 57–73, 238–54, and 395–401, and 34 (April and July 1888): 52–61 and 216–25.

77. The *Index-Catalogue of the Library of the Surgeon General's Office* (1892) lists 170 articles and 65 books on the subject.

78. John Laws Milton, *On Spermatorrhoea, Its Pathology, Results and Complications*, 11th edition (London: Henry Renshaw, 1881); M. L'Allemand, *A Practical Treatise on the Causes, Symptoms, and Treatment of Spermatorrhoea*, trans. Henry McDougall, 5th American edition (Philadelphia: Henry C. Lea, 1866); Robert Bartholow, *On Spermatorrhoea* (New York: William Wood and Co., 1866).

3 Marking Social Dis-Ease

1. And in some cases same-sex relations, as for example in the case of the famous Cleveland Street Scandal (discussed in the next chapter) in which post office boys were procured for the enjoyment of an upper-class male brothel's patrons, or more sustainedly, the Guardsmen who were notorious from the eighteenth century on as a plentiful source of male prostitutes in London. See Jeffrey Weeks, "Inverts, Perverts, and Mary-Annes: Male Prostitution and the Regulation of Homosexuality in England in the Nineteenth and Early Twentieth Centuries," *Journal of Homosexuality* 6.1–2 (Fall/Winter 1980–81): 113–34. Indeed, much of the controversy in Wilde's case derived from the working class origins of his sexual contacts, a stable boy, newspaper seller, valet, and bookmaker's clerk among them.

2. Keith Thomas, "The Double Standard," Journal of the History of Ideas 20 (1959), 197. A contemporary Victorian account by W. H. E. Lecky in his *History of European Morals from Augustus to Charlemagne* (1869) provides a similar argument, though couched in somewhat more spiritual terms:

> Herself the supreme type of vice, she [the prostitute] is ultimately the most efficient guardian of virtue. But for her, the unchallenged purity of countless homes would be polluted, and not a few, who, in the pride of their untempted chastity, think of her with an indignant shudder, would have known the agony of remorse and despair. On that one degraded and ignoble form are concentrated the passions that might have filled the world with shame. She remains, while creeds and civilizations rise and fall, the eternal priestess of humanity, blasted for the sins of the people. (Quoted in Sheldon Amos, *A Comparative Survey of Laws in Force for the Prohibition, Regulation and Licensing of Vice* (London: Stevens and Sons, 1877), 18)

3. Joseph Banks, *Victorian Values: Secularizing and the Size of Families* (London: Routledge and Kegan Paul, 1981). Also Geoffrey Alderman, *Modern Britain 1700–1983: A Domestic History* (London: Croom Helm, 1986), 161.

4. For the "familialist" formulation see Michele Barrett and Mary McIntosh, *The Anti-Social Family* (London: Verso, 1982).

5. See Peter Gay, *The Bourgeois Experience* (Oxford: Oxford University Press, 1984) in defense of nineteenth-century sexual fulfillment.

6. An excellent example of the eroticization of working-class women is found in the notebooks and photographs of A. J. Munby, whose texts are considered as such by Leonore Davidoff in her articles "Mastered for Life: Servant and Wife in Victorian and Edwardian England," *Journal of Social History* 7 (1974) and "Class and Gender in Victorian England," *Sex and Class in Women's History*, ed. J. Newton, M. Ryan, and J. Walkowitz (London: Routledge and Kegan Paul, 1983). Also see Helena Michie's discussion of Dante Gabriel Rosetti's poem "Jenny" in her recent book, *The Flesh Made Word: Female Figures and Women's Bodies* (New York: Oxford University Press, 1987) in which she claims: "Jenny is reduced, interestingly enough, to a cipher of *male* lust. Her sexuality and her body are denied her as, like her mirror, she becomes a reflection of other people's desires, a blank page on which a series of men can write narratives of her significance" (61, original emphasis). Here, Michie suggestively points to the effects produced by the displacement of middle-class male desire onto working-class women's bodies.

7. This difference was codified in laws regulating sexual intercourse with young women. Under legislation passed in 1849 "to protect women under twenty-one from fraudulent practices for procuring their defilement," the abduction of an heiress who had not yet reached the age of twenty-one was a felony, while it was merely a misdemeanor to abduct a young woman under sixteen with no title to property. Under this legislation the "age of consent" remained fixed at twelve, and while the age of consent was contested and ultimately raised for all women as a result of the events that will be recounted this chapter, there continued to exist a discernible difference in the perceptions of women's sexualities across class throughout the century. See Erna Reiss, *Rights and Duties of Englishwomen. A Study in Law and Public Opinion* (Manchester: Serrat and Hughes, 1934). The converse of this legislative inequity between women of different classes was, of course, that working-class women had relatively more latitude to define and experience themselves as sexual beings, which legislation increasingly sought to contain. This phenomena is most clearly attested to in the writing of moral reformers who sought to "save" young working-class prostitutes only to find that very often these women did not want to be saved and that the economic and personal advantages that prostitution afforded them made this occupation a positive choice for them. See Judith and Daniel Walkowitz, " 'We Are Not Beasts of the Field': Prostitution and the Poor in Plymouth and Southampton Under the Contagious Diseases Acts," *Feminist Studies* 1 (Winter 1973): 73–106.

8. Henry Mayhew, *London Labour and the London Poor* (New York: Dover, 1968), 4:34.

9. Henry Mayhew, *The Morning Chronicle Survey of Labour and The Poor: The Metropolitan Districts* (London: Caliban Books, 1980), 1:151–68 and 221–46. Of course, in Mayhew's version these women are quick to condemn themselves for having "fallen" in this way, even as they affirm the impossibility of their being able to conform to bourgeois standards of propriety. As one of Mayhew's informants puts it: "But no one knows the temptations of us poor girls in want. Gentlefolks can never understand it. If I had been born a lady, it wouldn't have been very hard to act like one. To be poor and to be honest, especially with young girls is the hardest struggle of all" (161).

10. For much more detailed considerations of articulations of class and gender in the (re)production of London's "underworld," see Judith Walkowitz, *City of Dreadful*

Delights (Chicago: University of Chicago Press, 1992) and *Prostitution and Victorian Society* (Cambridge: Cambridge University Press, 1980).

11. The first act, the Contagious Diseases Prevention Act, was passed in July 1864. It was superseded in June 1866 by the "Act for the better Prevention of Contagious Diseases at certain Naval and Military Stations," which was further amended and extended in August 1869. See below.

12. Frank Mort, *Dangerous Sexualities*, 126–36, provides a detailed history of the political negotiating and strategizing that lay behind the act's passage.

13. A lengthy discussion of the shifts in the legal status of sexual relations between men is provided in the next chapter.

14. In *Endangered Lives: Public Health in Victorian Britain* (Cambridge, Mass: Harvard University Press, 1983), Anthony Wohl provides the following statistics on urbanization:

> At the beginning of the [nineteenth] century roughly 20 per cent of the population of England and Wales lived in towns with over 5,000 residents; by 1851 over half the population (54 per cent) did so and by 1911 almost 80 per cent. By 1801 only London had a population of over 100,000; by 1851 there were ten such towns (with roughly one-quarter of the nation's inhabitants living in them) and by 1911 there were thirty-six towns of that size and 43.8 per cent of the nation dwelt in them (compared to 11.0 per cent in 1801). The movement from the countryside to the towns and the towns' natural growth were relentless throughout the century, In 1851 the nation had more town than country dwellers. In 1871 there were 14,041,000 urban dwellers and 8,671,000 rural residents; in 1901 the figures were, respectively, 25,058,000 and 7,469,000. (3–4)

Bruce Haley, *The Healthy Body and Victorian Culture* (Cambridge, Mass.: Harvard University Press, 1978), 5–12, provides the following paraphrased account of infectious diseases in the period: Beginning with the outbreaks of smallpox and typhus in the 1820s, there were frequent epidemics and high mortality and morbidity rates throughout the next twenty years. During the 1830s and 1840s there were recurrent episodes and overlapping series of contagion: from 1831 to 1833 there were two influenza epidemics and an outbreak of cholera (which alone claimed 52,000 lives); from 1836 to 1842, there were major epidemics of influenza (causing 16,000 deaths a year in each of the first four years), typhus, small pox, and scarlet fever; and from 1846 to 1849, there were occurrences of typhus, typhoid, and cholera.

15. For an excellent account of the political deployments of "public health," see Frank Mort, *Dangerous Sexualities*.

16. This account relies extensively on Anthony Wohl, *Endangered Lives*. See also F. B. Smith, *The People's Health 1830–1910* (London: Croom Helm, 1979); Bruce Haley, *The Healthy Body*; and W. M. Frazer, *A History of English Public Health, 1834–1939* (London: Baillière, Tindall and Co., 1950).

17. Wohl, *Endangered Lives* 155–56.

18. Michel Foucault, *The History of Sexuality*, trans. Robert Hurley (New York: Vintage, 1980), 1:135–59.

19. For a survey of competing statistical claims see F. B. Smith, *The People's Health*, 294–303. Also Judith Walkowitz, *Prostitution and Victorian Society*, 48–65. William Acton, in the second edition of his *Prostitution Considered in it Moral, Social and Sanatary Aspects, in London and Other Large Cities and Garrison Towns with Proposals for the Control and Prevention of its Attendant Evils* (London: John Churchill and Sons,

1870 (revised edition)), 50–72, provides a compilation of contemporary statistical tables from London hospitals which qualified earlier unquantified claims such as those of the *Lancet* which reported "on good authority, that one house in sixty in London is a brothel, and one in every sixteen females (of all ages) is, *de facto*, a prostitute" ("Prostitution—the Need for its Reform," 7 November 1857). Given the relative infancy of statistical methodology in the period, it is not surprising that the figures available are often incomplete, confusing, or contradictory; however, it is clear that the awareness of the incidence of both prostitution and venereal diseases was heightened by the application of these new techniques of information gathering and interpretation.

20. Keith Nield, "Introduction," *Prostitution in the Victorian Age. Debates on the Issue from 19th Century Critical Journals*, Keith Nield, ed. (Westmead: Gregg, 1973).

21. While stressing the historical importance of venereal infection as a symbol of cultural "degeneration," Elaine Showalter illustrates, in her essay "Syphilis, Sexuality and the Fiction of the Fin de Siècle," *Sex, Politics, and Society in the Nineteenth Century Novel*, Ruth Yeazell, ed. (Baltimore: Johns Hopkins UP, 1986), 88–115, the different developments that this archetype took in the writings by male and female authors at the end of the century.

22. W. R. Greg, "Prostitution," *Westminster Review* 53 (July 1850): 238–68.

23. Showalter, "Syphilis," remarks upon the way in which venereal diseases have been reterritorialized by larger social discourses: "Whereas in the Renaissance syphilis functioned as a religious symbol of the disease in the spirit, and during the Restoration became a political metaphor for the disease in the state, fin-de-siècle English culture treats it as a symbol of the disease in the family" (89).

24. Judith Walkowitz, *Prostitution and Victorian Society* 41.

25. Eric Hobsbawm, *The Age of Capital 1848–1875* (London: Abacus, 1975), 96.

26. F. B. Smith, "Ethics and Diseases in the later Nineteenth Century: The Contagious Diseases Acts," *Historical Studies* (University of Melbourne), 15 (1971): 122.

27. Brian Harrison, "Underneath the Victorians," *Victorian Studies* 10.3 (March 1967): 257.

28. For a description of the brutal repression suffered by men engaging in same-sex erotic practices in the British military during the nineteenth century, see Arthur Gilbert, "Buggery and the British Navy, 1700–1861," *Journal of Social History* 10.1 (Fall 1976): 72–98.

29. Myna Trustram, "Distasteful and Derogatory? Examining Victorian Soldiers for venereal disease," *The Sexual Dynamics of History: Men's Power, Women's Resistance*, The London Feminist History Group, ed. (London: Pluto Press, 1983), 156.

30. Ibid. 157. This figure, which includes all domestic and overseas forces, was much higher than those for forces who remained in the U.K. as indicated by the figures cited in the *Report of the Committee Appointed to Enquire into the Pathology and Treatment of the Venereal Disease with the View to Diminish Its Injurious Effects on the Men of the Army and Navy* (1868) which found that:

the admissions to the hospital on account of venereal diseases among troops serving in the United Kingdom, amounted in that year [1864] to 291 per 1,000 of the strength, that they constituted 29 per cent of all the admissions, that the average number of men under treatment for them was 19.1 per 1,000 of the Force, and that the loss of service arising from them was equal to that of the whole Force serving in the United Kingdom for an entire week. The Statistics of the Navy for 1862, show the number of cases admitted for treatment—for all diseases—throughout the service to have been 1,506 per 1,000 of the Strength. The average number treated for venereal diseases was 125.1 per 1,000, constituting 12.5 per cent. of all admissions. The daily loss from venereal diseases was about 586 men per day, or in the ratio of 9.9 per 1,000, which may be looked upon as equal to the loss of the whole complement of such a vessel as H.M.S. Royal Oak (iron-clad). (xxv)

31. The best accounts of the legislative history of the C. D. Acts are found in Walkowitz, *Prostitution* 73–85, and Smith, "Ethics and Diseases." The following narrative is culled from these sources as well as from the *Report of the Committee . . . [on] Venereal Disease.*

32. Greg, "Prostitution" 257. For a discussion of the significance of Greg's position, see Mary Poovey, "The Ideological Work of Gender," *Uneven Developments* (Chicago: University of Chicago Press, 1988), 1–23.

33. William Acton, *Prostitution* 162. All further references cited in the text.

34. William Acton who trumpeted his staunch support of the C. D. Acts in his own medical work *Diseases of the Urinary and Generative Organs* discussed in the last chapter, felt that this understanding was so commonplace that in his widely read *Prostitution* he dismissed even the need to discuss it: "How these [venereal diseases] are passed from sex to sex and back again, ad infinitum, it were superfluous here to illustrate" (50).

35. The *Report of the Committee . . . [on] Venereal Disease*, explicitly states: "These objections [to the genital examination of enlisted men] having been founded, not on any doubt as to efficient examinations affording facilities for the early detection of disease, but upon the feeling that they were distasteful to the men and derogatory to the character of the medical officers" (xxxii).

36. Trustram, "Distasteful or Derogatory " 162–3. This passage also turned up in the literature of the repeal movement as an example of the explicit double standard encoded in the C. D. legislation. See for example, *An Address to the Members of the American Legislature and of the Medical Profession from the British, Continental, and General Federation for the Abolition of State Regulation of Prostitution and The National Medical Association (Great Britain and Ireland) for the Abolition of State Regulation or Licensing of Prostitution* (London: F. C. Banks,1877), 43.

37. Trustram, "Distasteful or Derogatory" 163.

38. The phrase is Abraham Flexner's from his *Prostitution in Europe* (1914) quoted in Walkowitz, *Prostitution* 15. Walkowitz cites the following statistics to support Flexner's claim:

In one late Victorian study of London prostitutes interned in Millbank prison, the fathers of over 90 percent of the sample were unskilled or semiskilled working men. Over 50 percent of these women had been servants, largely general servants; the rest had worked in equally dead end jobs, such as laundering, charring, and street selling. (15–16)

39. Edward Bristow, *Vice and Vigilance: Purity Movements in Britain since 1700* (Dublin: Gill and Macmillan, 1977), 75–175; Judith Walkowitz, "Male Vice and Female Virtue: Feminism and the Politics of Prostitution in Nineteenth-Century Britain," *Powers of Desire: The Politics of Sexuality*, Ann Snitow, Christine Stansell, and Sharon Thompson, eds. (New York: Monthly Review Press, 1983), 419–38; Jeffrey Weeks, *Sex, Politics and Society: The Regulation of Sexuality Since 1800* (New York: Longman, 1981), 81–95; Paul McHugh, *Prostitution and Victorian Social Reform* (New York: St. Martin's Press, 1980).

40. Reproduced in Josephine Butler, *Personal Reminiscences of a Great Crusade* (1911; rpt. Westport, Conn.: Hyperion Press, 1976), 9.

41. Walkowitz, "Male Vice and Female Virtue" 422. The internal quotation is from Josephine Butler.

42. Sheldon Amos, *A Comparative Survey of the Laws in Force for the Prohibition, Regulation, and Licensing of Vice in England and Other Countries* (London: Stevens and Sons, 1877), 28 (original emphasis).

43. *An Address to the Members of the American Legislature* 42.

44. Brian Harrison, "State Intervention and Moral Reform in Nineteenth-Century England," *Pressure from Without in Early Victorian England*, Patricia Hollis, ed. (London: Edward Arnold, 1974), 289–322.

45. Quoted in Nield, *Prostitution* 187.

46. See Richard Carwardine, *Transatlantic Revivalism: Popular Evangelicalism in Britain and America 1790–1865* (Westport, Conn.: Greenwood Press, 1978), 159–197.

47. On religious involvement in the Temperance Movement, see Brian Harrison, *Drink and the Victorians, the Temperance Question in England 1815–1872* (Pittsburg: University of Pittsburg Press, 1971).

48. Bristow, *Vice and Vigilance* 83.

49. For a comparison of Butler and Hopkins, see Walkowitz, *Prostitution* 238–45. On Hopkins, see Mort, *Dangerous Sexualities* 119–26 and Bristow, *Vice and Vigilance* 94–121.

50. This is, of course, a radical simplification of Butler's and the L.N.A.'s position and distorts the class nature of the discussion. As Judith Walkowitz, "Male Vice and Female Virtue," argues, middle-class women in the repeal movements appealed to working-class men to support the anti-C. D. cause in defense of "their" women, thereby supporting "a patriarchal stance and a sexual hierarchy within the organized working class that feminists had vigorously challenged in other contexts" (424). However, this complexity aside, it still seems fair to say that Butler and her comrades were primarily concerned with articulating a feminist critique within the repeal movement, rather than suggesting a counter ideology for men.

51. Quoted in Walkowitz, *Prostitution* 238.

52. Quoted in Bristow, *Vice and Vigilance* 99–100. Unfortunately other than Bristow's well-documented but poorly analyzed text and Mort's excellent but brief consideration, little work has been done on the history of the social-purity movements in late-Victorian Britain.

53. This trope of the battle will emerge repeatedly throughout the texts produced by the chastity leagues, usually in the form of the male's "battle against himself" or more accurately against his sexualized body.

54. Bristow, *Vice and Vigilance* 102–4.

55. An example of a pledge card is found bound in vol. 19 of an uncatalogued collection of Victorian Sex pamphlets held in the Stanford University Special Collections. Hereafter all texts found in this collection will be referred to as "Victorian Sex Pamphlets" (VSP) followed by the volume number.

56. Quoted in a White Cross League Church of England Purity Society publication entitled "The Manual, Part II," VSP, 19.

57. VSP 21.

58. Bristow, *Vice and Vigilance* 131 and 138.

59. Ibid 131.

60. "To the Teachers in Elementary Schools," C.E.P.S. publication 10, VSP 19

61. "Helps to Purity of Life," *C.E.P.S. Shortpapers for Men* 4, VSP 19.

62. C. G. Wheelhouse, "The Special Temptation of Early Life. An Attempt to Solve the Difficulty of a Pure and Healthy Minded Child on the Subject of Solitary Sin" (Second edition, 1890) 17, VSP 21.

63. F. Le Gros Clark, "The Perils of Impurity: A few words of warning to Boys and Young Men," *White Cross League Church of England Society Papers for Men* (London, n.d.) 5:16, VSP 21.

64. Ibid 16.

65. H. T. B., "The Testimony of Medical Men," *C.E.P.S. Papers for Men* 6 (London, n.d.) VSP 21.

66. *Pall Mall Gazette*, 6–10 July 1885. On the "Maiden Tribute of Modern Babylon," see Judith Walkowitz's brilliant analysis in *City of Dreadful Delight*. Also see, Deborah Gorham, "The 'Maiden Tribute of Modern Babylon' Re-Examined: Child Prostitution and the Idea of Childhood in Late-Victorian England," *Victorian Studies* 21.3 (Spring 1978): 353–79. Also, Bristow, *Vice and Vigilance*, 106–11 and Mort, *Dangerous Sexualities* 126–30.

67. In the most comprehensive recent discussion of the act, Francois Lafitte in his article, "Homosexuality and the Law," *British Journal of Delinquency* 9.1 (July 1958), notes that "as applied to 'mankind,' case-law has long restricted its scope to a single sexual act—sodomy, whether with a male or a female (12)." This effective practice can itself be traced back to Sir Edward Coke's famous interpretation in the *Third Institute of the Laws of England* (1644): "Buggery is a detestable, and abominable sin not to be named among Christians, committed by carnall knowledge against the ordinance of the Creator, and the order of nature, by mankind with mankind, or with brute beast, or by womankind with brute beast."

68. Since the next chapter will take up the complexities of this transformation at length, I won't attempt to elaborate its significance here and rather simply note its legislative context.

69. This argument, first advanced, somewhat dubiously by Victorian journalist and Wilde biographer, Frank Harris, has been given new life by F. B. Smith, "Labouchere's Amendment to the Criminal Law Amendment Bill," *Historical Studies* (University of Melbourne) 17.67 (October 1976): 165–73. Unfortunately, Smith's essay (which provides an excellent account of the legislative history of section 11) relies exclusively on trying to elucidate Labouchere's motives in introducing the clause—comparing it to other statements he made on the subject of same-sex practices—and never attempts to contextualize the act as a whole within the sex/gender system of the period.

70. Weeks, *Coming Out: Homosexual Politics in Britain, from the Nineteenth Century to the Present* (London: Quartet, 1977), 16.

71. Ibid 12.

Part II. Pressing Issues

1. In the edition I use—the two-volume set of *Studies in the Psychology of Sex* (New York: Random House, 1942)—*Sexual Inversion* is included as "part four" of the first volume and thus this quotation appears on p. 63 of part four.

2. The Latin designation for sodomy was *crimen non nominandum inter christanos*— the crime not to be named among Christians. It is interesting to note here that while the translation of Krafft-Ebing's *Psychopathia Sexualis* constituted the first "official" use of the terms "homosexual" and "heterosexual," this text still used Latin to describe the specific sexual practices that fell under these headings. On the "unnameable" offense

itself, see Christopher Craft, "Writing Against Sexuality: Foucault, Homosexuality, and the Passions of Interpretation," *Another Kind of Love: Sodomy, Inversion and Male Homosexual Desire* (Ph.d. diss., University of California, Berkeley, 1989).

3. On the textual history of *Sexual Inversion* and its place in the discourse about "English homosexuality," see the introduction to Part I, "Against the Norm," above—especially n. 1.

4. In his recent article "Alias Bunbury," *Representations* 31 (Summer 1990): 19–46, Christopher Craft discusses the following Wilde allusion in *Sexual Inversion*, from case history 27 ascribed to "H. C., an American, aged 28, of independent means, unmarried, the elder of two children":

> Soon after this the Oscar Wilde case was bruiting about. The newspaper accounts of it, while illuminating, flashed upon me no light of self-revelation; they only amended some idle conjectures as to certain mystic vices I had heard whispered of. Here and there a newspaper allusion still too recondite was painstakingly clarified by an effeminate fellow-student, who, I fancy now, would have shown no reluctance had I begged him to adduce practical illustration. I purchased, too, photographs of Oscar Wilde, scrutinizing them under the unctuous auspices of this same emasculate and blandiloquent mentor. If my interest in Oscar Wilde arose from any other emotion than the rather morbid curiosity then almost universal, I was not conscious of it.
>
> Erotic dreams, precluded hitherto by coition, came now to beset me. The persons of these dreams were (and still are) invariably women, with this one remembered exception: I dreamed that Oscar Wilde, one of my photographs of him incarnate, approached me with a buffoon languishment and perpetrated fellatio, an act verbally expounded shortly before by my oracle. For a month or more, recalling this dream disgusted me. (19)

5. Stephen Humphries, *Hooligans or Rebels? An Oral History of English Working Class Childhood and Youth 1889–1939* (London: Basil Blackwell, 1981).

6. E. M. Forster, *Maurice* (New York: Norton, 1971), 159.

7. Flora Thompson, *Lark Rise to Candleford* (London: Oxford University Press, 1945), 569. I wish to thank Mary Klages for bringing this passage to my attention.

4 Legislating the Norm

1. This legislative account is taken from H. Montgomery Hyde's, *The Other Love* (London: Heineman, 1970) which provides the most detailed contextualization of sodomy's criminalization. Other corroborating narratives appear in Alex K. Gigeroff, *Sexual Deviations in the Criminal Law* (Toronto: University of Toronto Press, 1968), 3–36; and François Lafitte, "Homosexuality and the Law," *British Journal of Delinquency* 9.1 (July 1958): 8–19. Unfortunately this historical process has been underanalyzed by gay historians; note for example, the absence of the bill's consideration in Alan Bray's, *Homosexuality in Renaissance England* (London: Gay Men's Press, 1982), since this text reviews literature back to the very period of the law's passage in order to situate such a crystallizing moment in London's "molly-houses" of the late-seventeenth and early-eighteenth centuries

2. While to date there is no work that comprehensively traces the history of this nonnomination or its implications, John Boswell in his *Christianity, Social Tolerance,*

and Homosexuality (Chicago: University of Chicago Press, 1980) indirectly illustrates that by the thirteenth century it had entered ecclesiastical discourse when he quotes a letter from Pope Honorious III to the Archbishop of Lund (1227): "We have received a petition from you requesting that we deign to provide mercifully for the fact that numerous subjects of yours, clerics and laymen, frequently engage in prohibited sexual relations, not only with persons related to them but also by having sinful relations with dumb animals and by that sin which should be neither named nor committed, on account of which the Lord condemned to destruction Sodom and Gomorrah" (380).

3. On the "flock" see Michel Foucault, "Omnes et Singulatim: Towards a Critique of Political Reason," *Tanner Lectures on Human Values*, Sterlin McMurrin, ed. (Salt Lake City: University of Utah Press, 1981), 2:224–54; see also Boswell, *Christianity . . . and Homosexuality*, who explores this nexus from the origins of Christianity through the Middle-Ages. A much less rigorous but nonetheless interesting argument can be found in Arthur Evan, *Witchcraft and the Gay Counterculture* (Boston: Fag Rag, 1978).

4. Michael Goodich, "Sodomy in Medieval Secular Law," *Journal of Homosexuality* 1.3 (Spring 1976): 297. Boswell, *Christianity . . . and Homosexuality* 303–32, discusses the emergence of the rhetoric that described sodomy as "against nature" during the High Middle Ages.

5. On "truth" as a "system of exclusion" that arranges particular historical configurations of power/knowledge, see Michel Foucault, "The Discourse on Language," in *The Archeology of Knowledge*, trans. A. M. Sheridan Smith (New York: Pantheon, 1972), 215–37.

6. Hyde, *Other Love* 31. As Boswell, notes, "the word [sodomy] would not necessarily imply homosexuality since by the early seventeenth century 'sodomy' referred to 'unnatural' sex acts of any type and included certain relations between heterosexuals—anal intercourse for instance" (98).

7. The actual legal history of the offense is a bit more complicated as Gigeroff, *Sexual Deviations* makes clear:

> [T]he original statue of 1533 (25 Henry VIII, c. 6) was to endure only until the last day of the next parliament, . . . it was made perpetual in 1540 (32 Henry VIII, c. 3), . . . the penalty was altered in 1548 (2–3 Edward IV, c. 29) before being repealed in 1553 (1 Mary, c. 1) and revived in 1562 (5 Elizabeth I, c. 17). (8)

However, since the wording of the statute remains fairly consistent throughout these machinations, it does not seem pertinent to examine their legislative history in more detail here.

8. Sir James Stephen, *A History of the Criminal Law of England* (London: Macmillan and Co., 1883), 2:429. See also Hyde, *Other Love* 39. For an outline of the specific legal restrictions on papal authority generated during Henry's reign, see John Reeves, *History of the English Law* (Philadelphia: M. Murphy, 1880), 4:542–54.

9. For Hyde, the choice does appear arbitrary: "No doubt buggery appeared to Cromwell as suitable a subject as any other for the inauguration of this process which was to continue and eventually lead to the practical abolition of all ecclesiastical courts a century later . . ." (*Other Love* 39). However, given the range of possible choices, it seems highly unlikely that "sodomy" should be randomly singled out to initiate this strategy simply for lack of any better alternative.

10. The nature of the relation between the regent and the power of the state is, of course, very complex: see Ernst Kantorowicz, *The King's Two Bodies: A Study in Mediaeval Political Theology* (Princeton: Princeton University Press, 1957): "It is evident

that the doctrine of theology and canon law, teaching that the Church and Christian society in general was a '*corpus mysticum* the head of which is Christ' had been transferred from the theological sphere to that of the state, the head of which is the king" (15–16).

11. This movement provides an excellent example for Foucault's description of sovereign power as essentially "the right to *take* life or *let* live": "Power in this instance was essentially a right of seizure: of things, time, bodies, and ultimately life itself; it culminated in the privilege to seize hold of life in order to suppress it" (*History of Sexuality* 136). See also Gilles Deleuze and Felix Guattari's intriguing if somewhat abstruse suggestion that the social body collapses into the king's body becoming the recording surface for what they call the "barbarian despotic machine" in *Anti-Oedipus: Capitalism and Schizophrenia*, trans. Robert Hurley, Mark Seem, and Helen Lane (New York: Viking, 1972), 192–222.

12. Gigeroff provides the following brief biography of Coke: "Sir Edward Coke had been Speaker and later Attorney General in the House of Commons before becoming Chief Justice of the Common Pleas in 1606, and in 1613 Chief Justice of the King's Bench. It was at this time that he wrote the *Third Institute*, one of the first systematic accounts of criminal law since Bracton's treatise, *De Corona*, in the thirteenth century" (3–4).

13. Edward Coke, *The Third Part of the Institutes of the Laws of England* (London: E. and R. Brook, 1797). All further references to this book are included in the body of the text.

14. Foucault explains this displacement between ecclesiastical and civil codes:

Doubtless acts "contrary to nature" were stamped as especially abominable, but they were perceived as an extreme form of acts "against the law"; they were infringements of decrees which were just as sacred as those of marriage, and which had been established for governing the order of things and the plan of beings. Prohibitions bearing on sex were essentially of a juridical nature. The "nature" on which they were based was still a kind of law. (*History of Sexuality* 38)

15. In his *Byron and Greek Love* (Berkeley: University of California Press, 1985), Crompton remarks: "Henry VIII used accusations of sodomy to counter popular support for the monasteries he meant to pillage" (53–54) and then quotes a 1543 letter to Earl Arran, Regent of Scotland in which Henry directs that he send commissioners "most secretly and groundly to examine all the religious of their conversation and behavior in their livings, whereby if it be well handled, he shall get knowledge of their abominations" in order to provide the grounds for confiscating monastic wealth (53–54).

16. Bray, *Homosexuality* 19. Bray then goes on to gloss these characterizations:

With such propaganda—and it becomes wearisomely familiar—the Protestant party was doing no more than adapting to its own use the identification of heresy with sodomy that the Catholic Church had itself constructed during its confrontation with the heresies of the twelfth century, the identification of religious deviation with sexual deviation. (19)

17. This characterization of public execution derives from Michel Foucault's *Discipline and Punish*, trans. Alan Sheridan (New York: Vintage, 1979), 48–49.

18. Bray, *Homosexuality* 26.

19. A more careful consideration of the seeming contradiction between the description

of sodomy as *clamantia peccata* and *peccatum illude horrible non nominandum inter christanos* might offer an interesting addition to the understanding of the Catholic Church's definitions of sodomy during the period.

20. Bray, *Homosexuality* 19.

21. Ibid. 16.

22. Ibid. 37. Bray's anachronistic use of "homosexuality" is based on his supposition that it is "directly physical—and hence culturally neutral."

23. The following is based on an anonymous pamphlet published in London in 1699 entitled *The Tryal and Condemnation of Mervin Lord Audley, Earl of Castle-Haven, at Westminster, April the 5th 1631. For Abetting a Rape upon His Countess, Committing Sodomy with His Servants, and Commanding and Countenancing the Debauching of His Daughter* recently reprinted in Randolph Trumbach, ed., *Sodomy Trials* (New York: Garland Publishing, 1986). See also Caroline Bingham, "Seventeenth-Century Attitudes Towards Deviant Sex," *The Journal of Interdisciplinary History* 1.3 (Spring 1971): 447–68.

24. Bingham reports in addition to *The Tryal and Condemnation* several other narrative versions of Lord Audley's prosecution: Anon., *The Case of Sodomy in the Tryal of Mervin Audley, Earl of Castlehaven . . .* (London, 1708); Anon., *The Arraignment and Conviction of Mervin Lord Audley, Earl of Castlehaven . . . at Westminster on Monday April 25, 1631. As Also the Beheading of Said Earle Shortly After on Tower Hill* (London, 1642); *My Lord of Castlehaven, His Last Speache W^ch He Made att His Execution, uppon Satterday the 14th of May 1631*; as well as a variety of legal documents pertaining to the case.

25. In his book, *The Moral Revolution of 1688* (New Haven: Yale University Press, 1957), Dudley Bahlman—quoting Swift—notes that during the period the word "project" connoted an orientation of the individual toward the public sphere for the improvement of civil society: "The word 'project' was used at this time to mean some scheme, usually of an ingenious but simple stature, which would have a remarkable effect in bettering the lot of man" (101).

26. John Lacy, *A Moral Test* (London, 1704), 13.

27. Bahlman, *Moral Revolution* is the most comprehensive source on the Reformations Societies. See also A. G. Craig, "The Movement for the Reformation of Manners, 1688–1715 (Ph.D. diss., Edinburgh University, 1980); Edward Bristow, *Vice and Vigilance: Purity Movements in Britain Since 1700* (Dublin: Gill and Macmillian, 1977); and Peter Fryer, *Mrs Grundy: Studies in English Prudery* (London: Dennis Dobson, 1963).

28. Josiah Woodward, *An Account of the Rise and Progress of the Religious Societies* 63; quoted in Bahlman, *Moral Revolution* 38.

29. Bahlman, *Moral Revolution* 33.

30. Foucault, "Omenes et Singulatim" 245–50.

31. John Disney, *An Essay upon the Execution of the Laws against Immorality and Prophaneness* (London, 1708), iv. Bahlman succinctly summarizes the position taken by many reformers: "at a higher level morality would be a social cement, an instrument of civil peace" (42).

32. *Select Trials*, 2 vols. (London: 1734 & 1735); these texts provide synopses of numerous sensational trials and were originally sold as popular reading to a heterogeneous audience. While it is unclear exactly how many of these texts were sold and read, there is some indication that they were relatively popular. The (presumably) first edition appeared in 1734 in plain binding on rough paper with the inscription "Printed for J. Wilford, behind Chapter-House, in St. Paul's Yard." Eight years later another, three-volume edition, of the same text was issued by "J. Applebee in Bolt-Gate, Fleet Street,

For James Hodges of the Looking Glass over against St. Magnus Church, London Bridge." Completely reset with new page layout and typeface, the 1742 edition is printed on high-quality edged paper with a tooled furniture binding and engraved frontispiece illustrating seven scenes of crime and punishment. That the text was reprinted only seven years after its original imprint in a higher-quality edition seems to indicate that the market for the volumes was not exhausted by the earlier set and that there was still enough demand a decade later to warrant a subsequent, more costly, version.

Peter Wagner, "The Pornographer in the Courtroom," *Sexuality in Eighteenth-Century Britain*, Paul-Gabriel Boucé, ed. (Manchester: Manchester University Press, 1982), 120–40, discusses trials reporting as a popular genre that incorporated both the strategies and the audiences of various ephemeral forms such as chap books, gallows sheets, ballads, broadsheets, and even the quasi-official *Old Bailey Sessions Papers* (OBSP). Casting these accounts as precursors to the tabloid press of the nineteenth century, Wagner notes:

> [A] branch of trial reporting developed in the early eighteenth century which eventually eclipsed its competitors with the notable exception of the newspapers. This branch was represented by the separately published trial reports or collections of trials reports which drew on and enlarged or "embellished" the reports in the OBSP and the Ordinary's Account. It was this branch which developed a particular kind of trial reporting which was soon to turn into pornography. Concentrating initially on cases involving crime in combination with sex, such as rape, incest, or adultery followed by murder, the focus then slowly shifted to the sexual aspects of the trial. (122)

While we may be rightly suspicious of Wagner's facile conflation of various popular representations of sexual offenses with "pornography," his characterization of these texts as titillating does underscore the extent to which such literature could mediate between the "strictly legal" interpretation of particular acts as "crimes" and the public interpretation of such legal interpretation as entertainment. As such these accounts provide valuable insight into the strategies used to represent sexual offenses to a heterogeneous audience and thus into how public meanings were constructed around legal categories.

33. Using material largely culled from the *Select Trials*, Bray, *Homosexuality* argues that the seventeenth century saw the emergence of a "new identity," "the molly," that crystallized a variety of cultural meanings not applicable to earlier definitions of "sodomite" and "bugger": "The identity existed rather as a possible lifestyle that integrated homosexuality, to the extent that it was adopted, into a broad range of other experiences and forms of behavior, into the kind of person that you were; it had as palpable an existence over and against the individual as the conventions and life of the molly houses themselves, which it repeated on a personal scale" (99). While it seems quite probable that the subculture that produced and was (re)produced by and through the "molly houses" significantly transformed the meanings attributed to sexual acts between men—both by those who engaged in them and those who execrated them— Bray's conclusions are unfortunately based on highly problematic textual interpretations. Since he, first, ignores the cultural construction of the *Select Trials* as "popular fictions"— although he admits in a footnote that this is what they are—and then attempts to use them to produce a pseudophenomenology of what the molly's "experience" must have been like, his "fiction" interpolates a number of questionable assumptions about how these individuals made their lives meaningful in the context of a dominant culture that

seemed to exclude them. Thus, for example, Bray argues that the effect of raids on molly houses made the members of the subculture more aware of their "identity": "Someone who was a molly might well, probably would, avoid arrest and the horrors that followed, but what he could not avoid knowing was the constant possibility of this fate. And the implication of that? He could not avoid knowing—he could not afford to avoid knowing—what he was and what he was part of" (93). This subjectifying approach necessarily leads Bray to conclude that the "molly" was an "identity" based in a "lifestyle" and leads him to suggest that "the molly" was the prototype for—though not the same as—"the homosexual." Here the anachronistic usage of terminology derived from contemporary gay culture illustrates the circularity of Bray's project: in order to demonstrate the creation of a cultural category not unlike one produced in the past one hundred years, he uses the rhetoric of this category to describe an earlier set of experiences and then concludes that they are structurally similar. Randolph Trumbach in his article, "London's Sodomite: Homosexual Behavior and Western Culture in the 18th Century," *Journal of Social History* 11.1 (Fall 1977): 1–33, also uses the *Select Trials* to develop an account of what the "molly's" life was like, but he is much less speculative about the subjective aspects of this experience.

34. At the trial of Thomas Wright, Joseph Sellers, an informer, was reported to have testified:

> On Wednesday the 17th of November last, I went to the Prisoner's House in Beech-Lane, and there I found a Company of Men, fiddling and dancing, and singing bawdy Songs, kissing and using their Hands in a very unseemly Manner. I was introduced by P--- who was one of their members; but it seems they were jealous that he had made some discovery for they call'd him a *Treacherous, blowing-up Molly-Bitch*, and swore they'd massacre any Body that should betray them. But the prisoner taking P---'s part, the matter was made up. At going away the Prisoner kiss'd me with open mouth. (2, 197)

Sellers also later testified: "The prisoner was very fond of us and kiss'd us at parting in a very lewd manner" (2, 197).

35. Samuel Stevens reported at the trial of William Griffin that his accounts were accurate since "Every night when I came from thence, I took memorandums of what I had observ'd, that I might not be mistaken in dates" (2, 195).

36. Trumbach, "London's Sodomite" 17. It is interesting to speculate—if these observations were accurate—on the significance of this ritualized parody in the Molly subculture. Perhaps the reenactment of the key moments in the process whereby reproductive sexuality was institutionalized and its meanings fixed (e.g., betrothal, marriage, childbirth, baptism) allowed the men who sought each other as sexual or emotional partners to obtain a critical distance on a dominant discourse that excluded their sexual practices under punishment of death. The ironic reiteration of these cultural *point de capiton* within the context of a molly house, then, might have destabilized the apparent monovocality of the hegemonic order, opening up a symbolic space within which the subculture could pose its own meanings and practices over/against the larger culture. However, if this scenerio has any credibility, it is important to note that the subculture still posed its self-articulation in quasi-religious terms, suggesting that the ecclesiastical significance attributed to "sodomy"—which was also part of the same religious constellation *as its negation*—was to some extent operative for the subculture. Of course, until such time as there is any actual information on how participants in the subculture understood or represented their experience for themselves, the above remains highly fictive.

37. It is interesting to note that the defense more often than not consisted of character witnesses, sometimes the man's "bedfellows," who testified that the accused was not the kind of man who would engage in such practices. If appropriate, the accused's status as a married man or father was also invoked on his behalf. Although in the cases reported here this was seldom a successful tactic, it does seem to indicate the extent to which "character" was thought to mitigate the charge and therefore to suggest that the crime was increasingly perceived as a moral and not religious violation.

38. As Wagner, "Pornographer in the Courtroom" notes, the "Ordinary's Accounts" were initially a distinct genre written by the prison chaplain who held the post of Ordinary of Newgate providing "a moralizing tract on the backgrounds, the criminal careers, the behavior in prison as well as the execution of the convicts who had been condemned to death at the Old Bailey" (121). These "Accounts" were subsequently condensed and assimilated into the texts of the *Select Trials*.

39. The most significant counterexample to this claim appears in the *Select Trials* synopsis of Gilbert Lawrence's trial for sodomy in August 1730. Here the text notes the indictment as: "Gilbert Lawrence of the Precinct of St. Brides, was indicted for that he not having the fear of God before his eyes, but being moved by a devilish Instigation. . . ." The "Ordinary's Account" indicated that while awaiting execution Lawrence refused to confess his crimes even though the narrator/confessor told him: "It was to no purpose to deny the fact, since there was no hope of a Reprieve, and that he would glorifie God by a free Confession, which would also make him leave this World with greater peace of Mind, in taking Shame and Confusion of Face to himself, for so notorious, so heinous, so barbarous, so unnatural a crime" (375). However, this extended religious diatribe can to some extent be attributed to the indication that Lawrence was a French Catholic and therefore his execution merited this religious charge, while those of "good Protestants" did not.

40. Anon., *Plain Reasons for the Growth of Sodomy in England* (London, c. 1730).

41. The final chapter of the text, entitled "The Perfection of *Prudes*, and the Barbarities of Women to One Another," provides an interesting coda to the arguments against male effeminacy. Here the author argues that children born out of wedlock should be legitimized since, in the his estimation, so long as sex is procreative it is moral, while the immorality of sex lies in not providing for the children thus engendered. This advocacy of male sexual access to women beyond the constraints of (Christian?) marriage underscores the normative assumption upon which the attack on sodomy depends; i.e., that "manliness" is tantamount to virility with/against women.

42. The page references to this text which will follow in the body of the chapter are taken from a slightly later edition: William Blackstone, *Commentaries on the Laws of England*, vol. 4 (London: T. Cadell, 1791).

43. Gigeroff, *Sexual Deviations* 13.

44. Sir Leon Radzinowicz, *A History of English Criminal Law* (New York: Macmillan, 1957), 3:141–207.

45. Ibid. 202. This statement occurs during Radzinowicz's discussion of the attempts to criminalize adultery. While he never explicitly refers to sodomy in this context, it seems plausible to extrapolate the doctrine for this offense as well.

46. A. D. Harvey, "Prosecutions for Sodomy in England at the Beginning of the Nineteenth Century," *The Historical Journal* 21.4 (1978): 939–48. Radzinowicz, *History*, 4:72 and 330–31, also provides statistics concerning sodomy prosecutions during the first half of the nineteenth century.

47. Harvey, "Prosecutions for Sodomy" 939.

48. "As women became more and more confined to a narrow range of social roles,

and an exhaustive code of manly behavior and manly attitudes became more established, so sexual ambivalence became more and more outlawed. . . ." (Harvey, "Prosecutions for Sodomy" 946).

49. Clippings of these accounts along with Robert Holloway's sensationalistic pamphlet, *The Phœnix of Sodom or the Vere Street Coterie. Being an Exhibition of the Gambols Practiced by the Ancient Leechers of Sodom and Gomorrah, Embellished and Improved with Modern Refinements in Sodomitical Practices, by the Members of the Vere Street Coterie, of Detestable Memory* (London, 1813) are reprinted in Trumbach, *Sodomy Trials*.

50. The narratives of the crowd violence toward these men are truly horrifying. The most vivid account appears under the headline "The Pillorying of the Vere-Street Club," and, as the following excerpt indicates, it spares no pains to provide all the details to its readers:

> At an early hour the Old Bailey was completely blockaded and the increase of the mob around 12 o'clock put a stop to the business of the Sessions. The shops from Ludgate Hill to the Haymarket were shut up, and the streets lined with people, waiting to see the offenders pass. . . . Shortly after twelve, the ammunition waggons from the neighboring markets appeared in motion. These consisted of a number of carts driven by butchers' boys, who had previously taken care to fill them with offal, dung, &c. appertaining to their several slaughter-houses. A number of hucksters were also put in requisition, who carried on their heads baskets of apples, potatoes, turnips, cabbage-stalks, and other vegetables, together with the remains of divers cats and dogs. The whole of these were sold to the populace at a high price, who spared no expense to provide themselves the necessary articles of assault. . . .
>
> The miscreants were then brought out, and all placed in the caravan. . . . At the instant the church clock went half-past twelve, the gates were thrown open. The mob at the same time attempted to force their way in but they were repulsed. . . . The first salute received by the offenders was a volley of mud, and a serenade of hisses, hooting, and execration, which compelled them to fall flat on their faces in the caravan. The mob, particularly the women, had piled up balls of mud to afford the objects of their indignation with a warm reception. The depots in many places appeared like pyramids of a gun-wharf. These were soon exhausted, and when the caravan passed the old house which once belonged to the notorious Jonathan Wild, the prisoners resembled bears dipped in a stagnant pool. The shower of mud continued during their passage to the Haymarket. Before they reached half way to the scene of their exposure, they were not discernible as human beings.

The account then describes the second half of their trip to the pillory when "dead cats and dogs, offal, potatoes, turnips, &c. rebounded . . . on every side" and narrates their time in the pillory when "upwards of 50 women were permitted to stand in the ring, who assailed them incessantly with mud, dead cats, rotten eggs, potatoes, and buckets filled with blood, offal and dung."

51. *Hansard Parliamentary Debates*, New Series, 19 (1828): 350–60.

52. Ibid. 354 (my emphasis).

53. The concept "organic intellectual" derives from the work of Antonio Gramsci. See, "The Intellectuals," *Selections from the Prison Notebooks*, Quintin Hoare and Geoffrey Nowell Smith, trans. and ed. (New York: International Publishers, 1971), 4–23.

54. The 1861 "Act to consolidate and amend the Statue Law of England and Ireland

relating to Offenses against the Person," 24 & 25 Victoria, Chap. C, reiterates the definition of the offense and the required proof as specified in the 1828 act, amending the latter only by changing the penalty from death to "penal servitude for life or for any term not less than ten years." In addition, however, the 1861 statue defines a lesser crime, "the attempt to commit the said abominable crime," punishable by "penal servitude for any term not exceeding ten years and not less than three years, or any terms not exceeding two years, with or without hard labour." It is this last lesser offense that would seem to have provided the prototype for the 1885 criminalization of "acts of gross indecency," also punishable by two years imprisonment with or without hard labor.

55. *Hansard Parliamentary Debates*, New Series, vol. 300: 578.

56. Victor Turner, "Social Dramas and Ritual Metaphors," *Dramas, Fields, and Metaphors: Symbolic Action in Human Society* (Ithaca: Cornell University Press, 1974), 35.

57. While almost no work has been done on this type of historical event, the one recent text that does take up the subject is woefully inept at characterizing its field of inquiry. In the introduction to their book, *Scandal* (New York: Stein and Day, 1985)— which admittedly is intended as an "Encyclopedia of Scandal" and not as an analytical text—Colin Wilson and Donald Seaman provide a series of platitudes by way of definition: "A scandal is any event that 'lets the cat out of the bag' and provides material for interesting gossip"; "it [scandal] suggests that truth has finally triumphed and the hypocrite stands exposed"; "scandal is based on wishful thinking. The public wants to be shocked in order to confirm its own sense of virtue"; "what interests us is the contrast between myth and reality that becomes apparent when a scandal explodes"; etc. What these characterizations do suggest, however, is that scandal is constituted primarily by the public responses that it provokes and, indeed, to some degree is these responses themselves. (The authors of this text would probably vociferously deny this suggestion, however, since their project is designed specifically to provide a listing of those "events" that provoke such responses and does not address the responses themselves at all.)

58. Max Gluckman, "Gossip and Scandal," *Current Anthropology* 4.3 (June 1963): 313.

59. In passing it seems useful to mention Mikhail Bakhtin's discussion of "grotesque realism" in *Rabelais and His World* (Cambridge, Mass.: M.I.T. Press, 1968). Here Bakhtin suggests that the penetration of bodily imagery into representations of the official moral, social, and political order inverts the dominant ideology and opens up a space for proposing another ideology in place of the official one. This seems somewhat analogous to the press coverage of sexual transgression which both represents non-standard sexual practices within the privileged informational locus of the official culture and uses nonstandard—i.e., "low" culture—narrative forms to effect these representations (see above). Thus, one might perhaps consider the newspaper reporting of sexual scandals as both enabling and delimiting representations of marginal sexual practices. For related considerations, see also Peter Stallybrass and Allon White, *The Politics and Poetics of Transgression* (Ithaca: Cornell University Press, 1986).

60. Of all the late-Victorian "scandals," only the Cleveland Street affair has received even the most cursory attention. The following account is culled from two books, H. M. Hyde, *The Cleveland Street Scandal* (New York: Cowards, McCann andGeoghegan, 1976) and Colin Simpson, Lewis Chester, and David Leitch, *The Cleveland Street Affair* (Boston: Little Brown, 1976). The former, which attempts to reconstruct the chronology of events, relies on newspaper accounts, but, as in *The Trials of Oscar Wilde*, fails to provide any analysis of this coverage. The latter proceeds in much the same manner with

a somewhat more detailed account of the behind-the-scenes machinations which led to or did not lead to prosecutions.

61. On the effects of libel law on the press, see Pat O'Malley, " 'The Invisible Censor': Civil Law and the State Delegation of Press Control, 1890–1952," *Media, Culture and Society* 4.2 (1982): 323–37.

62. Saul is also reputed to be the anonymous author of a choice piece of Victorian pornography entitled *The Sins of the City of the Plain* published privately in 1882.

63. Simpson et al, *Cleveland Street Affair* 163–65, provides summary quotations of these texts.

64. A poem published in the *North London Press* makes these connections explicit:

> My Lord Gomorrah sat in his chair
> Sipping his costly wine;
> He was safe in France, that's called the fair;
> In a city some call 'Boo-line'
> He poked the blaze and he warmed his toes,
> And, as the sparks from the logs arose,
> He laid one finger beside his nose—
> And my Lord Gomorrah smiled.
>
> He thought of the wretched, vulgar tools
> Of his paederastian joys,
> How they lay in prison, poor scapegoat fools;
> Raw, cash-corrupted boys.
> While he and his "pals" the "office" got
> From a "friend at Court," and were off like a shot,
> Out of reach of Law, Justice, and "that—rot,"
> And my Lord Gomorrah smiled.

Quoted in Simpson, *Cleveland Street Affair* 117–18.

65. Quoted in Stuart Mason (Christopher Millard), *Oscar Wilde: Art and Morality* (1907; rpt. New York: Haskell House, 1971), 75–76.

5 Typing Wilde

1. Actually the handwriting on the card is so bad that it is difficult to make out exactly what the text says. Indeed, at the committal hearing the court was forced to ask the Marquis of Queensberry to read it aloud in order to verify the alleged libel. There is some speculation that the words may actually have read "For Oscar Wilde—Ponce and Somdomite" and that the marquis was encouraged by his legal representatives to interpret them as "posing as" in order to strengthen his case. Given the marquis's general infelicity with words and the incredible importance that the phrase "posing as" had for the defense case, it seems not implausible that this rendering of the libel's text was shaped by legal counsel.

2. Similarly, the plea also charged that Wilde's "Phrases and Philosophies for the Use of the Young" was a corrupting influence against which the public should be forewarned, in this case not because the work itself depicted "the practices and passions of persons of sodomitical and unnatural habits and tastes," but because it appeared in a magazine,

The Chameleon, containing another work, "The Priest and the Acolyte" (not written by Wilde), that did.

3. While *The Picture of Dorian Gray* has provoked allusions to its "immorality" ever since it was first published, few critics have bothered to consider how a text that (re)presents no sexualized relations between men has been so consistently (if not universally) understood to depict erotic intimacies between its male characters. For an analysis that attempts—without resorting to crude biographical reductionism—to specify how the text signifies its counterhegemonic sexual meanings, see my "Writing Gone Wilde: Homoerotic Desire in the Closet of Representation," *PMLA* 102.5 (October 1987): 801–13.

4. M. M. Bakhtin, *The Dialogic Imagination*, trans. Caryl Emerson and Michael Holquist (Austin, Tex.: University of Texas Press, 1981), 388–94. In his discussion of "the trial" as a "fundamental organizing idea in the novel" (388), Bakhtin is referring primarily to the word "trial" as a "test" or "challenge" that recoups the narrative structure of Christian hagiography or chivalric romance for modern genres. Yet Bakhtin's analysis also applies to the case of courtroom trials inasmuch as his usage derives the trial's narrative specificity from its "testing [the hero's] discourse" (388)—a definition that succinctly encapsulates the discursive function of the juridical trial. In Wilde's case, Bakhtin would seem to underscore the cultural intertext that made the trial's narratives accessible, if not marketable, when he writes that

> the testing of a strong personality who opposes himself on one ground or another, to the community, who seeks to attain complete self-sufficiency and a proud isolation, or who aspires to the role of a chosen leader; the testing of the moral reformer or amoralist, the trial of the Nietzschean man or the emancipated woman and so forth—these are all very widespread organizing ideas in the European novel of the nineteenth and early twentieth century. (389–390)

5. Peter Brooks, *The Melodramatic Imagination* (New Haven: Yale University Press, 1976), argues that as a "system of meaning" melodrama provided the nineteenth century with a "fiction[al] system for making sense of experience" that "has the distinct value of being about recognition and clarification, about how to be clear about what the stakes are and what the representative signs mean, and how to face them." If, as I suggested in the last chapter, sexual scandals constitute a liminal moment in cultural history during which normative values and practices are contested, then the melodramatic mode would seem to provide a highly effective means for resolving such cultural indeterminacy into clearly defined alternatives and for organizing the production of meaning around them. For a parallel consideration of melodrama apropos of the famous W. T. Stead scandal, "The Maiden Tribute of Modern Babylon" (discussed in Chapter 3), see Judith Walkowitz, *City of Dreadful Delights* (Chicago: University of Chicago Press, 1992).

6. In the following pages, I draw on the reports of *Wilde v. Queensberry* found in eighteen London newspapers: twelve dailies and six Sunday papers. Since the daily papers provided day by day accounts of the proceedings that took place from Wednesday 3 April through Friday morning 5 April 1895, followed by the reports of Wilde's arrest on Friday afternoon and subsequent indictment on Saturday 6 April, their narratives differ significantly from those in the Sunday papers appearing on April 7 (*Reynolds', The People, News of the World, Weekly Dispatch, Lloyd's Weekly Newspaper, Illustrated Police Gazette*). For, in the latter—whose circulations eclipsed those of the dailies by hundreds of thousands—the "story's" denouement (i.e., Wilde's arrest on charges of committing "acts of gross indecency") could always already be read back into its

beginning. In addition, the dailies themselves can be divided into morning (*Times, Morning Leader, Morning, Daily Telegraph*) and evening papers (*Evening Standard, Star, Echo, Evening News, Pall Mall Gazette, Westminster Gazette, St. James Gazette, Globe*), with the latter often providing less-complete accounts of the day's proceeding than the former in part due to earlier deadlines. This pattern is especially pronounced on Friday 5 April, when the events changed radically from morning to evening.

More significantly for my purposes, the newspaper accounts can be roughly divided into three distinct groups according to narrative mode. One group signaled by their manifestly unanalyzed "transcription" of opening speeches, examination, and cross examination, by their lack of narrative interruptions, and by their almost fetishistic attention to detail that they provided "verbatim" accounts of what had transpired in the courtroom (*Evening Standard, Echo, Daily Telegraph*). A second group, while also purporting to provide complete accounts of the proceedings, had a much more highly dramatized and intrusive narrative voice which both set the scene—graphically and interpretively—and foregrounded the significance of particular elements in the case with well-developed editorial asides and commentary, interpretive subheadings, and illustrations (*Evening News, Star, Morning Leader,* and all the Sunday papers). The third group, while not professing to provide detailed accounts, instead offered digests of the proceedings either with (*Pall Mall Gazette, Westminster Gazette*) or without (*Times*) editorial commentary. In all three cases, however, it is important to remember that the texts are always pastiches, comprised of direct and indirect quotation, paraphrase, description, commentary, and, quite crucially, omission, in varying proportions.

7. Stuart Mason (Christopher Millard), *Oscar Wilde: Art and Morality* (1907; rpt. New York: Haskell House Publishers, 1971) provides a selection of the critical reviews that appeared in the press after *Dorian Gray*'s publication. See especially Wilde's exchange with the reviewer from the *Scotts Observer*.

8. A show at the Metropolitan Museum of Art entitled "In Pursuit of Beauty: Americans and the Aesthetic Movement" displayed several trade cards and advertisements that played upon this very association to market their products. For example, the advertisement for Garland Stoves portrays a young woman (whose head is haloed by Wilde's floral familiar, a giant sunflower) aesthetically arranged in well-appointed interior complete with lily. The caption to the picture draws all these references together precisely by invoking Wilde's name: "Aesthetic stoves are all the style / Some very tame, some very 'Wilde,' / GARLANDS are always the best / Far excelling all the rest." I thank Peter Gibian for bringing these cards to my attention.

9. Regenia Gagnier, *Idylls of the Marketplace: Oscar Wilde and the Victorian Public* (Stanford: Stanford University Press, 1986), 51–99. Ellen Moers' classic work *The Dandy: Brummell to Beerbohm* (New York.: Viking, 1960), 294–308, also situates Wilde's "aestheticism" in relation to the ideological constructions of "the gentleman," but her approach is primarily anecdotal.

10. One might speculate that this parodic association of the "aesthetic" male with the "effeminacy" of the "female" domestic realm was predicated upon the anxiety generated in middle-class men by the Victorian ideology of "separate spheres." Since bourgeois men were supposed to be absent from the home during the day while engaged in their "productive" endeavors, they necessarily had little in common with their wives whose world was meant to be focused almost exclusively on this "private" arena. The figure of a male who took interest in the aesthetic of the domestic, then, necessarily threatened the precarious balance of such polar relationships and as a consequence was impugned as "unmanly"—i.e., "effeminate"—in order to recode this threat while maintaining the prevailing ideology of gender separation. The contradiction inhering in the image of the

"aesthete" as both "ladykiller" and "effeminate" would thus reproduce the strategic transformation of a (real?) fear into its (ideological?) antithesis and illustrate the means by which a dominant ideology recoups such interruptions within its structures of difference.

11. Moers, *Dandy* 296.

12. Roland Barthes, *Mythologies*, trans. Annette Lavers (New York: Hill and Wang, 1972), 109–59.

13. Roland Barthes, *S/Z*, trans. Richard Miller (New York: Hill and Wang, 1974), 9.

14. For Queensberry's biography, see Brian Roberts, *The Mad Bad Line* (London: Hamish Hamilton, 1981).

15. For an analysis of the cultural constructions of Victorian "etiquette," see Michael Curtin, *Propriety and Position: A Study in European Manners* (New York: Garland Publishing, 1987).

16. Ernesto Laclau, "Populist Rupture and Discourse," *Screen Education* 34 (Spring 1980): 87–93.

17. The point here is not that the newspapers were original in their development and deployment of these strategies but rather that they crystallized the signifying practices that had heretofore been diffuse. While it is beyond the scope of this analysis to consider, it would be interesting to compare the journalistic strategies with those of less standardized popular genres.

18. Hyde, *The Trials of Oscar Wilde* (New York: Dover, 1962), 12.

19. While it is far beyond the scope of this book to consider the social and historical construction of contemporary psychoanalytic categories, it does seem interesting to note in passing that Wilde's initial representation as a sexual subject by the press was organized around the question of his language *to the extent that it bore the trace of his (unnameable) sexual practices*. This implicit privileging of the relation between linguistic utterance and sexual desire suggests that the conceptualization of "the sexual" was undergoing a larger cultural transformation isomorphic to the shift from "activity" to "agency" precisely at the moment that Freud was beginning to hypothesize this connection in a clinical setting with his work on hysteria (e.g., *Studies in Hysteria* was published in 1895—the year of Wilde's trials).

20. For example, in the version that appeared in the *Evening Standard*, the exchange about what "kind" of book *The Picture of Dorian Gray* was appeared as follows:

Then a well written book putting forward certain views might be a good book? —No work of art ever puts forward views. Views belong to people who are not artists.

A ——— novel might be a good book? —I don't know what you mean by a ——— novel.

Then I will suggest "Dorian Grey" [*sic*] as open to the interpretation of being a ——— novel? —That could only be to brutes and illiterates.

An illiterate reading "Dorian Grey" might consider it such a novel? —The views of illiterates on art are unaccountable. I am concerned only with my view of art. I can't care twopence what other people think of it.

6 Dis-Posing the Body

1. The *Echo* quoting the *Morning*, glosses the charges against Wilde by saying:

[I]t may be said, by way of parenthesis, that the maximum punishment for the full offense is penal servitude for life or any other term not less than ten years; and the punishment for the attempt to commit the offense is punishable with penal servitude for from three to ten years. Incidentally, it may be mentioned that in Scotland until 1887 the offense was a capital offense.

The confusion here between "the full offense," "the attempt to commit the offense," and the unmentioned new legal category, "acts of gross indecency," illustrates the extent to which the residual effects produced by the legal and cultural meanings of "sodomy" often adumbrated the emergent category. Yet as the ensuing trials will make clear "sodomy" is not specifically at stake in Wilde's case, so that the meanings associated with this uninvoked charge will be refigured in the narrative accounts as part of the signifying constellation through which "Oscar Wilde" comes to represent a new type of sexual actor.

2. The variations of this description were innumerable throughout the two months of the trials. To use just one other example from the *Evening News's* report of the same day's proceedings: "Taylor, two years ago took at a rental of £3 a month, the upper rooms over a closed baker shop in Little College-street. The rooms he furnished in a remarkable manner, draped and furnished in a curious way, perfumed and always lighted by artificial light." Here the generalizing adjectives "remarkable" and "curious" serve to underscore the anomaly of Taylor's lodgings without specifying the details that render them anomalous, while the references to "perfume" and "artificial light" simultaneously connote both that which needs to be hidden (i.e., cannot he held up to the light and must be masked by scent) and the essential "un-Englishness" of the milieu.

3. Except in the case of Alfred Woods who alleged that Wilde had taken him to his home when Wilde's family was absent, in which case the incident was rendered doubly transgressive precisely because it violated domestic sanctity.

4. In its coverage of Wilde's committal hearing, the radical weekly *Reynolds' Newspaper* (7 April) provided the following account of C. F. Gill's questions to Charles Parker concerning what transpired after he and his brother dined with Wilde and Taylor at Kettners:

> What took place afterwards? —He asked me into his bedroom, which opened off the sitting room. We went there.
> Mr. Gill: Did you undress? Yes.
> Both of you? yes.
> Sir John: Did you take them all off? Witness (bluntly): Yes.
> Mr Gill: I don't propose to take this further, Sir John, in any detail. (To the witness) Acts of indecency took place between you in the bed? —Yes. I was there about two hours. He gave me £2 and told me to come again in about a week.

This is the most explicit any account gets and it is not repeated in any of *Reynolds's* subsequent coverage of the trials themselves. Indeed, even later in the same report *Reynolds'* describes Alfred Woods's testimony which was apparently more revealing than Parker's by noting: "The evidence given was of course unreportable, and the witness excused himself by saying that he was the worse for drink at the time."

5. Throughout the months of legal proceedings the editorial references to Nordau's *Degeneration* that accompanied the reporting of these trials underscore the extent to which the notion of "degeneration" framed both the writing and the reading of these journalistic accounts. For example, in the concluding sentence of its article "The Wilde Case" on April 14, the *News of The World* opines, "The present unsavory phase of English social life is foretold and dissected in [Dr. Max Nordau's] work entitled

'Degeneration.'" Similarly, *Reynolds's* front-page editorial "Oscar Wilde's Case" appearing after the indecisive conclusion of *Regenia v. Wilde and Taylor* comments:

> [I]t is certain that this whole case has stamped as pernicious the kind of literature with which Wilde's name is closely identified. That literature is one of the most diseased products of a diseased time. Indeed, so far as English writers are concerned, we do not know where we should find all the worst characteristics of our decadent civilization—its morbidity, its cold heartless brilliance, its insolent cynicism, its hatred of all rational restraint, its suggestiveness—more accurately mirrored than in the writings of Oscar Wilde. In his powerful book on "Degeneration," Max Nordau has dissected Wilde's absurdities with great ability.

As the rhetoric of this passage suggests, the delineation of transgressive behavior as "diseased" metonymically collapses this metaphoric description of the body politic with a biological etiology for Wilde's "characteristic[ally]" "decadent" "absurdities" that grounds these social practices in a mode of embodiment. Other comparable uses of "degeneration" can be found on 27 May in both the *Daily Chronicle* and the *Westminster Gazette.*

6. While there was not much social concern with male prostitution during the late nineteenth century, the arguments against female prostitution were often organized around the issue of the corruption of working class "girls" by wealthier and older men. As discussed in chapter 3 above, it was precisely this concern as it was mobilized in Stead's "Maiden Tribute" scandal that lead to the passage of the Criminal Law Amendment Act containing the clause under which Wilde was charged here. Thus, while the connection between cross-generational relationships between men and cross-generational relationships between men and women was only tangentially raised during the trial it seems clear that the cross-class, cross-generational characteristics of both these pairings was central to the effectiveness as symbolic transgressions. [In the committal hearing Charles Parker's brother William was asked if he knew what Taylor's intention was in introducing him and his brother to Wilde and he apparently replied "The same as women" (*Morning*, 14 April).]

7. Unfortunately, almost no historical work has been done on male prostitution in the period. The only essay that I am aware of is Jeffrey Weeks' "Inverts, Perverts and Mary-Annes: Male Prostitution and the Regulation of Homosexuality in England in the Nineteenth and Early Twentieth Centuries," *Journal of Homosexuality* 6.1/2 (Fall/Winter 1980–81): 113–34. Here Weeks attempts to explore the coincidence that "writings on male prostitution began to emerge simultaneously with the notion of 'homosexuals' being an identifiable breed of persons with special needs, passions, and lusts" (113).

8. The one exception to this pattern, and in fact the only paper to mention male prostitution explicitly, was the radical weekly, *Reynolds' Newspaper.* On 26 May, the day after Wilde's conviction and sentencing, *Reynolds'* ran a front-page editorial under the headline "MALE PROSTITUTION" in which it stated: "Every person with any feeling will be profoundly sorry that a man of such eminent parts as Oscar Wilde could have so far degraded himself and outraged the ordinary instincts of humanity, as to seek an outlet for his passions in male prostitution." The editorial then went on to excoriate the men who testified in the case whom it labeled "this particular gang of harlots" as follows:

> The extent to which male prostitution has invaded our social life is evidenced by the existence of the infamous crew who admitted at the Old Bailey their intercourse with Oscar Wilde for monetary consideration. These unsexed blackguards are the

putrid spawn of civilization. It did not require Wilde to degrade them. They were brutes before he ever set eyes upon them. It is appalling to think that the conviction of any man should depend upon the testimony of such loathsome creatures.

9. Indeed, so avid was Lockwood in pursuit of his goal that Wilde's attorney, Sir Edward Clarke, himself a former solicitor-general, had cause to remark to the court that it was his understanding from his own experience that the role of this office was to seek the ends of justice and not to persecute any individual—a remark that set off one of the many heated legal exchanges that punctuated the newspaper accounts of the proceedings.

Epilogue

1. Michel Foucault, *The History of Sexuality*, trans. Robert Hurley (New York: Vintage, 1980) 1: 43.

Index